# How to Parent Your

# TEEN

# Without Losing Your Mind

## Questions & Answers for Parents from today's top experts

from the editors of
*Christian Parenting Today & Campus Life*,
a Christianity Today International Publication

Cartoons by John McPherson

HOLMAN
REFERENCE

Nashville, Tennessee

# How to Parent Your Teen Without Losing Your Mind

0-8054-9362-X


Dewey Decimal Classification: 248.8'45
Subject Heading: Parenting
Library of Congress Catalog Number: 01-037523

Unless otherwise indicated, Scripture quotations are from:
*The Holy Bible*, New International Version (NIV)
© 1973, 1978, 1984 by International Bible Society,
used by permission of Zondervan Publishing House.

Additional Scripture quotations are taken from the:
*Holy Bible*, New Living Translation (NLT) © 1996,
used by permission of Tyndale House Publishers, Inc.,
Wheaton, Illinois 60189. All rights reserved.

**Library of Congress Cataloging-in-Publication Data**

How to parent your teen without losing your mind/ Carla Barnhill,
    general editor p.cm.
From the editors of Christian parenting today & Campus life: questions & answers
for parents/ with cartoons by John McPherson. Includes bibliographical references.
ISBN: 0-8054-9362-X (alk. paper)
    1. Parenting—Religious aspects—Christianity—Miscellanea. 2. Parent and
Teenager—Religious aspects—Christianity—Miscellanea. 3. Christian teenagers—
Religious life—Miscellanea. I. McPherson, John, 1959- II. Christian parenting today.
III. Campus life (Wheaton, IL).


BV4529.H69 2002
248.8'45—dc21

# CONTRIBUTORS

**Gregg Lewis** is an award-winning author and coauthor of more than 40 books. Former Editor of *Campus Life* magazine and a member of the founding editorial staff of *Marriage Partnership* magazine, Gregg enjoys writing on youth- and family-related themes.

**Deborah Shaw Lewis** holds a Master's Degree in Early Childhood Education from the Erickson Institute in Chicago, Illinois, and is the author of ten books, including *Motherhood Stress, Stressbusters for Moms, Mother in the Middle,* and *When You Were a Baby.* In the books *Seven from Heaven* (with Bobbi and Kenny McCaughey) and *Celebrating the Wonder of Motherhood* (with Bobbi McCaughey) the Lewises helped tell the amazing story of the Iowa septuplets.

Gregg and Deborah are the parents of five children ranging in age from 12 to 21. The Lewises reside in Rome, Georgia.

**Karen Dockrey** is an educator, a youth minister, and a parent of teenagers. She has been working with and writing for youth for over 26 years. She has authored more than 28 books including *When a Hug Won't Fix the Hurt, Growing a Family Where People Really Like Each Other,* and *The Youth Worker's Guide to Creative Bible Study.* She has served two churches as minister with youth and currently spends her professional time writing for youth and their leaders. She leads workshops across the country on parenting and creative Bible teaching. She received her Master of Divinity from Southern Baptist Theological Seminary and works with youth at First Baptist Church Downtown in Nashville, Tennessee.

**Jim Burns** is the President of YouthBuilders, formerly the National Institute of Youth Ministry. His passion is communicating to young people and adults practical truths to help them live out Christian lives. Highly respected for his expertise in the area of youth ministry, family and parenting issues, Jim is the author of many books and speaks to thousands of young people across the nation. He is a frequent guest on television and radio, dealing with parenting issues and youth culture. He has a Master's Degree in Christian Education and Pastoral

Theology from Princeton Theological Seminary and a Doctoral Degree in Religious Education from the Greenwich School of Theology in Great Britain. He and his wife, Cathy, and their children Christy, Rebecca, Heidi, live in Dana Point, California.

**Dave Veerman** was born in Chicago and reared in Rockford. He graduated from Wheaton College (class of '65) and received his Master of Divinity from Trinity Evangelical Divinity School ('69). Dave worked for 26 years with Youth for Christ, in the Campus Life ministry in Illinois and Louisiana and at YFC headquarters as the National Campus Life Director. He has authored 37 books including *Youth Evangelism, Reaching Kids Before High School, From Dad with Love, Getting Your Kid to Talk, How to Apply the Bible, Parenting Passages, Understanding Your Teenager, Tough Parents for Tough Times*, and *Dave's Complete Guide to Junior High Ministry*. In addition, he was one of the senior editors of the *Life Application Study Bible* and was the senior editor of the *Student's Life Application Bible*. Dave is a founding partner in The Livingstone Corporation, a company that helps produce books, Bibles, and other resources for a wide variety and number of publishers. Dave also presents *Understanding Your Teenager* seminars across the country. Dave and his wife, Gail, live in Naperville, Illinois, and are active in the Naperville Presbyterian Church. They have two daughters, Dana (22), and Kara Conrad (26).

**Carla Barnhill** is the Editor of *Christian Parenting Today* magazine, as well as a former associate editor for *Campus Life* magazine. She also served as co-editor of the *Teen Devotional Bible* (Zondervan). Carla's passion for teenagers grew out of her work on staff at Trout Lake Camp in Minnesota where she saw teens struggling with everything from broken ankles to broken homes. As an editor, Carla has met with both teens and their parents to find out what matters most to them as they seek to build better family relationships. Carla earned a Bachelor's Degree in English and Philosophy from Concordia College in Moorhead, Minnesota, and a Master's Degree in Literature from the University of Edinburgh in Scotland. She has also completed work toward a Masters in Theology from Fuller Theological Seminary.

# CONTENTS

# Contents

# The Middle TEEN: Ages 15-17 . . . . . . . . . .163

# Contents

# Contents

# INTRODUCTION

Here at *Christian Parenting Today* magazine, we hear from parents all over the world. They want help. Some are desperate for help. And they want it *now*. Surprisingly, many of our readers are the parents of young children. As they look around at society, they find the thought of raising a teenager in this environment quite sobering. Despite the fact that their children's teen years are a ways off, they are scared to death of what those years will bring. That's why we've joined with our sister publication for teens, *Campus Life* magazine, to create this resource for the parents of teens. We've gathered some of the most respected youth experts in the country to help parents acquire knowledge and build the skills for handling their toughest questions about the spiritual, social, physical, and emotional development of children from ages 10 to 19.

Tragic school shootings, the increase in sexual activity and drug use among teens, and a general feeling that today's teenagers are in trouble have led to a new look at what teenagers really need in order to make it through adolescence. The answer is surprisingly simple: Teenagers need their parents. Ironically, teenagers are notorious for pushing their parents away. But a recent survey by the National Center on Addiction and Substance Abuse (CASA) at Columbia University noted that, when asked, teenagers say they wish their parents were more involved in their lives. Teenagers want their parents to talk with them about sex, drugs, alcohol, and violence. While they might never admit it to you, your teenagers desperately need you and want you to take an active role in their lives.

Your role will change as your child moves through his or her teen years. In the preteen years, you need to lay the groundwork for what lies ahead. Experts say that between the ages of 10 and 12, your child actually goes through a biological change that's very similar to what toddlers experience. The "terrible twos" are thought to be the result of a toddler's brain and body developing at a rapid pace. All this development can make your young child tired, overwhelmed, and easily frustrated, especially when she lacks the language skill to talk about what she's feeling. As the hormones of puberty set in, the mind and body of a young teenager also experience all kinds of sudden shifts and changes. Those changes can be confusing and overwhelming. Most pre-teens lack the emotional maturity to understand what they're feeling, so they lash out in fits of anger or frustration—a preteen tantrum.

How you deal with these changes will have a strong impact on how you and your growing teen get along. As you read through the pre-teen section of this book, you'll find that Gregg and Deborah Lewis come back to one major point over and over: This is the time to set the stage for a strong parent/teen relationship. The work you put in during these years will have a major payoff down the road.

As your child hits the early teen years, peer pressure and puberty combine to create major challenges both for your teen and you. Around 13 and 14 your child will make some huge decisions about who she is and who she wants to be. The choices she makes during these years—how she spends her time and who she spends it with—will have significant consequences now and in the future. Karen Dockrey, our early teen expert, sees these years as a tremendous opportunity for parents to instill their values in their teenagers. Your involvement is vital in these years.

When the CASA study looked at high-risk behavior in teens, such as sexual activity and drug use, they found that most kids started experi-menting with these behaviors in their early teen years. Not surprising-ly, they have also found that the kids most at risk for these behaviors are those whose parents are the least involved in their lives. Your pres-ence, your support, and your input may not be openly encouraged and will likely be resisted. But your involvement is an essential part of your early teen's social and spiritual development. These are the years when teenagers want and need to know how to make their own decisions. They need your guidance as they discover what's right and wrong.

The middle teen years are marked by the tension between your child's growing desire for independence and your desire to guard him from the dangers that independence can bring. Jim Burns, who answers your questions about this age group, notes that teens between 15 and 17 are discovering the ramifications of their actions. That makes this a great time to instill in them a sense of responsibility. As your teen gains more freedom, he may begin to resent your involvement in his life, but Burns points out that your presence is needed more than ever.

Once your child hits 18, you might think you're home free. But as Dave Veerman points out in the late teen section, your child still needs your help as he grows from a teenager into a young adult. These late teen years can be some of the most difficult for parents. If you have a good relationship with your teenager, it's tough to loosen the apron strings and send your "baby" out into the world. If your teenager has made some poor choices, it's hard to watch him pay the price for those mistakes without jumping in to save him. As you learn to let go and watch your child move into the adult world, keep in mind that this transition isn't easy for your child either. As she tackles the realities of adulthood—learning to do laundry, paying rent, or just getting along with a college roommate—she'll need your advice and support.

Throughout this book, you'll not only hear from these respected experts but from teenagers themselves. You'll find out what they think and feel about the changes they're going through and maybe get some insight into your own child's emotions.

You'll also find words of wisdom from some well-known Christians like Stuart Briscoe, Rebecca St. James, and Chuck Colson as they look back on what their parents did right. Their words are a tremendous source of encouragement for parents who wonder if they're really making an impact on their hardheaded teens.

The bottom line is that your teenager needs you now as much as when he was a baby waking up in the middle of the night to eat. Now the needs may not be physical but they are emotional, spiritual, and social. As challenging as they are, your child's teenage years will also be some of the most wonderful, rewarding times of your life. You may find you have formed one of the most enduring friendships of your life. Most of all, you will see the fruit of your parenting labors peek out at you bit by bit as you watch your teenager grow from a child to an adult. At times you will have a sense of awe at this person God is creating. With prayer, patience, and perspective, you can make these years a time to cherish.

**Carla Barnhill**
*Editor*
*Christian Parenting Today*

# The
# PRETEEN
## Ages 10-12

### by Gregg and Deborah Shaw Lewis

# The PRETEEN
## Ages 10-12

When your child turns ten, you might think you still have a few years before you have to deal with "teen" issues. But what parents do during the preteen years sets the tone and lays the ground rules for the teenage days ahead. Now is the time to sit down with your child and talk about the changes that will take place in the coming years.

You're entering a time of incredible transition. But not everything will or should change. You are still the parent. Your child still needs you, your unconditional love, your gentle guidance and direction, your discipline, your protection, and your affection.

During the next ten years the framework of your relationship will change from one of adult-to-child into one of adult-to-adult. That process is beginning now. Expect the shift to be slow and uneven. When our oldest son was going through his teen years, we concluded it was like living with two different people, one still a child and one a mature young man. The difficult part was never knowing which one would walk into the kitchen each morning!

The first way you can prepare for these changes is to discuss them with your child at the beginning of his preteen years. Explain to your child that surviving the teen years will require a partnership between the two of you. His job will be to learn to handle independence and responsibility. Your job will be to teach him how to deal with life on his own and to know when to let go. As you talk with your child, be honest. Tell him you expect to make some mistakes, just as you expect him to make some mistakes. It is, after all, a learning process for both of you. Set up guidelines with your child: what the rules are and what the consequences will be if he breaks a rule. Let your child have input into both.

Your guiding principle during these years should be to gradually grant privileges and independence. As your child demonstrates his trustworthiness in handling those privileges, you may grant him further freedom.

It's much easier to grant new privileges than to take certain freedoms away from your child. Too many parents start out wanting to be the "good guy" and allow freedoms their preteens are unprepared to handle. That puts those parents in the awkward position of having to become more restrictive. And they have a hard time coming up with new privileges with which to reward their children when they prove they have matured.

On the other hand, parents who have begun the teenage years with fairly restrictive limits on their children's behavior are in the position to have a positive relationship with their children. When their children demonstrate maturity, these parents can grant appropriate new freedoms.

Teenagers have an innate drive to challenge your authority. That's part of their job at this point in life. If you have set your limits restrictively, they will challenge those limits. If you have set more permissive limits, they will still find a way to challenge you. The difference is that your children may have to find more outrageous behavior with which to shock you.

During this process of growing up, your child must experience the consequences of his or her behavior. If his behavior is trustworthy, he should have the positive consequence of new responsibilities and freedoms. At the same time, you should set specific negative consequences for misbehavior, then enforce those consequences fairly and consistently.

Your protection is also crucial to your preteen's well being. So many parents resign from their parenting role at the first sign of rebellious behavior. "They've got to grow up sometime!" these parents tell themselves. They give their teenage children independence and responsibilities for which their children are woefully unprepared. They back out of their child's world, just at the point their children are making life-changing decisions and need their parents' input the most. In doing so, they allow their children to be vulnerable to harmful forces in our world.

The best way to protect your children is to know them, to stay involved with them and their world. Know their friends and the parents of their friends. Get to know some of the parents well enough that you can call them and ask questions about the parties, events, and other kids your child is involved with.

But your most important responsibility as a parent, no matter what age your kids are, is to love them, unconditionally.

Tell them you love them every day. Give them affection every day. And back up those demonstrations of love by caring enough to be there for them. Stick with them through the changes and stay involved enough in their lives to know them and appreciate the adults they are becoming. In other words, let them know you love them enough to be their parent forever.

— *Gregg and Deborah Shaw Lewis*

# STARTING JUNIOR HIGH

*I'm worried about the transition from grammar school to junior high. I remember middle school as a tough time, and that was 20 years ago! How can I prepare my child for the kinds of pressures and challenges that lay ahead?*

One of the best decisions we ever made as parents was this: When each of our kids turned 10 or 11, we took them on a trip to talk about sex, the coming teenage years, and our changing roles as parent and child. It was time with just Mom or Dad, no siblings or friends allowed. Gregg took the boys, usually on a camping fishing trip. Our daughter went away with Debi for a weekend of shopping. The kids got to pick the destination.

We, however, got to pick the homework. We went to our local Christian bookstore and found some books we liked on the topics we planned to cover. Both parent and child were required to read them ahead of time.

Then, while we traveled to and from our destination, while we were alone in the hotel room or the tent, and off and on during the day, we discussed the facts of life and the emotional side of adolescence.

We warned our kids about the emotional and physical changes they would experience. We asked about their feelings on the changes ahead. We answered their questions as honestly as we could.

Later, when the struggles of adolescence hit, we could remind them, "This is what we were telling you about. Remember when we told you you'd feel this way?"

We also laid a foundation of honesty and openness about these personal matters, so that later, our children knew they could talk to us about anything. The experience proved invaluable to our family. We think it can work for you, too.

## ACTION STEPS:

1. Plan a weekend trip just for you and your child. Let him choose the place.

2. Pick up Christian books on sex, friendship, or any other subject you want to talk about. Make time before the trip for both parent and child to read the books you've chosen.

3. Spend the weekend talking through the issues your family will face as your child enters his teen years.

"My camp counselor last year said junior high is the worst because everyone just judges you on your clothes, how you look, and what you do. I'm afraid people are going to be like, 'You wore that yesterday! You're really stupid.'" — Taryne, 11

# HOMESCHOOLING

*We've been homeschooling our son all through the elementary grades. Now that he's junior high age, we're not sure we should continue. Should we move him into public schools? How do we make this decision?*

There are no hard and fast rules when it comes to your child's education. You need to do what seems best for him at this time. To figure that out, ask yourself these questions:

• How comfortable are you with the local public junior high?

• Do you belong to a strong homeschool group that provides some social interaction with other kids his age? Does he have social interaction elsewhere: at your church, in a club, or with his hobbies?

• Are sports an issue? If your son wants to play sports, are there teams affiliated with your homeschool organization, the local recreation authority or YMCA? Can he participate on public school teams as a homeshooler?

• Is he interested in band or other extracurricular activities that could enrich his life and make him a more well-rounded person?

• What does your son want to do? He's old enough that he should have some say in the decision. If he's happy with homeschooling and doesn't want to enter a public school, there's probably no reason for him to switch.

If he's unhappy, sit down with him and start with a prayer for wisdom in making this decision. Then write out the pros and cons for each alternative—public school, private Christian school, or homeschool—letting him contribute to the list. He isn't old enough to make this choice on his own, but he should have a voice. Often, once the issues are written down on paper, the best decision will be clear.

**ACTION STEPS:**

1. **Pray for wisdom as you make your decision.**

2. **Determine if homeschooling is still meeting your child's spiritual, social, and academic needs.**

3. **Write out the pros and cons of your school options. Then use these lists to make your decision.**

BOB TRIED IN VAIN TO GET THROUGH THE LIVING ROOM WITHOUT SHOWING HIS REPORT CARD TO HIS PARENTS.

# ACADEMIC CHALLENGES

*As my son gets older, schoolwork seems to get harder and harder for him. He's always had a tough time learning, and I'm worried that he'll never be able to keep up with the academic challenges of middle school. What can I do to help him?*

Your best bet is to keep track of what your son is doing in school. Ask if the school has a regular progress report halfway through the first grading period. If not, ask his teachers for a midterm report or parent-teacher meeting so you can address problems early on. You'll also need to sit down with your son each day to look through his schoolwork and monitor test scores and homework grades.

"What I worry about is that I'm not going to get all my homework done and I'll get in trouble a lot and have to go to the principal." — Daniel, 10

If you find that your son does indeed struggle with middle school academic pressures, get him a tutor right away. Ask his teachers or the principal to recommend a tutoring service. You can also ask them about the following tutoring options:

• Does the school system have a "homework hotline"?

• Can they recommend a college student or teacher who tutors after school?

• Some schools and/or teachers offer free informal tutoring the half hour or so before school starts or right after school. Is that available?

• Does your school encourage study teams: groups of students who work together and help each other?

• Does the school have a "study-buddy" program that matches a student who is doing well with another who needs help?

If you haven't already, talk to your son's teachers about having him tested for a learning disability. If he does have one, it's best to find out now and start working with the school professionals trained to help your son succeed.

Finally, be careful of your attitude toward your son's schoolwork. Academic success, while valuable in our culture, is not the only measure of a person's worth. God created each of us with many gifts and abilities, only some of which can be measured by a letter grade. Encourage your son's effort and reward him for doing his best—even if his best results are C's. Help him find other areas of life in which he can feel more successful. Most of all make sure he knows that you love him and are proud of him no matter what his report card looks like.

**ACTION STEPS:**

1. Get to know your child's teachers early in the school year and talk with them often.

2. Consider finding a tutor for your child.

3. Make sure your child knows he's loved and valued by you and by God.

# SKIPPING A GRADE

*Our 10-year-old daughter is ready for an academic challenge that we don't think our public middle school can offer. Her teacher suggested a private school, but that's something we can't afford. Another option is letting our daughter skip a grade. Could that affect her natural emotional and social development? Are there other options?*

Talk to your school counselor and explore what your options are. Is there a program for gifted students in your school? Could your daughter take some advanced classes? If she is gifted in math, perhaps she could stay in sixth grade for her other classes, but go to a seventh grade math class. Express your concern to the counselor or principal; they might also have some ideas for adapting their programs to meet your daughter's needs.

If they can't help, you might have other options. Do you live close to another school system that has a higher academic standard? Do they take out-of-district students? We moved two of our children to a neighboring school district in order to meet their academic needs. We drive them farther and we pay $20 a month in tuition for each child. But we are very pleased with the arrangement.

If having your daughter skip a grade seems to be your best option, some things to ask yourself are: How old is she? We have a niece who's a gifted student, and her September birthday made her one of the oldest children in her grade. So, when she skipped a grade, she just went from being one of the oldest to one of the youngest in her class. Her parents would have been reluctant to make that change if she had been one of the youngest in her original grade.

How mature is your daughter, socially, emotionally, and physically? It might help to take an hour or so to walk through the school, observing the classes a year ahead of your daughter. Do you think your daughter could fit in with these kids? Are they considerably more mature-looking? Do they seem to act significantly different from your daughter?

Private school could still be an option as well. Talk to the principal about scholarship opportunities. Some employers also offer financial help to private school students.

Most importantly, start your process with prayer. Just as you, her earthly parents, are concerned, her Heavenly Father also cares and has promised to give you wisdom.

**ACTION STEPS:**

1. **Consider ways to supplement your child's education through a gifted student program or advanced placement classes.**
2. **Think through your child's emotional, social, and physical readiness to move to a higher grade level.**
3. **Look into other ways to finance a private school education.**

# SCHOOL

*Our 12-year-old son hates school. He never wants to go. He'll even fake an illness to stay home. But when we ask him why, he just shrugs. How can we get him to open up?*

Get to the bottom of this as soon as possible. And since your son isn't talking, you'll probably need to do some investigating.

A parent-teacher conference would be a good place to start. During the meeting, express your concerns and ask the teacher for advice. He or she may have some insights into what is going on or offer some information your son hasn't told you. If that doesn't get you anywhere, enlist the help of other adults who know your son well—the youth director at your church, a friend's parent. Ask them to describe your son's behavior in certain social situations. Encourage them to flesh out any concerns or potential problem areas they see.

Information you've gathered from your discussions should help you have a productive and helpful conversation with your son. Obviously, the point of this conversation isn't to put him on the defensive. It's simply to help him through whatever it is that is troubling him about school.

When talking about difficult issues with our children, we've found it helpful to take the conversation to a neutral place. Get permission to take your son out of school at lunchtime and head to his favorite restaurant. ("Hey, buddy, let's do lunch today. I want to catch up on what's going on with you.") Something about that atmosphere encourages them to open up.

Also, consider having this conversation with just one of you present. Sometimes the presence of both parents can make a child feel "ganged up on" and more likely to clam up. With just one parent there, he may feel more comfortable speaking his mind. If you are both close to him, Dad might have better luck getting your son to open up, especially if there's a sensitive issue—like teasing in the locker room—involved.

Then, listen. This is one of the hardest parts of parenting. It's always a challenge for us to keep from offering too much advice. But doing so only causes our kids to tune us out. But when we've actively listened to what they're saying, we've discovered that they naturally want to talk.


**ACTION STEPS:**

1. Talk to your child's teacher and other adults to gain their insights.

2. Find a neutral place to talk, like a favorite restaurant.

3. Consider having a one-on-one conversation with your son, rather than having both parents present.

"I was deadly afraid that I was going to get stuffed in my locker, but now that I'm there, no one's planned to stuff me." — Scott, 12

# SEX EDUCATION

*Our public school will be teaching sex education next semester. We've talked with our 11-year-old about sex, but we're concerned our Christian views of morality might be undermined by what he learns at school. How can we handle this?*

The sex-ed curriculum used by your school will have been picked by educators and parents willing to take the time to serve on a committee. So your first step is to get involved in your son's school, if you're not already. Go to the principal and ask about opportunities for parents to be involved in the local school system.

Since your child will be in sex ed next semester, you're too late to change the curriculum for this year. Instead, ask to preview the sex-ed materials. If you still have concerns, you have a choice. You can ask that your child not be included in the class. Or you can let your child take the class, then talk with him about the problems you see in the materials. Even if you agree with the school's approach, this is another good opportunity to discuss the subject with your child. We also suggest you meet with the person who will be teaching the class. Find out what he or she plans to talk about and be clear about any concerns you have.

It might encourage you to know that several public school sex education materials are abstinence-based. Our schools use Choosing the Best, an abstinence curriculum written by a Christian for use in public schools. This program is honest about the fallacy of "safe sex" and presents abstinence until marriage in a positive light.

Some sex-ed curriculums are called "abstinence-based" but are actually a combination approach. These programs encourage abstinence until young people are "more mature," but assume that most teens will be sexually active and should be taught how to have "safe sex." Postponing Sexual Involvement (PSI), the national program promoted by Jane Fonda, is an example of this combination approach. Unfortunately, PSI is offered to schools free of charge. Other programs, like Choosing the Best, while not expensive, do cost the schools some money.

Your involvement can go a long way toward helping you feel better about what your child will be learning. And if the school officials know you and trust that you have the students' interests at heart, they'll be more apt to listen to your concerns.

**ACTION STEPS:**

1. **Volunteer to serve on the committee responsible for choosing the sex ed materials and talk with the sex ed teacher.**
2. **Continue talking to your child about what he or she is learning in class.**
3. **Pay attention to the subtle messages in the material and make sure your child knows where you stand.**

# WORRYING

*Some of my friends who have teenagers tell me I worry about my kids too much. They tell me I need to lighten up and gain some perspective. I guess I'm not sure how to do that. Do you have some suggestions?*

Without knowing you, we don't want to merely assume that your friends are right. It's been our experience that far too many parents these days don't worry about their kids enough. They have abdicated their authority and responsibility for teaching and raising their children to educators, the media, and a host of other influences. They don't seem to ever stop and think about what they're doing or how those forces are shaping their kids (1 Sam. 3:13).

But there is a real difference in being concerned and being overly worried and protective. If that's what your friends are getting at, you may need to listen. And honestly, the only way to worry less is to pray and trust more. Pray with your spouse about specific concerns you have for your kids; ask God for his sensitivity and wisdom in knowing how to handle the coming years. He's a better parent than any of us, and he's willing to help us. Pray with your kids about your concerns—and theirs. Your heart-felt prayers will let them know you care and remind them that God does, too.

"My parents don't usually get involved in my problems—they just leave me alone. Sometimes I wish they'd care more, and that they'd come to me and try to help, but then I think about it and realize, why would I want them to come? How could they really help me? Even when I want to tell them something, I'm afraid they'll react wrong or get upset." — Ashley B., 11

Find other parents in your church or community who have kids the age of yours, or who have already successfully survived their kids' teen years. Using others for practical advice, encouragement, and prayer support can do wonders to reduce your worry.

Most of us do need to lighten up and enjoy our parenting experience. Look for things you can laugh about. Don't get so focused on the tensions and the troubles we all face that you forget to appreciate or even notice the positive things happening in your family. Deliberately look for things to be thankful for each day. The hands-on parenting years pass too quickly. You really do need to enjoy them while you can.

**ACTION STEPS:**

1. **Continue to pray and ask God to give you wisdom and relief from your worries.**
2. **Develop a network of other parents you can turn to for advice and support.**
3. **Remember to enjoy parenting and be thankful for the gift of your children.**

# ENCOURAGING KIDS

*We've started to feel like all we do is point out the things our kids do wrong, and we don't like it. Can you give us some tips on how we can build them up?*

You may have taken the most important step: You're being sensitive to what we feel is one of the most significant issues of parenting. One of the most important indicators of a young person's emotional health is his or her sense of parental approval and unconditional love. Children get both when we regularly affirm them.

So how can you do that? The old "sandwich strategy" is a good one to keep in mind—begin with something positive, make the criticism or suggest the correction that needs to happen, then close with another positive, affirming comment.

In addition, make it a goal to personally affirm each of your children with a compliment or positive observation at least once a day. Before long it should become a habit that happens so naturally and easily you don't even have to think about it. What a difference that could make in the atmosphere of your home and in the life of your children!

One further suggestion: It's certainly important to praise your children for what they do. And sometimes you may need to provide them with experiences and opportunities that allow for the kind of behavior and

"YOU KIDS DRIVE ME NUTS! ALL DAY LONG YOU PESTER ME ABOUT ICE CREAM AND NOW YOU AREN'T HUNGRY!"

success you can compliment. But you need to be careful that in your well-meaning praise you don't fall into a trap of only affirming them for what they do. That can lead them to believe you only accept them for what they achieve and that your love is performance-based. You need to be just as careful to praise your children for who they are and the positive Christian character traits you see in their lives.

There's certainly nothing wrong with noting and praising performance, such as a nice hit in a baseball game or improved grades on a report card. But remember to be just as quick to note the thoughtfulness demonstrated toward a younger sibling or the patience shown in a potentially irritating situation.

In his grace, God puts more emphasis on who we are than on what we do. As parents, we do well to apply the same principles to our children.

**ACTION STEPS:**

1. Try the "sandwich strategy": Sandwich correction and criticism with words of affirmation.
2. Give each of your children at least one compliment every day.
3. Focus your praise on who your kids are, not just what they do.

"My family jokes around a lot, and they're really sarcastic. It's OK at home, but when they do it in public, like at a restaurant, it's embarrassing. My parents don't know they embarrass me, but they do."

— Jenny, 12

# OTHER PARENTS' RULES

*My son's friends are allowed to watch movies my husband and I think are inappropriate for preteens. How can we talk to the other parents about this without sounding judgmental or superior?*

This is an issue where parents can feel like they're in a battle against the entire world. Our own children have had friends who, even as preteens, were allowed to watch R-rated movies. If you feel it's necessary to talk to other parents about the movies they allow in their home, simply tell them there are some movies you're not comfortable having your son watch.

Our most important principle has been to know what our children are watching, either movies or television. If we let the kids watch anything with questionable content, we watch with them and discuss what troubles us. We've explained to our kids that movies and television are food for our brains. Just as we would never let them eat spoiled or rotten food that would make them sick, we don't want them to watch shows that give them a "sick" or mistaken perspective on the world. Research indicates that kids who watch violent movies and television are not only more likely to resort to violence, but they also become more fearful of the world, greatly overestimating their own risk of being a victim. We don't want our children to be afraid of the world; we want them to boldly step out into life.

Movies and television also portray a smooth, well-rehearsed, blemishless version of sex. We've told our sons, "One day you will be married. You will love your wife, but she will not look like Pamela Anderson—with her hair and makeup professionally done and every flaw airbrushed away. Watching a Hollywood version of sex may leave you with unrealistic expectations or a false sense of how it ought to be or of how you should perform—and rob you of the joy of real sex."

We've given the same speech to our daughter—using Leonardo DiCaprio's name, of course. You could try a similar conversation about your concerns with your son. By offering him a higher view of life and of sex, you might find that he'll say no to unacceptable movies on his own. If that fails, host a weekly movie night at your house and encourage your son to invite his friends.

**ACTION STEPS:**

1. Be clear and calm as you explain your concerns to other parents.

2. Equip your children to make godly choices on their own by talking about the messages mature movies send. Talk about objectionable content and the reasons it goes against God's plans for his people.

3. Help your child be a positive influence on his friends by hosting "movie night" at your home.

# TRUSTING OTHERS

*We've always taught our daughter to respect people in authority, like pastors and teachers. But with the way things are today, I'm afraid for her to trust anyone too much. I can't bear the thought of her being taken advantage of—she's so young and impressionable. Am I paranoid, or are my fears legitimate?*

One of our jobs as parents is to protect our children's innocence. And that has become very difficult in recent years. It seems like we have only two choices: We can be careless of our child's safety with other adults and let someone take advantage of our child; or we can be so suspicious of the adults around our children that we instill our own fears in the hearts of our children. That destroys their innocence by making them distrust all other adults.

But there is a way to find a middle ground. The key is to stay involved in your daughter's life and to know the other adults she encounters. In general, no other adult has a reason to spend a lot of time alone with your child. Teachers, youth ministers, and other adults spend time with small groups of students, and those relationships should be encouraged. But only rarely should an adult be alone with one child. If another adult began to spend a lot of time alone with one of our children, I would want to know that person very, very well. And I'd want to know exactly what was going on and why they needed to be alone with our child.

Teach your daughter to respectfully assert herself if an adult ever says or does something that makes her uncomfortable. Let her know it's OK to say no to someone. Until she's older and can make better decisions about who's trustworthy and who isn't, insist that she introduce you to any adult she spends time with.

**ACTION STEPS:**

1. **Make sure you know all the adults in your child's life.**
2. **Ask questions of any adult who wants to be alone with your child.**
3. **Encourage your child to respectfully say no to anything that makes her uncomfortable.**

# LETTING GO

*My husband says I baby my children, who are 11 and 12. But I'm just trying to do what's best for them. I think my husband is too harsh with the kids. The way I see it, if we don't show them unconditional love, who will?*

As parents, your job is to meet your children's needs. Your kids still need for you to love them, to supervise them, to know what's going on in their lives. But they need to begin making more of their own decisions. As they do, they need your gentle guidance and involvement, perhaps more than ever.

A good example: A friend told us about the time her daughter was 11 and desperately wanted a pair of designer jeans. This friend drove her daughter to an outlet mall where the jeans could be purchased at a discount, handed her daughter her clothing allowance, and let the child make the decision on how to spend her money.

The girl tried on the coveted jeans. She looked at the price tag: This one pair would take all her clothing allowance. Then she tried on some other jeans. The mother looked them over and agreed that the other jeans were well made, fit her daughter nicely, and were a good buy. The girl could buy three pairs of those jeans for the same price as one pair of the name-brand jeans.

My friend said it was one of the hardest things she's ever done, but she bit her tongue and let her daughter make up her mind. Finally, after agonizing over it, the girl went home with three pairs of jeans. And the mother told her she'd made a good choice. The family never heard about those designer jeans again.

"I really like the mall, and whenever I
go there, I always see something I
want. My mom always says, 'Save
your money for something else.' But
one time I bought something, and I
spent a lot of money on it, and I
never really wore it. My mom was like,
'I told you to wait until you really
wanted something.'" — Taryne, 11

Too many parents take a "time to let them make their own choices" approach to parenting too far, too fast. They resign from the decision-making process suddenly and completely, instead of making a graceful, slow exit. The better option is to allow children to make their own choices while offering them a safety net of guidance and support.

## ACTION STEPS:

1. Start allowing preteens to make some choices on their own with your guidance.
2. Help your child assess her choices, and give her the tools she'll need to make a wise decision.
3. To avoid "babying" preteens, let them live with the consequences of their choices and help them learn from their mistakes.

# FAMILY ACTIVITIES

*Our son refuses to eat out with us or go to the movies or do any other family activities. We try talking about it, but we just end up arguing. Is this normal for a 12-year-old? What can we do about it?*

It's common for adolescents to want to establish their own identities apart from their parents and families. Different kids do this in very different ways. You need to be careful how and at what point you try to resist this natural drive.

On the other hand, you clearly believe family time and strong family relationships are important. And you're right. So how do you find a balance and avoid unpleasant battles over the seemingly conflicting goals of you and your son?

You say you've tried talking. We encourage you to try again. Avoid talking about it when you're ready to walk out the door to do something your son doesn't want to do, or even when there is a specific activity you have in mind.

Instead, order a pizza and hang out at home for a night. Let him know you're bothered by the conflict. Tell him you want to understand his feelings and would like him to understand yours. He may need to hear you acknowledge that he's growing up and that his relationship with the family is changing. Let him know these changes are hard for you because your role as parent is changing at the same time. Finally, explain that family relationships are still important and you want to do what you can to maintain those ties.

"Sometimes I like going out with them, but sometimes I don't. They embarrass me when they do stuff like have personal conversations out in public. If they just wouldn't talk about me in front of other people, that would solve the problem." — Alison, 11

Be open to rethinking your family traditions. Let's say, for instance, your other children are younger than your son. He may feel current family activities are no longer age-appropriate for him. Consider giving your son a voice in suggesting some new activities he thinks would be acceptable. You can even offer him the option of not coming along on some outings.

Control may be another underlying issue. If you allow him to have some input, he's more likely to be willing to come along. You might also look for opportunities where you and your spouse could do some one-on-one activities with your son; family activities don't always have to include the entire family.

Be willing to compromise. You might even get him to agree to a basic tradeoff. For every "family activity" he chooses, you get to choose one. If you can show respect for his growing independence and his feelings, the chances are a lot better that he'll respect your wishes to keep family a priority.

**ACTION STEPS:**

1. **Understand your child's growing desire for independence.**

2. **Talk with your child about your reasons for wanting to build family unity. Listen to his reasons for wanting to skip family activities.**

3. **Work out a compromise that carefully considers your child's changing needs.**

# BIBLE READING

*We want to encourage our kids to start reading the Bible on their own. Though we've read Scripture to them consistently until now, we think it's important for them to take responsibility to do it individually. How do we do that?*

The first step is to give each of them a new, age-appropriate Bible. Any Christian bookstore should have a wide selection of youth Bibles. Take your children shopping; browse through what's available. Feel free to point out the features you think are important, but let them pick out their favorite. At the same time, look for devotional books for them to follow as they study.

Your kids are old enough to begin taking some responsibility for individual Bible readings and devotion times. So don't underestimate their ability to stick to a schedule and develop good, long-lasting habits. Encourage them to spend five minutes reading the Bible every day. Every month or so, ask them how it's going.

Also encourage your kids to join Bible study groups. If youth Bible studies aren't available at your church, investigate what you need to do to get one started. Even as adults, the encouragement and support of an organized Bible study group is important to our personal walk with Jesus, and now is a good time to get your kids in the habit of belonging to one. Our church youth director conducted a youth Disciple Bible Study group when our oldest sons were in their middle teens. That Bible study laid a good foundation for our sons to understand how and why to study the Bible.

Our children have also attended Chrysalis, a Christian youth leadership group that begins with an intensive spiritual retreat and continues with monthly get-togethers. You can look for similar organizations (such as Youth for Christ and Young Life) and encourage your child to get involved.

"I used to not like church because I felt like I didn't understand what was going on. My mom said that if you go you'll learn more and you'll have fun because you'll know more. Also, God is God—he's the one who made us and you should learn more about him."

— Daniel, 10

**ACTION STEPS:**

1. Help your child pick out a new, age-appropriate Bible and devotional book and encourage him to read on his own a few minutes each day.
2. Encourage your child to join, or start, a youth Bible study group at your church.
3. Look for other discipleship opportunities such as retreats, seminars or Christian clubs in your area.

# PRAYING OUT LOUD

*My 11-year-old daughter doesn't like to pray aloud, even if it's just with our family. We want to encourage her to feel free to talk to God, but we don't want to force her. What should we do?*

This is not uncommon for an 11-year-old, so don't pressure her. If she's shy in other areas, this may just be a result of that personality trait.

She might just need a little help finding ways to communicate with God that are natural for her. Your local Christian bookstore should have (or could order) books on devotions and personal prayer time that are written for girls her age. You might let her pick out a book that interests her and encourage her to keep a prayer journal. Doing so would give her an opportunity to share her feelings with God in a more private way.

If you suspect there's a deeper, more serious spiritual reason your daughter doesn't like talking to God—she's upset with God about something or feels guilty or somehow unworthy—now is a good time to talk with her about God's unconditional love. Help her see that God wants to hear from her and speak to her no matter what's going on in her life.

Finally, continue being a good example for your daughter in this area. Make sure she doesn't see praying as some rigid, formal formula. We not only pray with and for our kids at bedtime and mealtime, but often before they go to school in the morning, asking God's blessing on whatever specific things they have scheduled that day. From time to time we ask each person to pray specifically for one other member of the family so everyone prays and is prayed for. Sometimes we ask one of our children to pray for us one-on-one about some challenge we're facing. When kids see praying as a normal part of life, and something meaningful they can do for another family member, they feel more comfortable praying out loud.

**ACTION STEPS:**

1. **Help your child find a devotional book that suits her personality and needs.**

2. **Talk about any fears or insecurities that might be getting in the way of her relationship with God.**

3. **Integrate informal prayers into every aspect of family life.**

## Thanks...

I was 9 years old and living in England when the Second World War broke out. I well remember the worried look on my parents' faces as they heard the news. They, too, had been about 9 years of age when the First World War had started, so they understood my youthful anxieties. But they understood something else. Having lived through one catastrophic war, they had learned that in the midst of fear and anxiety it is possible to trust God so implicitly that fears are diminished and anxieties become manageable.

As the war progressed, our small town became a war zone. We lived just a few miles away from a major shipyard where aircraft carriers and submarines were being built for the Royal Navy. This meant endless bombing when the ships were nearing completion.

Night after night the sky was red with the light of fires. The windows rattled, the foundations shook, and the chimes on our grandfather clock clanged incessantly throughout the night. And through it all my parents never wavered in their confidence that the Lord was in control of our lives. They did not assume we would not be hurt, neither did they pretend that they were not anxious. But they did instill in me by word and example an unshakable confidence that nothing would happen to us outside the benevolent permission of a gracious God. He would either protect us from all physical harm or he would call us home, as my mother would say with a wry smile "on the bosom of a bomb." Today, so many years later, my own confidence in God is a testimony to the example given to me by my godly parents.

Stuart Briscoe — pastor and author

# RESPONSIBILITY

*Now that our son is 11, we want him to start being more responsible for himself and his actions. How can we teach him responsibility?*

You're wise to ask this question. A major goal for every parent should be to eventually send our children into the world as independent and responsible adults. Any parent who isn't already deliberately working toward that goal needs to start today. Young people don't automatically become responsible adults the day they turn 18, or even 21. It's a gradual process. Sometimes progress is so gradual that you could swear your kids are regressing.

Communication is an important ingredient in the parental cupboard no matter how old our children are. But it can be especially beneficial when it's used at the beginning of adolescence. Now is an ideal time to sit down and talk to your son about your excitement and pride in his growing maturity. (Most kids love to talk about growing up and to hear your recognition of what is, and will be, happening to them.) Let him know you expect and want him to become more independent.

Then let him know independence and trust require increased responsibility. Ask him to help you make a list of all the various responsibilities and expectations he has now—from school work to family chores to church and community involvement. Once you have what you feel is a pretty complete list, ask him to go through it and indicate which ones he thinks are reasonable, which ones might need to be adjusted for his current age, and what additional responsibilities might be added.

Next, talk with him about his finished list. You'll both need to compromise a bit to agree on a working list of reasonable responsibilities. Then, discuss possible rewards for fulfilling those responsibilities as well as reasonable consequences for failing to carry them out. Now it's time to put everything into a written "contract." Then stick to your agreement. You can always make adjustments and agree to change or add to your list in the future.

Keep in mind that as your son accepts more responsibility for his schedule, his behavior and other aspects of his life, he'll still need your interest, presence, and guidance. So stick with him and keep talking!

**ACTION STEPS:**

1. Talk openly with your child about independence, trust, and responsibility.

2. Work with your child to create a list of age-appropriate responsibilities, rewards, and consequences.

3. Stay involved in your child's life as he learns to handle more responsibility.

> "I don't get an allowance, but I do get money from babysitting. My parents want me to spend my money wisely, but because I earned the money myself, they let me do what I want with it. I think it's good that they don't give me guidelines, because that way I learn on my own without them pushing me."
> — Ashley B., 11

# ALLOWANCES

*We'd like to start giving our 10-year-old an allowance, but we're not sure how to do it. How much should we give him? Should he have to do things to earn it? Should we set guidelines on how he can spend it?*

We know lots of good parents who take very different approaches to allowances. So there is more than one right way to do this.

We do feel strongly that kids should have an allowance to spend as they wish. That's how they learn to manage money. And they definitely need to have chores to do around the house. That's how they learn to do household tasks and assume regular responsibilities.

However, we decided to keep chores and allowance separate. Our children do chores because that's part of being a family. And they receive an allowance because they are a part of our family. But one does not depend on the other. We have friends who have worked out a system of paying their kids for doing their chores, and that seems to work well for their family.

We chose to pay our children a monthly allowance. And they receive one dollar for each year of their age. Our 10-year-old gets 10 dollars a month; our 14-year-old gets 14 dollars.

We expect our kids to tithe—to pay one-tenth of their allowance to our church. And they have to save 20 percent. If they want to spend money from their savings accounts, they have to consult with us. Other than that, their money is theirs to spend. We still pay for necessary clothing and food, of course. All of our kids have found ways to supplement their allowances with babysitting, mowing lawns, etc.

"I have to save some of my allowance for church, then my dad helps me set short-term, medium-term, and long-term goals for the rest. Long-term is like college, medium-term is like a bike, and short-term is spending money. It's really helping me learn to think for the future." — Ben, 11

For us, the overriding monetary philosophy was this: We wanted to give kids enough that they learned some financial discipline and money management skills. We didn't want to give them so much they wouldn't have to learn the value of frugality. Most of all, we didn't want them to sacrifice too much of their time, energy or youth just to earn money.

**ACTION STEPS:**

1. **Come up with a system that works for your family and stick with it.**

2. **Encourage your children to tithe 10 percent of their allowance and save 20 percent.**

3. **Give kids some freedom to spend the rest of their money as they like.**

# STEPFAMILIES

*I recently remarried after a painful divorce, and my 10-year-old son won't have anything to do with his stepfather, even though my new husband bends over backward for him. What's going on, and what should we do?*

Your son is probably grieving. No matter how unrealistic or unlikely, children of divorce hope against hope that their parents will reconcile. So when one parent remarries and the chance for reconciliation is gone, they experience a loss. It's as if they've lost their original family all over again. It's common for children to then direct these negative feelings toward their new stepparent.

Most children have a hard time understanding these feelings, much less articulating them. They don't understand why they have feelings of sadness and loss, perhaps even anger. We attended a wedding recently that was a second marriage for both bride and groom. The newlyweds were beaming with joy. Their six children all stood there looking bewildered, unhappy, numb, or angry. None of the adults seemed to realize what the children were going through. They were just disappointed that the kids weren't getting into the spirit of things.

Your first step is to try to understand what your son is dealing with. Check out your local Christian bookstore or public library for a book you can read with your child about these issues. It might also be good for your family to meet with your pastor to talk about the situation. Finally, find a regular time to just spend time with your son. But you shouldn't do all the talking. Be willing to listen to how he feels.

During this time of grief, your child still needs you and your husband to be the authority figures in his life. So, make sure that in "bending over backward," your husband isn't allowing your son to break family rules or be disrespectful to him.

With patience, understanding, and prayer, your family can survive this difficult transition.

**ACTION STEPS:**

1. **Understand that your child is probably grieving.**

2. **Find resources—your pastor, friends, books—that can help you work through this issue.**

3. **As a couple, remain a strong, consistent source of authority and structure for your child.**

"My stepsister picks on me all the time and makes me feel bad, like I'm not wanted. I'll tell my dad about it, and he'll usually talk to her and then talk to me. He and I talk about personal stuff, like my sisters and my mom and my dad's remarriage. It makes me feel better, because he teaches me a lot."

— Kristan, 11

# GRANDPARENTS

*My mother-in-law can no longer live on her own and recently moved in with us. We all love her, but caring for her has put a physical and emotional strain on all of us, especially our 12-year-old. He feels we no longer have time for him, and in some ways, he's right. We need help making this transition. How can we balance the needs of our parents with the needs of our children?*

More and more families are facing this "generational squeeze." And striking that balance between the needs of the two generations is never easy.

One of the first things you need to realize is that this cloud does have a silver lining. For your son, having his grandmother around can enrich his life and give the two of them a chance to develop a stronger relationship. Grandparents, even those who are ill and needy, can play a wonderful role in the lives of children. They are adults who love the child unconditionally, but who have no obligation to discipline him. That combination can make a grandparent an ideal confidant and friend.

In addition, exposure to an older person can increase your son's sensitivity to the problems faced by the elderly. And, since your mother-in-law's health has deteriorated, that presents your son with an opportunity for service.

On the other hand, as you already know, this situation does present serious challenges and problems. Be honest and acknowledge that with your son. Articulate your love and motivation for providing care to his grandmother while you reemphasize your love for him.

Let him know you realize he has reason to feel the way he does. Ask him for suggestions on how to help compensate for the reduced time, energy, space, privacy, family time, and money you may have as a result of this new living arrangement. Part of his frustration is probably due to his feelings that this is completely out of his control. At least give him a sense that you're listening and willing to cooperate with him in working through the challenges.

Kids generally demonstrate a great capacity for flexibility and compassion. If you can make a little time for him, give him understanding, and offer a measure of hope that you'll be able to work this out together, we expect he'll soon adjust and surprise you with a new attitude.

**ACTION STEPS:**

1. Encourage your child to see this as an opportunity to really get to know his grandparent.

2. Talk with your child about the changes and acknowledge his frustrations.

3. Ask your child for his input in helping your family adjust to this living arrangement.

# ARGUING IN FRONT OF KIDS

*My wife and I disagree about whether or not we should fight in front of our kids. I think they should see how a real marriage works and how we resolve conflict. She thinks it will make them feel like their home life is unstable. What do you think?*

We think that any child, no matter how old, is greatly impacted by the atmosphere of the home. Does that mean it's best to pretend everything is perfect and keep any conflict or disagreement hidden behind closed doors? Not necessarily.

On the one hand, there's a lot to be said for openness and honesty where everyone knows where everyone else stands. On the other hand, there's also real benefit from an atmosphere of peace and quiet, where children are protected from unnecessary worry or conflict.

Every marriage is going to have conflict. How comfortable you feel dealing with yours will depend on a variety of factors—your own personalities, the family models you grew up with, your personal convictions, and even your children's ages and personalities.

Kids do need to be reassured that disagreement (or even conflict) and love are not mutually exclusive. Explain this to your children. But also make sure there's enough love talked about and demonstrated to far outweigh any conflict.

We know one couple whose policy is this: If their kids see them disagree or argue, they make sure the kids also see them work it out, apologize, and make up. If some of that reconciliation takes place behind closed doors, they reenact or at least talk through the resolution in their kids' presence, so they'll all learn from what happened. Perhaps more of us ought to consider this strategy.

At the very least, you and your wife need to come to an agreement about how you'll deal with conflict. Then, do your best to show your love by trying to abide by that agreement.

**ACTION STEPS:**

1. **Make sure there's enough love talked about and demonstrated to far outweigh any conflict.**

2. **If you argue in front of your kids, resolve the conflict in front of them, too.**

3. **Come up with a policy on dealing with conflict, and then stick to it.**

# BORED WITH CHURCH

*My son never seems to pay attention in church. He seems bored and disengaged. What can I do to help him show more interest in worship?*

Start by asking your son why he's bored in church. It might be that he's tired and a later service would be better for him. He might be more engaged if he could sit with his friends from the youth group. His boredom might be something that's easy to cure with a few adjustments.

We live in a time when church worship is changing. Many churches now have "contemporary worship" or "praise" services. And in some towns, churches work together to sponsor occasional non-denominational, community-wide worship events. Young people often enjoy these services because they tend to be less formal than more traditional services. See what you can do to help expose your son to some of these "youth-friendly" worship styles he may find more interesting.

"Some parts of church are boring, like the songs. But when the pastor starts talking, he tells a lot of cool stories. I'd like church better if the songs were more rock 'n' roll and they didn't sing all of them in a row." — Ryan, 11

If this contemporary worship service style seems to connect with your son, investigate what you can do to add a similar type of service at your church. Our congregation has recently begun having a contemporary service once a month on Sunday evenings. That has been such a big hit with our youth and with the younger couples in the church that there's already talk of doing it more often. This certainly doesn't replace the traditional service, it only offers one more way for people to worship.

Finally, help your son find ways he can be involved in the service. Talk to your youth pastor about planning a "youth Sunday" where the young people assist in the service by reading Scripture, singing a worship song, or putting together a dramatic piece. If nothing else, talk to your son about the different elements of the worship service. Help him understand what's going on, and he might find it easier to pay attention. You might even encourage him to take notes about the service, then talk about them afterward.

**ACTION STEPS:**

1. **Participate in a community worship service or prayer event.**

2. **Work with the staff of your church and other families to add an optional contemporary service once a month or so.**

3. **Help your child get involved in the service.**

# IMMATURITY

*Our son doesn't seem to want to grow up. He's 11, but he still plays with children's toys and seems so immature. Should we be worried? Is there anything we can do to help him act his age?*

Chances are your son *is* acting his age. There's an incredible range of "normal" behavior all through adolescence. Visit any middle school in the country and you'll see students who look like they belong in an elementary classroom walking alongside others who could blend in on a high school campus. Talk to middle school teachers and they'll tell you they see that same range in kids' intellectual, emotional, and social development.

As long as you're giving your son age-appropriate choices and responsibilities, he's happy, and his interests and behavior aren't causing him social embarrassment, you can probably relax and enjoy these last days of his "innocence." He'll grow up soon enough, and you'll wonder what happened to those days when you needlessly worried if it was ever going to happen.

**ACTION STEPS:**

1. **Recognize that there's a broad range of "normal" behavior in the preteen years.**
2. **Make sure your child has age-appropriate responsibilities and opportunities.**
3. **Check with your child to find out if he's happy and has friends who enjoy his company.**

# STAYING OVERNIGHT WITH FRIENDS

*Our 11-year-old daughter has trouble spending the night at friends' homes. She always ends up getting "sick" and calling us to come and get her. Is this normal? Should we try to push her to get past her fears or wait until she's ready to spend the night away from us?*

In the great scope of life, whether or not your daughter spends the night away from home really isn't a very big deal. Be careful not to make it one.

Our question for you is: How much does this bother your daughter? Is she embarrassed about having to come home? Is the fact that she's missing out on sleepovers causing her to lose friends? If she's unhappy about the situation, see if she can articulate why this happens. Try to find out what worries or frightens her. Then, if there's an underlying problem, you can address it. If she seems unconcerned, and you're the only one who's bothered by those late night pick-ups, let it go and stop worrying.

Is this behavior consistent with your daughter's personality? Is she usually reluctant to try new experiences? Is she generally the fearful, worrying sort?

If that's the case, you might look for less stressful (or at least different) ways to provide new, stretching experiences for her. Find out what she's interested in and encourage her to pursue those interests. As she discovers her abilities, her self-confidence will grow.

Some practical strategies: Why not host some overnight get-togethers at your house? Or you could go with your daughter and one or more of her friends on some overnight outing, like a camping trip. A few positive experiences such as those may get her past this problem.

**ACTION STEPS:**

1. Determine whether or not this issue bothers your child. If not, let it go.

2. If your child is unhappy, talk about the reasons she might be reluctant to be away from home overnight.

3. Help build her confidence by arranging less stressful social activities for her and her friends.

"If I'm feeling bad about something, I usually go up to my room. Then my dad comes up and tries to make me feel better by telling jokes and stuff. But I wish he wouldn't do that. I just want to be alone." — Ryan, 11

# EARLY PUBERTY

*Our 11-year-old daughter hit puberty before most of her friends. She's very self-conscious about wearing a bra and developing hips while her friends are still skinny little girls. She's already being teased about being "fat," and she's become the subject of gossip for the other girls. How can we help her survive this difficult time?*

We suggest Mom and daughter spend a weekend alone to talk about the physical and emotional changes of adolescence. Let your daughter pick the destination and activity. As you talk, explain that this is part of becoming a woman and that all of her friends will soon be going through the same growing process, albeit at different rates. Answer her questions honestly and be as straightforward as you can.

When our daughter suffered through much the same situation, we felt like it would last forever. But this problem really is short-lived. Your best course of action is to spend plenty of time with your daughter. Remind her often of how beautiful she is—inside and out. Reassure her that she is not fat, just perfectly healthy. Discourage her from dieting. Help her focus on her positive accomplishments.

Help your daughter arrange activities that allow her to spend time with her friends, one at a time. If it's just her and one friend, that friend likely won't tease or make fun of her. And that girl will be less likely to gossip about your daughter.

**ACTION STEPS:**

1. **Plan a mother/daughter weekend to talk about the coming changes and answer her questions.**

2. **Reassure your daughter and help her focus on her inner beauty.**

3. **To keep other girls from ganging up on your daughter, encourage her to spend one-on-one time with her friends.**

WALLY NORTMAN WAS A MASTER AT
BEATING CURFEWS.

# CURFEW

*My son refuses to listen and follow the rules we establish. If his curfew is to be home by 5, he "forgets" and comes home at his leisure. We've tried phoning his friends' parents, walking over to get him, etc. His behavior is constantly contrary to what we ask of him.*

It sounds like you need to have a family conference to discuss what the rules are in your home and what the consequences will be if the rules are broken. Start with the rules that are most important to you. Instead of coming up with a big list, talk only about those rules you are prepared to enforce on a consistent basis, such as curfew. Be sure you also talk about your reasons for setting this rule. Then, ask your son to contribute to the list, adding rules he thinks are important for him to follow.

Next, set logical consequences for each rule. Let him make suggestions there, too. Be specific, and explain exactly what will happen if he forgets to obey the family rules. For example, if he forgets to come home on time, he could be grounded from going to his friends' houses for two or three days. If he forgets again, the grounding increases to four or five days. If he forgets to do his homework, you might have him do the forgotten work, even if he cannot turn it in at school. If he doesn't do his chores, he gets to do extra chores for several days. But don't simply talk with him about the rules and consequences for breaking them. Write them down and leave a space at the bottom of the page for each of you to sign. This "contract" will serve as a reminder of what behavior is expected from your son.

Then stand your ground. This won't work unless you're diligent in enforcing the consequences, with no exceptions. If he misses a birthday party because he's grounded, that's sad—but necessary. If he has been able to disregard your rules with little consequence in the past, expect this to take a while and to be unpleasant. This is the part of parenting that requires determination and courage. But the importance of consistent, unwavering discipline can't be overstated. If the behavior you describe is allowed to continue, you and your son are in for some truly rocky years.

**ACTION STEPS:**

1. **Plan a meeting with your child to talk about family rules. Decide together what rules are important.**

2. **Set out clear, logical consequences for breaking the rules.**

3. **When a rule is broken, apply the consequences consistently.**

# FLIRTING

*My 12-year-old daughter has already become flirtatious with boys. While this might be part of her natural development, I don't want her to get involved with boys too early. What do I do?*

Sometimes it seems every segment of our culture is conspiring to persuade teenage and preteen girls that being attractive to the opposite sex is the most important (if not the sole) measure of their self-worth. Look at any teen magazine and note the number of articles and advertisements that convey this message—over and over and over.

With all that pressure to attract boys, it's no wonder girls start flirting at an early age. But we as parents may be able to reduce the emotional need for flirtation by making sure our daughters are getting plenty of personal affirmation elsewhere. There's nothing wrong with telling our daughters how beautiful they are. But it's a good idea to find other characteristics to praise as well.

When your daughter does something thoughtful or selfless, let her know you respect her for it. Praise her intelligence and initiative as much as you do her appearance. Do the same in pointing out role models. If you make this a habit, eventually, the message will sink in. Even if it doesn't seem to make a difference to her right now, this kind of praise is vital to the development of a strong sense of self worth.

Look for activities and opportunities where she can use and develop a variety of gifts. The more recognition she receives and the greater sense of accomplishment she feels from different sources, the less affirmation she will need from any one source (like boys).

"If I do like somebody, my mom doesn't really care because she knows I'm just in fifth grade and I haven't even grown up, really. So she knows it's just a little stupid thing." — Ashley A., 11

But perhaps the best proactive strategy we'd suggest is this: Make sure your daughter continues to receive a generous supply of appropriate physical affection from her father. Too many young girls fall victim to a sometimes tragic developmental dilemma. At this critical stage in their lives, they find themselves on the uncertain, awkward verge of womanhood and first begin to consider and question their attractiveness to the opposite sex. At the same time, a father's own sense of awkwardness regarding his daughter's growing maturity causes him to change the entire nature of their physical relationship and especially the pattern of how he displays affection to his daughter. (This happens with boys too, to a lesser degree.)

As a result, just when she needs more assurance of her attractiveness to the opposite sex, the most important male figure in her world is pulling away physically. This sudden deprivation of affection can create confusion and a deep sense of rejection. That can lead to a desperate search for male affection.

Even so, you don't need to overreact to flirtation. A certain degree of flirting is normal and healthy. Just make sure that doesn't become the primary source of your daughter's self-esteem. And dads, hug and kiss and hold your preteen and teenage daughters every chance you get. Give them more affection than ever, not less. Be sure they know you think they are beautiful—inside as well as out.

**ACTION STEPS:**

1. **Help build your daughter's sense of worth by praising her accomplishments in many areas. Focus on character and maturity as well as physical appearance.**

2. **Keep the father/daughter relationship strong by maintaining appropriate physical affection.**

3. **Remember that some flirting is normal.**

"When sixth graders have boyfriends and girlfriends, we just say we're 'going out' and walk down the hall together. No one really goes anywhere. So my parents don't care if I say I'm going out with someone, but if we went to the movies or something, then I'd be in trouble." — Ryan, 11

# DATING

*Our 12-year-old has some friends who have started going on "group dates." She's asked us when she can start dating, and to be honest, we aren't sure what to say. We feel like 12 is too young, but other than wanting her to wait a few years, we're not sure what dating guidelines we should establish. Can you help us?*

Now is a good time to make some of these decisions. Talk to some couples in your church or community whom you respect, whose children are in their mid-to-late teens, and ask them how they handled this with their children. Pray and ask for wisdom. Set some guidelines and communicate them clearly to your children.

What you won't find is some foolproof formula. Every family needs to do what makes sense to them. Our children were allowed to go on group dates at 14 and single dates at 16. We started talking to our kids about dating around age 11. We told them these rules and explained why they were important.

We also decided not to have a curfew for our children. Instead, we expect courtesy. Courtesy means that our children tell us where they are going and what they plan to do. Then we determine a reasonable time for them to be home. They arrive home before that time, or they call us to explain why they're taking longer than expected. If their plans change in the middle of the evening, they give us a quick call, just to let us know where they are. We are then courteous and thank them for the call.

For example, if our son, a high school senior, and his girlfriend are going to the movies and the movie ends at 9:30 p.m., we figure that they'll go for something to eat afterward—10:30 p.m.—and then head home. It takes him about 30 minutes to drive her home and get back to our place. So, he agrees to be home by 11 p.m. That's a pretty early curfew for most 18-year-olds! But it fits the evening's plans. And they don't end up driving around—or not driving around—for an extra hour, just because the curfew is midnight.

We would also like to recommend the book *I Kissed Dating Goodbye*, by Joshua Harris. We have listened to some of his audiotapes with our children and discussed what he has to say about dating and boy/girl relationships. We didn't always agree with Mr. Harris, but he presented a fresh, thought-provoking view of the issues that stirred up a lot of good conversation with our kids.

**ACTION STEPS:**

1. Seek advice from other parents you trust.
2. Discuss your dating rules with your children before they start dating.
3. Take a look at Joshua Harris's book *I Kissed Dating Goodbye* for a different perspective on dating.

"My mom always asks me, 'Who's going out with who now? Has anybody asked you out lately?' Then I ask her what she'd say if I did go out with somebody, and she says, 'Personally, I don't want you to go out with anybody.' So I'm like, 'But Mom, you talk about it all the time!' And she says, 'Well, I wouldn't mind if boys called you or anything. I just don't want my daughter growing up too fast.'"

— Jessica, 11

# Thanks...

I was 12 years old when I begged my parents to let me go to a party with a boy named Ned. My parents were very strict and would not allow their children to have boyfriends or girlfriends. Dating was definitely out. But since the party was going to be at our church, they thought my going with a boy would be pretty innocuous.

When the night of the "big event" arrived, Ned showed up at my door, met my parents, and walked me to the church. Everything was going just fine until near the party's end. The other kids decided to sneak away from the adults and have a kissing game. I looked at Ned and said, "Well, it's time for us to go home." Ned didn't put up a fuss. He knew I meant business. In a moment, we were out the door and heading up the street toward my house. After I said goodnight to Ned,

I told my parents why we left the party. They were pleased I'd done the right thing. I believe my mother said something like, "Good for you, Bets!"

I made the right decision that night because of certain realities around my home. First, my parents made sure all six of their children understood what behaviors were proper and what behaviors were improper. A kissing game was simply something you did not do. Second, authority was perfectly clear in my family. We children knew our no-nonsense mother and father were in charge. Third, my parents taught us God's Word and lived what they taught. Their example clearly showed us how a Christian should conduct himself or herself. They set the pace and established the framework for godly values that have guided me throughout my life.

Elisabeth Elliot—author and speaker

# FRIENDS

*Our daughter's friends have started leaving her out of certain things. Yesterday, they "forgot" to tell her they were all wearing their hair a certain way, and she came home in tears. I feel so bad for her, but I'm not sure how to help.*

Friendships between adolescent girls are complex and difficult. We wish we could tell you we have all the answers on this one, but we just don't. The same person who is a girl's best friend one day can be cruel to her the next. And the reverse is true: These friends who are unkind to your daughter today may be completely different tomorrow. We experienced this repeatedly with our daughter, but never with any of our sons.

The first question we'd like to ask you is this: Do you feel good about your daughter being friends with these girls? Or would you just as soon she developed different friendships?

Whatever your answer, a good approach to solving friendship problems is to arrange for your daughter to spend some time alone with each of her friends—or with some girls you'd like for her to develop friendships with. Have your daughter invite one girl to the movies, a play, a concert, a ballgame or whatever. Then a week or so later, she can invite another friend on a similar occasion. This one-on-one time will allow your daughter to renew her friendships with each girl.

If your daughter really clicks with one particular girl, go ahead and encourage them to spend more time together. Knowing she has one trustworthy ally can help your daughter survive the other girls' seeming rejection.

Another approach might be to host some events at your home. Let your daughter invite two or three other girls to spend the night, or to watch a video or to bake brownies—let her pick the activity. There's a certain degree of status and acceptance that comes with being the hostess or organizer of group activities. Giving your daughter that edge may be all she needs to get her through this time.

ACTION STEPS:

1. **Encourage your daughter to spend one-on-one time with these girls to help them rebuild their friendships.**

2. Help your daughter find an ally—one friend she can always count on.

3. Work with your daughter to plan parties or special times for her and her friends at your house.

"I don't mind going some places with my parents. But when I'm going to a movie I'd rather go with my friends, because then I can talk. My parents don't like it and tell me to be quiet. It's just more fun to go with my friends." — Glenn, 11

# MAKEUP

*Our 12-year-old daughter wants to wear makeup. Do you think she's too young?*

Now that your daughter is almost a teenager, it's a good time to set some guidelines about her appearance. Contact some parents whose children attend your daughter's school and whom you respect to find out how they've handled this. Then sit down with your daughter and come up with an acceptable timeline for wearing makeup. Let her express her opinion, then work out an agreement together.

As you talk, keep these tips in mind:

• Remind her that she's beautiful just the way she is. It's bothersome to see beautiful teenage girls who feel like they need to spend 40 minutes "getting ready" each morning so they feel presentable in public. Makeup seems to be a part of our culture, but girls shouldn't feel like they're unacceptable without it.

• Try not to make a big deal about it. Some issues are worth setting your foot down on; this isn't one of them. As long as your daughter isn't wearing too much makeup, look on it as a learning experience. Maybe Mom can even go with her to the cosmetics department to get a facial and a lesson on how to wear makeup. Odds are, if you don't make an issue of this, your daughter won't pick this area as one to rebel about.

• Your daughter's request isn't unusual. Most of the families we know let their daughters start wearing makeup at 12 or 13. While this may seem early, it's actually a good time to tackle this issue. This is a stage where you still have a good deal of influence on how much and when your daughter wears makeup. A year or two from now, your daughter might not be as willing to accept your advice.

ACTION STEPS:

1. Get insight from other parents of teenage girls.
2. Work with your daughter to come up with some guidelines for when she can wear makeup and how much is appropriate.
3. Keep emphasizing her natural beauty.


# HYGIENE

*Our 12-year-old son won't take a shower more than once or twice a week. Because of this, his hair looks dirty, his skin is greasy and he has a definite odor. He doesn't see the problem, so how can we get him to pay attention to his personal hygiene?*

Your son sounds like a pretty normal preadolescent boy. Our youngest son, who is 11, walks out the door in the morning and dirt jumps on him. That's the only explanation we have for how the same kid whose Sunday morning outfit seems so presentable leaving home can look like the sole survivor of a natural disaster by the time he gets into the sanctuary.

Most boys this age seem to have been endowed by God with an unexplainable affinity for dirt. They love being in it. And they certainly don't mind it being on them. Very few of them see any point in worrying about dirt or voluntarily taking showers more than once or twice a week (if that often). We wouldn't worry too much about trying to change such common preadolescent male instincts. Our experience has been that boys' seeming aversion to soap, showers, deodorant, and basic hygiene disappears about the time they discover girls.

Still, you don't have to wait for that to happen. You can explain to your son that part of growing up and becoming a man (which most 10- to 12-year-old boys want very badly to do very quickly) means that his maturing body sweats more and he actually needs to bathe more (not less) than when he was little. If necessary, make better personal hygiene an absolute prerequisite for some of his favorite activities. Tell him he can only go to the mall or a friend's house after he's made himself presentable. He'll soon get the idea.

**ACTION STEPS:**

1. **Recognize that this is a normal stage in a boy's life.**

2. **Explain that frequent bathing is a necessity for young men.**

3. **Determine times when showering is a must—before church or an activity with friends.**

# THE INTERNET

*I've discovered that our 12-year-old son has been visiting pornographic sites on the Internet. I'm so disappointed! I want him to stop immediately, but I don't want to cause a break in our relationship or encourage him to be more secretive about this problem.*

This is a problem that should be addressed immediately. Sit your son down, alone, and let him know what you have discovered and how you discovered it, opening the door for him to explain.

Do not ask him if he has done this. When we were new parents, a wise friend gave us some excellent advice: If you know your child has done something wrong, don't ever ask him if he did it. That creates the opportunity for him to lie. In fact, you are tempting him to lie. And if he lies, you've got a second problem on your hands, which makes it difficult to ever discuss the first issue. It's better to talk about what you know and how you know it and let your son take it from there.

There is a real possibility that he got onto the sites by accident. Some porn sites have Web addresses only one letter off from frequently visited children's sites. We know plenty of adults, including ourselves, who have inadvertently found porn sites while doing research on the Internet.

So start out assuming the best. Once you've told your son what you found, listen to what he has to say. His explanation should give you a sense of how serious the problem is. Whatever the case, take this opportunity to talk to him about Internet safety and about the dangers of pornography.

Many Internet service providers include "parental controls" where you can set limits on what your child can—and can't—do online. Whether your son found these pornographic sites by accident or on purpose, using these controls or installing filtering software is one way to make sure it doesn't happen again. In addition to that, it's appropriate to pay closer attention to what he's doing when he's on the Internet. Make sure your computer is not in an office area or a bedroom where your son can easily spend countless hours wandering around the cyber-world unsupervised, ending up in places seedier than most of us can even imagine. Instead, set up the computer in a public area of the house.

The Internet presents all kinds of issues our parents never had to face—some good, some not so good. It's essential that we do all we can to educate ourselves about the new problems created by our quickly changing society.

**ACTION STEPS:**

1. **Present the information you have calmly and matter-of-factly.**

2. **Listen to your child's explanation and determine how serious the problem is.**

3. **Reduce the temptation by keeping the computer in a public room in the house.**

# POOR CHOICES

*We think our 12-year-old is in with the wrong crowd. He listens to hard rock with questionable lyrics, and we're pretty sure he's been smoking. We don't want to make all his decisions for him, but he seems to be choosing so poorly.*

This is a confusing age. Kids are pushing for independence, yet survey after survey shows that young teens wish their parents were more involved in their lives. The trick is finding the balance.

You can and should maintain a deliberate and active role in his life while recognizing his growing need for independence by giving him limited and acceptable choices. Sure it takes time and effort on your part, but abdicating all control to a 12-year-old is asking for much bigger trouble in the years ahead.

Set some hard-and-fast rules on those things you feel most concerned about—like smoking—and talk with your son about consequences and penalties for crossing those lines. Then stick to your word. To keep him from feeling completely powerless, be willing to show some flexibility in other areas. But talk through your expectations and his as you set reasonable guidelines and consequences for crossing the line.

Your son might also benefit from some one-on-one time with Dad or another adult male he trusts. Plan a guys' getaway at a location of your son's choice. Use the time together to talk about his recent decisions. Talk about possible situations where it's essential that your son think for himself rather than follow the crowd. Share your concerns, fears, and uncertainties about this stage in his life. Let him know you'll be learning to let go at the same time he's pushing for independence, and admit you'll both make mistakes. Ask him to be forgiving and to feel confident about approaching you with problems. Pray together and ask God to guide him as he makes decisions.

Perhaps the most important point to remember is this: All teenagers will be involved in some risk-taking behavior. It's one way they stretch themselves to prove their growing maturity. The challenge for those of us who love those teenagers is to help direct them into healthy independence and risk-taking activities, like roller-coaster rides or skateboarding.

Allowing and even helping our kids take acceptable risks and try new experiences is one of the hardest things parents ever do. But if we want our kids to become independent, it's a job requirement.

**ACTION STEPS:**

1. Lay out ground rules and consequences for acceptable and unacceptable behavior.

2. Take a dad and son retreat to talk about the changes in your son, your concerns, and ways to get through the coming years together.

3. Encourage healthy risk-taking to help build your son's sense of maturity and independence.

"My mom knows the boys at my school because I've been friends with a lot of them for a long time. So she wouldn't care if I was going out with someone she knew and liked, but if I brought over some punk and said, 'This is my new boyfriend,' I think she'd be like, 'Don't go out with him.'"
— Brittany S., 11

## Thanks...

As Dad's car crunched the gravel of our driveway at the end of his workday, I ran to greet him. I didn't give him time to shed his mechanic's overalls before I dragged him to the back yard. He knelt beside me to look into a plastic ice cream bucket.

It held five springtime frogs.

With pride, I recounted where and how I had captured each frog along the creek. Dad's full attention was much more of a compliment than any words he might have offered.

Dad watched patiently as I showed my frog skills. I set a frog on the ground, gently touched it with a finger and caught it as it leaped. Then the next, and the next. After the last frog had performed, Dad spoke his soft words: "Now, son, let's walk down to the creek and let them go."

Let them go? I had lined the bucket with grass. Put a rock in the bucket. Added water. Punched air holes in the plastic lid.

There was room for the bucket on a shelf in my bedroom. Let them go?

"I don't want to," I said. "I caught them. They're mine."

"No," he said, his voice still soft. "They don't belong to you. Letting them go is something you have to do. And I'll help."

More than 30 years have passed since that spring afternoon. I remember it so clearly because of its impact on me. Not only because of the implicit lesson about respecting God's creatures, but because of my father's guidance.

By his attentiveness he allowed me to be the boy that I was; by his firmness he pointed me toward growth. Even though I protested his decision that day, I still remember the grudging, intuitive sense I had that my father was right. And part of me was relieved that I wasn't allowed to do what was wrong.

Sigmund Brouwer—author

# SWEARING

*I've heard my son swear casually a couple times in the last week. I'm sure he's picked it up from school and movies, but I don't like it. How can I show him that it's not cool to curse?*

The first thing you need to do is tell him what you heard and explain that you're concerned. (Don't ask him what he said, because this invites him to lie to escape punishment.) Tell him how you feel about swearing and why. The Bible is clear in its instruction that we are not to take the Lord's name in vain (Ex. 20:7). And it has much more to say about the use of our tongues and the significance of what comes out of our mouths (Ps. 39:1; Col. 3:8; James 1:26).

Swearing isn't only against God's will, it's a crude, undignified, and uncreative means of communication. Let your son know that few people will be impressed by his swearing—those who do it all the time will think nothing of it, and those who don't might be offended and think less of him. So from a practical social standpoint, there is nothing to be gained from swearing, but much that can be lost in terms of respect.

Of course, no amount of lecturing will do any good unless you are a good example in this area. If you don't swear, point that out, and you'll have a much easier time holding your son to a high standard when it comes to language. If you do swear, even occasionally, you'll need to work on your own problem before you'll have any credibility in this area.

Once your son knows what you expect and why, set some appropriate consequences for any offensive language you hear. Reinforce your beliefs by commenting on and discussing offensive and inappropriate language when you hear it—whether it's in a movie or TV show you watch together or just something you overhear. Part of the reason bad language has become so common is that so many of us don't even notice it anymore. When we ignore it, we may actually be adding to the problem.

**ACTION STEPS:**

1. **Tell your child you're concerned about swearing and explain why you feel the way you do.**

2. Set a good example with your own language.

3. Help your child become aware of inappropriate language by pointing it out and discussing it when you hear it.

# DIETING

*My son just wants to eat all the time. He's gaining weight and is starting to look a little heavy. Should I put him on a diet?*

We wouldn't recommend it. Your son is probably just going through a growth spurt. A lot of children gain weight, then grow in height to match the weight—it's a normal pattern of growth, particularly at this age. If you're concerned about his health, talk to your family doctor.

If the doctor feels your child is healthy, we would suggest you worry less about how much he's eating and monitor *what* he's eating instead. If he's pigging out on potato chips and sugar-filled soft drinks, that could be a problem. Kids this age do a lot of growing and need a lot of nutritious food. If they fill their stomachs with junk food, they probably won't get their nutritional needs met. Then they'll just keep eating.

So provide your son with lots of snack options that taste good and have some nutritional value. For example, corn chips and salsa are more nutritious than potato chips and dip. Animal crackers are lower in fat than candy bars. Ice cream has some nutritional value and frozen yogurt even more. Fruit smoothies are a big trend right now, so keep plenty of fresh or frozen fruit on hand and show your son how to make himself a healthy, satisfying snack.

You know what your son likes to snack on; it's up to you to provide him with healthier alternatives.

**ACTION STEPS:**

1. Talk to your family doctor to rule out any health problems.

2. Pay attention to what your child is eating, rather than how much he's eating.

3. Provide healthy snacks and lots of 'em.

# VIDEO GAMES

*Our 11-year-old is obsessed with violent video games and slasher movies. We don't allow these things at our house, but he has access to them at friends' homes and the local arcade. Is this normal? What can we do about it?*

Normal? Lots of folks might say yes. But that doesn't mean you have to like it, or allow it.

There is a pile of evidence showing the detrimental effects of viewing violent movies and television, and yet the violence in our entertainment keeps getting more prevalent and graphic. And research on violent video games is in some ways even more disturbing—one expert has stated that these games to a better job of training killers than military exercises do.

Most kids will say things like, "It's just entertainment." "It's fun." "I know it's not real." "I'd never do anything like that in real life. I know better!" You need to let your son know that's not the point. Research also overwhelmingly shows that the more exposure our society has to violent images, the more desensitized people become to it. Even the gentlest and most balanced individuals can become more tolerant and accepting of violence (both real and simulated)—to the point that it's no longer so upsetting and may be viewed almost fatalistically as "unavoidable."

So let your son know it's not so much that you're worried exposure to violent entertainment will turn him into a copycat homicidal psychopath. Explain that this is more than a moral issue; it's a serious social problem on which you want to take a stand. And if enough people took such a stand, the entertainment industry would have to change.

Talk about God's view of peace and his desire that we strive to love life and seek peace (see Ps. 34:14 and 1 Pet. 3:8-12).

Hold to your principles at home. And let your son know how strongly you feel about it by limiting his outings to arcades and the homes of friends whose parents don't share your values. Help your son think up activities he and his friends can do that you can feel good about.

You can't shelter your son from every bad influence society throws at him, but you should never shrug your shoulders and give up.

**ACTION STEPS:**

1. **Recognize that violent images have an impact on children.**

2. **Talk to your son about your feelings and your desire to promote peace.**

3. **Encourage your son to find alternative forms of entertainment.**

# PLAYING FOOTBALL

*My 12-year-old son wants to play tackle football at school next year. My husband thinks it will be a good experience for him, but I'm not so sure—it seems pretty rough, and I don't want him to get severely injured.*

All of our kids have played organized sports. But only two of our four boys played football—and then for a limited time. When our oldest son first went out for football, we were worried sick about possible injuries. But that was never a problem. The problem we did find was that his school all but worshiped football players. As a member of the team, our son's social status changed radically. Cheerleaders who'd never paid any attention to him were suddenly decorating his locker every week. His name was called out during pep rallies. Everyone in the school soon knew who he was. Girls began to notice him.

After two years of football, our son quit. He was better at other sports and enjoyed them more. He didn't like the false attention. And we were relieved.

In order for your family to make a decision, one of you should go with your son to the try-outs. Look the competition over. Is your son significantly smaller than the other boys? If so, you might need to encourage him to wait another year. But if your son wants to play and doesn't seem to be out-sized by the other players, you probably should let him try out for the team.

You can also talk to other parents about the coaches. Do they have a balanced attitude toward winning, or are they fiercely competitive? Do they encourage and teach their players or merely yell and scream at them?

In our sports-crazed society, being an athlete can give a child a false sense of what's important in the world. Yet sports also can provide positive experiences in which your son can learn the value of teamwork and relationships, the price of success, the effort required to achieve excellence, self-control, accountability to authority, humility, perseverance, performance under pressure, how to handle success and failure, and endurance in the face of pain and hardship.

The positive value of sports is more apt to come through when parents stay involved to support, affirm their children's efforts, and closely monitor the situation. So let your son try out and reevaluate his involvement often.

## ACTION STEPS:

1. Take a look at the other kids to determine if your child is physically ready to compete.

2. Talk to other parents about the coach's style. Make sure you're comfortable with the example the coach sets and the level of competitiveness he or she expects.

3. Stay involved in your child's sport to help him get the most from the experience.

## Thanks...

When I was 11 years old, I dreamed of becoming a famous singer. So when I heard about a local talent show, I just knew I had to enter. In my young mind, it would be my first "big break." But the problem was, I had to attend six consecutive rehearsals on Monday nights. And my dad would have to take me. I begged, "Dad, please, I just have to do this!"

Without a whole lot of hesitation, my father said yes and committed himself to driving me several miles every Monday night for six weeks in a row. Not only that, but he had to sit for a couple of hours while the other kids and I went through our less-than-exciting rehearsals.

This experience may sound like such a little sacrifice, but my dad worked 12-hour days as a telephone repairman. He came home exhausted—and hungry. A few Monday nights he got home so late that I met him at the door and insisted that we leave immediately. He'd willingly miss his supper so I could chase my crazy dream.

Seemingly insignificant experiences like this one show just how involved my father was in my life. He had his eye on me. In his own quiet way, he somehow connected with the hopes, dreams and longings of his 11-year-old daughter.

Margaret Becker—singer and songwriter

# QUITTING

*Our daughter is on the school soccer team, but she's not one of the best players and always sits on the bench. She wants to quit the team because she never gets in the games. We want her to stick it out for the rest of the season. It's caused quite a bit of tension around the house. Any ideas?*

Learning to finish what you start is an important lesson. One of our family rules is that once we have made a commitment, we see it through.

When our son was in middle school he joined the band. After a few months, he wanted to quit. We sat him down and talked to him about the importance of persistence, the value of sticking with a commitment. We told him that at the end of the year, he could choose something else but he couldn't quit in the middle of the year. He was very unhappy and thought we were being unreasonable. But by the end of that year, he signed up for another year! And he has stayed in the band throughout junior high and high school. He is glad now that we were "mean" and insisted that he stick with it.

On the other hand, one time another of our sons won a small role in a community play. The director's demands and excessive practice hours took their toll. Finally, after several weeks of rehearsals, the unreasonable schedule was affecting our son's schoolwork and his sleep. We not only allowed him to quit, we encouraged it. While we wanted him to learn to see things through, we also wanted him to learn to balance priorities—and the play was simply not worth the time and energy he was putting into it.

While sitting on the bench can be discouraging, your daughter can learn from the experience. Help her see that she can still play an important role by supporting her teammates and doing her best when she does play. She can be a great example of good sportsmanship to others.

This whole experience can teach your daughter one of life's most valuable lessons: No one gets to be the star all the time. Supporting roles are important, too (1 Cor. 12:14-26).

**ACTION STEPS:**

1. Encourage your child to finish out her commitment.

2. If the activity is interfering with school or affecting your child's well being, determine if the activity is really worth the sacrifice.

3. Help your child see the positive side of her involvement.

"My parents don't really notice when I'm depressed. I just go to my room and listen to music. I don't really involve my parents in my personal life. I like it that way." — Jenny, 12

# DEPRESSION

*Our 12-year-old daughter has suddenly withdrawn from us and stays locked in her room most of the evening. I'm afraid she might be depressed. What can we do to help her?*

Moodiness is a common characteristic of kids approaching and going through puberty. If this is a fairly new problem, you might want to give it a few days to see if it passes.

If the behavior persists, or if your child has very suddenly gone from a happy, outgoing child to a sullen, withdrawn one, you need to pay close attention. Sudden changes in a child's behavior are often signals that something significant has happened or is happening in his or her life. Parents need to note these things, so this is definitely worth your attention. Your first step, then, is to try to identify what may have triggered your daughter's withdrawal. Start by reaching out to her. She can choose to withdraw, but that doesn't mean you have to leave her alone to feel isolated. Go into her room, or better yet, take her to some neutral place like a restaurant or park. Let her know you've noticed the change, that you love her, and that you are concerned about her.

Merely giving her the opportunity to talk may open the floodgates. Just knowing you care and are there for her might be enough to draw her out of her emotional doldrums.

If she can't or won't articulate what's bothering her, if her withdrawal continues for more than a couple of weeks, or if she shows additional symptoms of depression (dropping grades, lack of appetite, sleeplessness, wildly fluctuating emotions, isolation from friends, etc.), we recommend taking her to a counselor. If you sense any morbid fascination with or talk of death, or if you hear her even mention the subject of death or suicide, get her professional help immediately. Depression among young people is becoming more and more common. It can result from emotional causes, but sometimes it's chemical or physical. Whatever the cause, clinical depression calls for more help than parents should attempt to give on their own.

## ACTION STEPS:

1. Look for a sudden or lasting change in behavior to distinguish real depression from normal preteen moodiness.

2. Take the initiative to talk to your child and find out what's bothering her.

3. Consider professional counseling if your child won't talk about her feelings or shows other signs of depression.

"If I get depressed, my mom and dad usually talk to me and share a verse from the Bible. Like once when I was worried about doing bad on a test, they showed me where it says to cast all your worries on God. It helped."

— Ben, 11

# DISABILITY

*Our child has a disability that affects the way she walks. She's already struggled with issues of self-esteem, and we think her struggles will only get worse as she enters junior high. How can we help her feel more confident?*

The junior high years are hard for anyone. They are especially hard for those who are considered different, particularly a child with a disability.

To get some ideas on how to help your daughter, we talked to our friends whose college-age daughter has cerebral palsy and walks with the aid of leg braces. Here's their advice on how to guide a child successfully through these deep waters:

• Encourage your child to pursue something she does well. For their daughter, this was band. It took a caring band director who encouraged her and made the necessary accommodations for her to really do well. Her parents saw her potential in this area and hired a band tutor who helped their daughter excel. She even marched with the marching band!

• Be positive. In every situation, there is a bright side. For everything your child cannot do because of her disability, there are things she can do. Focus on what she can do and on the wonderful person she is. Praise her efforts and her personal strengths. Take every opportunity to affirm her.

• Keep the lines of communication open. With our friends, it was Dad who teased their daughter in a good-natured way and got her to laugh at her problems. Mom was the one she could go to for a shoulder to cry on. There is no substitute for taking time to listen to your child and to talk with her.

• Do what you can to make it better. Our friend and her daughter spent hours shopping for shoes, looking for something she could walk in that didn't look too out of style. Mom knew that this mattered to her child, so she spent time on it.

• Accept the things you cannot do. No matter how much you try to protect your daughter, she will undoubtedly face some rough days.

All teenagers do. Your child has the opportunity to build her self-esteem by tackling these challenges and overcoming the problems.

**ACTION STEPS:**

1. **Help your child find areas where she can succeed and build her confidence.**

2. **Encourage your child to talk about her struggles.**

3. **Do what you can to help your child take on the challenges of adolescence and overcome them.**

# SEXUAL ABUSE

*Our daughter just confided in us that a family friend has been molesting her. We are devastated and confused. We have known this man for years and have a hard time believing he could do something like this. But we don't want to dismiss our daughter's claims if they are true. We just don't know what to believe or what to do next.*

Devastation and confusion are very reasonable reactions to what you've been told. You clearly don't want your daughter further victimized or to feel as if you aren't responsive to her cry for help; but neither do you want to see your friend hurt, his reputation damaged and your relationship destroyed. So if you honestly don't know what or who to believe (and even if you do), you have a horrible dilemma that you need to address now.

Several things need to happen right away—perhaps simultaneously. You need to discuss this with your daughter. Ideally, it would be good for her to talk with both you and your spouse. But chances are she may feel more comfortable talking about such a difficult subject with just one of you. Let her make that call.

Tell her you realize what a difficult thing this is for her to talk about. Also affirm her for making the decision to tell you. Assure her that your first concern is her welfare, that you love her, that this is in no way her fault, and that you intend to make sure that nothing like this ever happens to her again.

You need to be honest with her. Let her know how shocked you are. Explain that this is why you need to hear from her some details as to when and what exactly happened—so you'll be able to make certain it does not occur again. But you need to be careful about demonstrating or acting out your emotional reaction to what you hear. Your daughter has come to you in hopes you will be able to exert some control and protection; if you go out of control, she may clam up or decide she made a mistake by telling you.

A long heart-to-heart talk about what has been happening will most likely help clear up any doubts or questions you have. We know of cases where false accusations have been made, but you need to be prepared for the greater likelihood that what your daughter is telling you is the painful truth. You'll have a lot better sense of that after you talk with her.

No matter what your conclusion, two other things need to happen right away. For the time being, you need to make sure there is absolutely no private contact between your friend and your daughter. And if it's at all possible, you should avoid even any public contact between the two. Doing this protects them both.

In addition, you need to find a professional Christian counselor for your daughter. Any child who has been molested is going to have issues to work through that parents just aren't equipped to deal with. And in the off chance your daughter's accusations are false, she will need an experienced counselor to get to the bottom of that behavior. Also, if you still don't know what to believe, a good therapist may be able to clarify things for you. Don't just pick a therapist's name out of the yellow pages. Get a recommendation from your pastor or some other trusted professional who knows the therapist's experience.

Even after you've taken those crucial first steps of listening, protecting, and seeking professional help, you're still going to be left with a terrible dilemma. How will you present this to the authorities? When should you talk to a school counselor to get help on that end? What else do you need to do to protect your daughter? To protect others who could be future victims? To see justice done?

Different families will answer those questions differently. They are never easy. Just be sure to include your daughter in some of those discussions. She needs to sense a measure of involvement and personal determination as well as your protection and control.

Take these first steps right away. The best course of action will become clearer after that.

ACTION STEPS:

1. Talk to your child to find out what happened and when. Make sure your child knows you love her and that the abuse isn't her fault.

2. Avoid any contact with the accused abuser.

3. Seek professional Christian counseling immediately. Don't try to deal with this on your own.

# SASSINESS

*Our 11-year-old daughter has started to take a very sassy attitude with us. She talks back, uses a lot of sarcasm, and even makes fun of us sometimes. We'd like to stop this problem before it's too late. What can we do?*

Confront this as soon as it happens. Calmly explain that part of your job as her parent is to teach her courtesy and manners. Let her know that sarcasm and disrespect will not be tolerated at home because she needs to learn that they won't serve her well out in the world. Explain that there will be consequences if she continues with this negative behavior.

What should the consequences be? That depends on what's important to your child. Does she really like television or video games? You can ground her from one or the other. You could ground her from friends for a day or two, if that is what matters to her. Another possibility is to take away her phone privileges, again for a day or two.

This approach addresses the immediate problem, which needs to be handled directly and promptly. But there is a more subtle issue at work here. This behavior may signal that your relationship with your child needs some work.

Spend some time thinking and praying about your child's needs. Could she be feeling neglected and looking for attention—even negative attention? Is she being given an appropriate degree of independence? Perhaps her new behavior is a misguided effort to pull away from you and establish herself as her own person. If so, look for ways to give her new choices and new responsibilities that are acceptable. Or could she feel like she is being allowed too much freedom? That's scary for a kid this age; preteens sometimes feel they are in over their heads. Finally, take a close look at her friends. Are they contributing to the problem? If so, talk to your daughter about their influence.

If you're not sure what's going on with your daughter, ask her. Spend some time with your daughter and investigate this behavior.

**ACTION STEPS:**

1. Make it clear to your child that disrespectful behavior has to stop.

2. Set out consequences for sassiness and disrespect.

3. Talk to your child about what's going on and find out why she's expressing herself this way.

"If I want something, my mom's like, 'You're not buying that.' And I'm like, 'But I have my own money!' And she's like, 'No.' I don't get a choice."

— Ashley A., 11

# RESPECT

*Our daughter and her friends sometimes say mean things about their teachers and make fun of older people at our church. They would never do these things to the person's face, but we're bothered by the mean-spirited attitude. How can we teach her to show more respect to adults?*

First, address the issue directly. Tell your daughter you're disappointed in her behavior and concerned about her attitude toward adults. You might consider doing a little Bible study on the subject ahead of time and pointing out Scripture that talks about respecting our elders and people in authority (look at Titus 3:1-5).

The Bible also tells us that the way we treat "the least of these" (people who are poor, weak, ill or disadvantaged in any way—which would include the elderly) is viewed by God as a measure of how we would treat Jesus (Matt. 25:31-46). As Christians, we are supposed to be known by the love we show. It sounds like your daughter and her friends are falling short in this area and need to rethink their attitudes.

You might also remind your daughter that no matter what her peers do, she has a choice: she can be a follower who goes with the crowd, or she can be a leader who stands up for what she believes and helps influence others.

The second dimension of your strategy would be this: Look for ways to give your daughter more experience interacting with older people in your church or community. One friend of ours saw it as his Christian service and a valuable parenting tool to be a volunteer. He spent time helping elderly people in his community with household chores and repairs. And he made a point to take his two children along to help. They not only learned the importance of selfless service, they became much more empathetic and sensitive to the needs of the elderly folks who became their friends.

Perhaps there are even service projects the young people in your church could do to assist some of the older members of your congregation. A little more cross-generational interaction could benefit your daughter and her friends. We're guessing their attitudes would change pretty quickly if they could only get to know the folks they're making fun of.

**ACTION STEPS:**

1. Talk to your child about the biblical basis for respecting adults and people in authority.

2. Encourage her to influence her friends, rather than be influenced by them.

3. Provide opportunities—service projects or volunteering—for your child to get to know older people.

# CRUELTY TO ANIMALS

*Our son gets some kind of sick pleasure in being cruel to animals, to the point of sometimes killing some small, helpless ones, like mice. How can we teach him to respect life?*

At the risk of sounding like alarmists, we think you need to do more than look for ways to teach your son to respect life. The kind of behavior you describe is often indicative of deep emotional problems that most parents simply aren't trained to deal with. To be sure your son gets the help he needs, as well as for your own peace of mind, we strongly recommend professional counseling. It's essential to deal with this problem before the situation becomes more serious.

Cruelty to animals is a warning flag that demands some sort of response. Don't ignore it.

**ACTION STEPS:**

1. Be aware that this is deeply disturbing behavior.

2. Know that this is a problem parents really can't deal with on their own.

3. Seek professional counseling.

# ANGER

*My son is prone to sudden outbursts of anger, and I'm concerned he could become violent. How can I help him control his anger?*

Lots of kids—preteens in particular—have problems controlling their tempers. Better, more mature management of their emotional life is something all kids this age need to learn.

As is often the case in communicating with young people, the best time to discuss the issue of your child's outbursts is not at the time of the explosion. Instead, find a quiet, non-threatening setting (preferably during or right after some positive experience or interaction) when you can express your concern. As you talk about your concerns, it's important to deal with both aspects of this issue—your son's feelings of intense anger, and the behaviors he exhibits as he deals with these feelings.

Start with the anger itself. There's nothing wrong with anger. It's a perfectly normal feeling. Scripture speaks of anger not as a sin, but as an emotion that can quickly lead to sin if not controlled (Prov. 29:11; James 1:19). Psychology tells us that anger is usually a natural reaction to one of three things: pain, frustration, or fear. You and your son may or may not be able to identify the cause of his anger, but it won't hurt to try. Any insight he offers might help you identify practical strategies for channeling his anger. Has he been, or is he being, hurt by some person, experience, or circumstance in his life? Is something frustrating him—something going on in his life that he feels helpless to do anything about? Is he worried or fearful about something?

Even if you can answer these questions and understand the reasons behind your son's anger, the problem still isn't solved. Of equal concern is the expression of his anger. You'll need to come up with a plan of action for helping him manage his anger. Many school counselors have resource material to help with anger management. Ask your son's school for a copy of such resources. Your youth pastor might also have access to these kinds of materials.

Please realize there is a real difference between anger and violence. If your son's angry behavior already has reached the stage where he's being violent and actually endangering himself, you, or others, we'd recommend taking additional steps right away. Get him in to see a professional counselor who can help all of you get a better grip on this problem.

**ACTION STEPS:**

1. **Find a time when your child is calm and in a good mood to talk about your concerns.**

2. **Ask your child about possible reasons for his intense anger.**

3. **Talk to a school counselor or youth pastor about anger management.**

# SCHOOL VIOLENCE

*Our son recently got beat up at school, and we're not sure what to do about it. Should we tell him to fight back, turn the other cheek, tell a teacher? We just don't know what approach is best.*

Our experience tells us you first need to find out exactly what happened. Have your son describe the details of the incident and the events that led up to it. If you can, talk separately to others who witnessed the altercation—your son's friend, a teacher, or another adult. Be sure you let your son know that you aren't discounting his version, but that you want to get as complete a picture as possible in order to know how to respond.

No matter what the situation, we would emphasize that fighting, even in self-defense, is seldom a productive solution to conflict. Most schools these days take a hard line on violence. Students who get into fights, no matter how the fight starts, will very possibly be severely disciplined. So you would do well to review the incident with your son and talk about things he might have done to avoid the fight.

That doesn't necessarily mean your son has to accept the role of victim. Encourage your son to go to a teacher on his own any time he feels threatened. Because schools are more sensitive to the issue of violence today, most teachers and administrators will be responsive.

Finally, whatever the circumstances of this first incident, you need to go talk to the teacher or administrator yourself. Let them know you don't want your son to get in any more fights. Let the school officials know you'll be glad to do whatever you can to make sure it doesn't happen again, and let them know you'd like to enlist their help as well. By doing so, you'll demonstrate you're a concerned parent who supports their own concern over school violence. Most importantly, your involvement and continued concern for your son's well-being will be yet another way to show your love for him.

**ACTION STEPS:**

1. Talk to your son and anyone else who may have witnessed the incident to get a full picture of what happened.

2. Encourage your child to talk to a teacher whenever he feels threatened.

3. Meet with school administrators to seek their input and involvement.

"I'm afraid I'll have trouble with my locker and that my older brother and his friends will make fun of me. My parents try to help, but they're not really very helpful because they just don't get the situation. They talk about when they were in school, but they went to school a long, long time ago." — Alison, 11

# LISTENING IN:

*Here's what 10-to 12-year-olds have to say...*

### ... about allowances:

"I have to save some of my allowance for church, then my dad helps me set short-term, medium-term, and long-term goals for the rest. Long-term is like college, medium-term is like a bike, and short-term is 'spending money.' It's really helping me learn to think for the future." — *Ben, 11*

"I don't get an allowance, but I do get money from babysitting. My parents want me to spend my money wisely, but because I earned the money myself, they let me do what I want with it. I think it's good that they don't give me guidelines, because that way I learn on my own without them pushing me." — *Ashley B., 11*

"My parents told me I have to put a certain amount of money aside for church and for my savings account every time I get my allowance." — *Kelly, 11*

"If I want something, my mom's like, 'You're not buying that.' And I'm like, 'But I have my own money!' And she's like, 'No.' I don't get a choice." — *Ashley A., 11*

"I have to put 50 percent of my allowance in my savings, and I'm told to save it up for something important in the future." — *John, 12*

"I really like the mall, and whenever I go there, I always see something I want. My mom always says, 'Save your money for something else.' But one time I bought something, and I spent a lot of money on it, and I never really wore it. My mom was like, 'I told you to wait until you really wanted something.'" — Taryne, 11

### ... about junior high fears:

"I was deadly afraid that I was going to get stuffed in my locker, but now that I'm there, no one's planned to stuff me." — *Scott, 12*

"I'm afraid I'll have trouble with my locker and that my older brother and his friends will make fun of me. My parents try to help, but they're not really very helpful because they just don't get the situation. They talk about when they were in school, but they went to school a long, long time ago." — *Alison, 11*

"Drugs. I know there's a big problem with drugs at my middle school because my older brother gets offered a lot of drugs. My parents say that if I just say no I won't get bothered, but I don't know." — *Brittany N., 11*

"My camp counselor last year said junior high is the worst because everyone just judges you on your clothes, how you look, and what you do. I'm afraid people are going to be like, 'You wore that yesterday? You're really stupid.'" — *Taryne, 11*

"What I worry about is that I'm not going to get all my homework done and I'll get in trouble a lot and have to go to the principal." — *Daniel, 10*

"I was afraid of forgetting my locker combination. So over the summer, my parents got extra locks and I had to open each one 20 times a day for practice. I got used to combinations." — *Jenny, 12*

### ... about church:

"My parents just say it's God's rules that you have to go to church." — *Jessica, 11*

"Some parts of church are boring, like the songs. But when the pastor starts talking, he tells a lot of cool stories. I'd like church better if the songs were more rock 'n' roll and they didn't sing all of them in a row." — *Ryan, 11*

"I used to not like church because I felt like I didn't understand what was going on. My mom said that if you go you'll learn more and you'll have fun because you'll know more. Also, God is God—he's the one who made us and you should learn more about him."
— *Daniel, 10*

"I don't like the service. The sermon's fine, but all the singing and stuff ... you just stand there and look stupid. Last time, my dad said that if I didn't sing in the service, he'd take $20 off my allowance."
— *A.J., 11*

"Our old church was really boring, so we switched to a different one. They sang songs that sounded like you were singing in a funeral, they were so slow. I like our new church, but sometimes when I wake up in the morning I'm like, 'Why do we have to go?" and Mom's like, 'Because we do'--that's her reason. I don't get much say in that."
— *Kelly, 11*

### ... about dating:

"When sixth graders have boyfriends and girlfriends, we just say we're 'going out' and walk down the hall together. No one really goes anywhere. So my parents don't care if I say I'm going out with someone, but if we went to the movies or something, then I'd be in trouble." — *Ryan, 11*

"If I do like somebody, my mom doesn't really care because she knows I'm just in fifth grade and I haven't even grown up, really. So she knows it's just a little stupid thing." — *Ashley A., 11*

"My mom knows the boys at my school because I've been friends with a lot of them for a long time. So she wouldn't care if I was going out with someone she knew and liked, but if I brought over some punk and said, 'This is my new boyfriend,' I think she'd be like, 'Don't go out with him.'" — *Brittany S., 11*

"My mom's always telling me what to do if someone likes me—to go ask them questions about their life and to find out if they're OK. But she wants me to wait until I'm a teenager to start dating." — *Daniel, 10*

"My mom always asks me, 'Who's going out with who now? Has anybody asked you out lately?' Then I ask her what she'd say if I did go out with somebody, and she says, 'Personally, I don't want you to go out with anybody.' So I'm like, 'But Mom, you talk about it all the time!' And she says, 'Well, I wouldn't mind if boys called you or anything. I just don't want my daughter growing up too fast.'" — *Jessica, 11*

### ... about feeling depressed:

"If I'm feeling bad about something, I usually go up to my room. Then my dad comes up and tries to make me feel better by telling jokes and stuff. But I wish he wouldn't do that. I just want to be alone." — *Ryan, 11*

"If I get depressed, my mom and dad usually talk to me and share a verse from the Bible. Like once when I was worried about doing bad on a test, they showed me where it says to cast all your worries on God. It helped." — *Ben, 11*

"My parents don't really notice when I'm depressed. I just go to my room and listen to music. I don't really involve my parents in my personal life. I like it that way." — *Jenny, 12*

"My stepsister picks on me all the time and makes me feel bad, like I'm not wanted. I'll tell my dad about it, and he'll usually talk to her and then talk to me. He and I talk about personal stuff, like my sisters and my mom and my dad's remarriage. It makes me feel better, because he teaches me a lot." — *Kristan, 11*

"My parents don't usually get involved in my problems—they just leave me alone. Sometimes I wish they'd care more, and that they'd come to me and try to help, but then I think about it and realize, Why would I want them to come? How could they really help me? Even when I want to tell them something, I'm afraid they'll react wrong or get upset." — *Ashley B., 11*

### ... about being embarrassed by their parents:

"Sometimes I like going out with them, but sometimes I don't. They embarrass me when they do stuff like have personal conversations out in public. If they just wouldn't talk about me in front of other people, that would solve the problem." — *Alison, 11*

"It depends on where we are. Like at the movies, if they see someone they know, they stand there and talk forever and it gets really boring. But other places are fine because they never see anyone they know." — *Brad, 12*

"My mom is not always fun to be with. Like at skating parties, after all the other parents have left, she's just sitting there, watching. Or when we go to the pool, she'll honk the horn at any boy she sees. She is so embarrassing." — *Brittany N., 11*

"I don't mind going some places with my parents. But when I'm going to a movie I'd rather go with my friends, because then I can talk. My parents don't like it and tell me to be quiet. It's just more fun to go with my friends." — *Glenn, 11*

"My family jokes around a lot, and they're really sarcastic. It's OK at home, but when they do it in public, like at a restaurant, it's embarrassing. My parents don't know they embarrass me, but they do." — *Jenny, 12*

# The Young TEEN

## Ages 13-14

by Karen Dockrey

# The Young TEEN
## Ages 13-14

Mention young teens, and many adults recoil in terror. They cite horror stories and claim the best way to parent middle schoolers is to lock them in their rooms. The tragedy of this bad press is that parents miss the delight of these years. They overlook the strength and wonder of young teens. They forget that if young teens could parent themselves, they wouldn't need us. Consider that:

- Young teens are so animated that you don't have to generate energy or interest. They eagerly express contagious amounts of fascination in whatever's going on.

- Young teens tell you their feelings shamelessly. Their feelings of loneliness, alienation, failure, and fear can rip your heart right out. But because they honestly tell you what's up, you can face it with them head on. Then when they're happy, you can delight in the joy that bubbles over into the entire family.

- All parents have been through the angst of adolescence, so we can honestly assure our young teens that there are better days coming.

- Your young teen will be unique from any other young teen, and you are uniquely privileged to parent him or her. Your daughter may have the ability to see a situation from 15 sides. Rather than be aggravated by her pleas of "Couldn't it be this way instead?" prompt her to use her creative perspective to solve problems. Your son may remember every detail of each video he sees. Rather than grow bored when he shares details, affirm his magnificent memory and daily cite a new way he can use it.

The down side of all of this is:

- Young teens become so socially conscious that they may betray or be betrayed by lifelong friends for the sake of status. Some push aside genuine friendship for surface chatter. Then they wonder why they're lonely. They need your help to determine which friends are worth keeping and which ones will only cause them pain.

• Young teens experience a surge of hormones that is unfamiliar and powerful. This tends to push them toward outbursts of tears, rage and moodiness. Their usual good qualities get masked behind the confusion. But look deep—the God-given good is still there.

• The insecurity of middle schoolers tends to tap into our own insecurities, no matter how deep they lie. Our emotions get triggered at the very time our teenagers need our stability. So watch for this, ask God's power to bolster you up, and then proceed with his promise to manage whatever comes your way (Phil. 4:12-19).

As you parent these wonderful people, adopt a posture that is different from crisis management. Rather than think, "What will get us through this?" focus on, "What skill can I teach that will equip my teenager to manage life as a caring Christian?" By keeping your focus positive and really learning to enjoy your blossoming teen, you'll someday look back on these years as some of your family's best.

— *Karen Dockrey*

"My parents have always wanted me to listen to Christian music, and I didn't really think that was different from anyone else. Now it's just a habit to listen to Christian music. But if I ever want to get something that isn't Christian, my mom will go through the words to make sure they're clean, and if they aren't, I can't listen to it." — Kim, 13

# QUESTIONS ABOUT FAITH

*Our 14-year-old has started asking us some difficult questions about God, questions we just can't answer. How can we handle them?*

First, rejoice! When teenagers start asking questions about God, it shows they're ready for a deeper relationship with God. They demonstrate their eagerness to make the family faith their own. Congratulate your son for his wise questions.

Then, assure your son that questions are never bad. God himself urges us to ask, search, and knock (Matt. 7:7-8). Any belief that cannot be questioned is not solid enough to stand on. Asking God questions shows that we trust him, not that we don't. Use this stage of your son's spiritual growth to caution him against any religious leader who says to "just believe" or urges him to swallow something without evaluating it.

Together with your son, seek answers to the questions he's asking. Find books. Find Bible verses. Find resource people who can help. Be cautious of easy answers to hard questions or short solutions to complex struggles. Finally, be honest with your son about what you know and don't know. This communicates that you, and your son, can believe in God while struggling to understand him better. Explain that no Christian knows all the answers, and that we can continually discover more answers during this adventure called life. It's part of growing closer to God and learning how to honor him.

**ACTION STEPS:**

1. **Affirm your son's desire to really understand his faith.**

2. **Help your son seek answers to his questions through research, Bible study, and talking with other Christians.**

3. **Demonstrate that belief doesn't mean we have all the answers, only that we're always seeking God.**

Thanks...

When my parents became Christians, after they were married, they decided they wanted a different kind of home than the homes in which they'd been raised. Without having the slightest idea how to do that, they began studying the Bible and praying continually. They depended on God to care for them and us. My parents not only taught us what was right, they lived it. As a result we fell in love with the Lord ourselves.

Because my parents loved us, they made us abide by their rules--and that kept 10 children out of trouble in inner-city Detroit. They effectively took peer pressure off us by insisting we spend time reading our Bible, praying, and attending church activities.

CeCe Winans—recording artist

# FAITH AND FEELINGS

*Our 14-year-old daughter went on a church retreat last summer where she really experienced God. Now she's complaining that she doesn't feel God's love any more, and she's beginning to wonder if he even exists. What should we say?*

Start by telling her she has plenty of company, including the great prophet Elijah. After standing up to 450 prophets of Baal in the spiritual victory of the millennium, Elijah tucked his cloak into his belt and ran. After a threat to his life, Elijah whined, "I have had enough, Lord....Take my life" (1 Kings 19:4).

Why the drastic change? Elijah was exhausted, and he faced a problem he didn't know how to handle. He knew how to dramatically challenge the prophets of Baal. But he didn't know what to do about a pushy woman named Jezebel.

Our lives are similar. While we're in church or at a retreat, we know what to do. We know the feelings to feel. We're surrounded by other Christians who affirm all those great feelings. But when we get back into everyday life, where temptation hammers at us constantly, we feel alone and don't know what to do.

What your daughter needs to know is that God isn't a feeling; he's the steady presence he promised to be. God was with Elijah in the triumphant times and the tired times. He was with your daughter during the triumphant retreat and he's with her now.

Assure her that God remains close during her doubts and struggles. Sometimes she'll feel his presence. Sometimes she won't. But he will always be there. Together, search the Bible for promises that remind her of this: Psalm 23; Matthew 28:20; Revelation 21:1-4 and more. Then assure her that just like God took care of Elijah, he will take care of her now and for all of eternity.

**ACTION STEPS:**

1. Together, read the story of Elijah, who also felt a spiritual letdown.

2. Help your teen discover that God isn't a feeling, but a powerful presence.

3. Assure her that God promises to be with her for eternity.

# OTHER RELIGIONS

*Our 13-year-old has friends from all kinds of religious backgrounds — Buddhist, Jewish, Hindu, and even an atheist. While we're glad he's reaching out to others, we don't want him to get sucked into the idea that all "truths" are equal. How can we encourage him to care for his friends but continue to stand up for God's truth?*

There is indeed a tension between influencing others and letting them influence you. That's why time spent reaching out to non-Christians must be balanced by time spent with Christians. If your son's not already involved in a youth group or Christian club, help him find one where he can keep his own faith strong.

In an effort to avoid offending his friends, your son might hesitate to talk about the truths of his faith. So help him see that he doesn't have to preach at his friends to be a good witness. Instead, help him learn the facts of his faith so he can express those truths in love when his friends' beliefs contradict his own.

Encourage your son to talk to you about his friends and their beliefs. If their influence brings up questions about Christianity, offer to help him study books like *Mere Christianity* by C.S. Lewis and *True for You But Not for Me* by Paul Copan. But don't center all your discussions about these friends on their religious differences. Your son likes these people for lots of reasons. Find out what they are. Your love and openness toward his friends can also have a positive impact on them. As an added plus, your son will see that you trust him and will be much more honest when he does feel a little over his head.

Above all, affirm your son for caring about his friends. Genuine friendship and love are the best examples of God's love for us. If your son is a consistent, caring friend, he won't always need words to show Jesus to his friends.

**ACTION STEPS:**

1. **Make sure your son has solid Christian influences in his life to balance the influence of his non-Christian friends.**

2. **Use Christian resources to help your son feel confident about expressing his beliefs.**

3. Encourage your son to be a caring friend, reflecting God's love in his relationships.

# WITNESSING

*Our daughter is a committed Christian. But when it comes to sharing her faith, she's very timid. She has several non-Christian friends to whom she could be a wonderful witness, but she clams up whenever the subject of God comes up. How can we encourage her to be more open about her faith?*

If she's a committed Christian, she may already be giving a wonderful witness. If she is a faithful friend who genuinely cares about others, her actions will speak much louder than any words.

Still, it's important that your daughter be able to articulate why she believes in Christ as her Savior. Your daughter's fears about sharing her faith are typical of many Christians. Because faith is so important to us, talking about it is difficult. It's easy to talk about the weather. If someone disagrees, it's no big deal. But if your daughter shares her faith in Jesus and the listener rejects what she's saying, she'll likely feel like she's failed God.

Invite your daughter to tell you about her fears. Let her know it's normal to feel awkward about sharing something so personal. And let her know that if she wants to be more vocal about her faith, you'll help her find ways to overcome her fears.

Also recognize that your daughter cannot "fix" non-Christians. No matter how much she talks about her faith, her words won't force them to change. Each person makes his or her own choices, and one of those choices is to accept Jesus as Lord and Savior. That's a decision that comes from the leading of the Holy Spirit, not the pressure of a Christian friend.

If your daughter is looking for ways to be bolder in talking about her faith, use Jesus as a model. The Gospel of John offers some great examples of Jesus sharing the truth with others. My favorite is his conversation with the woman at the well in John 4:7-26. He started with what she understood and used those words to teach her about spirituality.

Help your daughter think of a non-Christian friend who might respond well to this approach, then encourage her to try it out. Maybe she has a friend who loves sports. Your daughter could use that to talk about the way God wants us to "run in such a way as to get the prize" (1 Cor. 9:24-25).

And don't forget prayer. Together, pray for your daughter's friends and ask God to open their hearts to the gospel.

One more thing: Make sure your daughter has some Christian fellowship in her life. She needs the love and support of other believers to ensure that she influences her non-Christian friends and not the other way around.

**ACTION STEPS:**

1. **Recognize that your daughter can witness effectively simply by being a caring, faithful friend.**

2. **Talk with your daughter about any fears she has about sharing her faith.**

3. **Make sure your daughter has the support and friendship of other Christians.**

# MISSIONS

*Is 13 too young for a mission trip? Our church's youth group is going to Honduras for two weeks this summer, and our daughter really wants to go. But we hesitate to send her so far away when she's so young. What do you think?*

Typically, middle schoolers do better with shorter mission trips closer to home. So talk to your youth leader about setting up a shorter trip for middle schoolers—maybe a weekend working at a homeless shelter —and letting the two-week trip be a rite of passage for the senior highers. If it's too late to do that this year, you can still consider letting your daughter go on the Honduras trip, as long as you think about a few key factors.

First, ask your daughter why she wants to go. The energy and momentum of the isn't-it-great-to-serve-God missions pitch can make even the most hesitant teenager claim she can hardly wait to go. But mission work is physically, emotionally, and spiritually draining.

Make sure your daughter understands that she will be asked to sacrifice a great deal (sleep, good food, hot showers) if she goes. And think about her spiritual needs, too. Is she ready to be confronted with abject poverty, or with people who might not be receptive to her faith? Mission trips often cause those who serve to ask some deep questions of faith. Is your daughter prepared to do that this year, or would a later year be better? Don't make her feel badly if she's not ready.

If she still wants to go, find out if you can go along. Talk to the youth leader about being a sponsor. Serving God together will be an experience neither you nor your daughter will ever forget.

Even if you decide to be one of the chaperones, look closely at the sponsor team and the preparations the leaders are making. If you hear too much of "We aren't worried about that because God will provide," be wary. God gets blamed for a lot of human irresponsibility. But if you see God-honoring attention to detail, you can be more confident that the leaders are being conscientious and that your daughter is likely to have a positive experience.

You've got to let God guide. If he guides you to wait a few years, you're not less spiritual. In fact you would be clearly dishonoring him to send your daughter on a trip that does not match her age, spiritual needs, or ministry focus.

**ACTION STEPS:**

1. **Talk with your daughter about her reasons for wanting to go on the trip.**

2. **Consider going along as a sponsor, especially with your daughter being so young.**

3. **Find out what preparations the leaders are making; then let God guide your final decision.**

# ANGER AT GOD

*Our son's best friend was killed in an automobile accident about a year ago. At first, our son said he hated God and didn't want to have anything to do with Christianity anymore. We thought that was a reasonable part of the initial grieving process. But now that it's been a year, he still feels the same way. He says he can't follow a God who could be so cruel. How can we help him?*

Who would want to follow a cruel God? The good news is, our God isn't cruel. The automobile accident, not God, killed your son's friend. So begin by agreeing that your son has a right to be angry. It's not right or good that a young man was stolen from this world by an early death.

Then help your son direct his anger at the source: Satan. Early death is a result of Satan's influence in this imperfect world (Gen. 3). One driver may have been drinking, an employee who constructed the brakes may have slacked off and not tightened them properly, or something else. But a human factor, prompted by Satan, caused the accident. Let your son rage at the devil that brought evil into the world.

Refusing to express anger keeps it inside where it can boil into depression. Letting it out too fast leads to explosiveness. So give your son a safe way to vent his feelings. Your son might write out his anger, tell you about it, compose a song, punch a punching bag, or shoot hoops with fury. Whatever helps him get those feelings out without hurting himself or someone else is OK. The anger won't be over in a single episode, but it will heal as it is given attention. Later help him turn the energy fueled by his anger into something that gives tribute to his friend, perhaps by doing things his friend might have done if he had lived.

You're right that anger is a part of the initial grieving process. But it needs help to heal. Through actions like the above, God can give your son that help. Your son needs to understand that God grieves with him and knows what it is to feel pain. He also needs to know that God is in control of the world. While we don't know why God allows evil to happen, we do know that God promises to bring good out of all things (Rom. 8:28). Pray for and with your son. Even if he doesn't want to pray for a while, let your son hear you asking God for healing. Encourage your son to give his pain to God and allow God to comfort him.

**ACTION STEPS:**

1. Allow your son to be angry, but help him direct his anger at Satan, not God.

2. Help your son find safe ways to deal with his strong emotions.

3. Pray for and with your son to help him heal.

# GRIEF

*Our youngest child died from leukemia about a year ago. His death has obviously been extremely difficult on all of us, but our 13-year-old has never really talked about his feelings. A year later, he still refuses to say his brother's name or go into his brother's old room. When we try to talk to him about this, he tells us to leave him alone. What can we do to help him heal?*

Let me begin by saying that my daughter fought leukemia from age 8 on. So I speak not just from clinical knowledge, but with heart understanding of how these tragedies impact siblings.

Because his experience with tragedy has been limited, your son probably hasn't learned how to grieve. All he knows is that his feelings are painful and he wants to push them away. So show him a better way to handle his emotions. First, go ahead and call the death sad. Don't try to turn it into a spiritual lesson. Refuse to say that God took your child. The leukemia did that. And it's not right. Your son misses his brother every day. Acknowledge this pain as real and an expression of love (Eccles. 3:4).

With these truths in mind, find a private time and place to invite your son to talk. Agree that it is hard to speak about his brother. When he tells you to leave him alone, say, "I know you don't want to talk about him. But as a family we walk through this together. I want you to say three sentences. After you say three sentences, we can stop." Of course you won't stop him at three sentences if he wants to keep talking, but you'll insist on at least three. Each week, find a time to talk and invite three more sentences. You'll hear sadness, anger, fear, loneliness, and more. Let him pour it all out, knowing that as he talks, he will begin to heal. Don't push away the angry feelings—

his or yours. They matter as much as the positive ones.

If your son won't talk to you, get your pastor or another trained person to sit down with the two of you and help you talk. Eventually, he'll start to talk and realize that it helps.

In addition to regular conversations, give your son a journal, art materials, or other private ways to express his grief. My daughter's story in my book *Facing Down the Tough Stuff* includes some of her sister's reactions and more ideas for walking through the pain as a family.

ACTION STEPS:

1. Talk with your son and ask him to say three sentences about his feelings.
2. Meet each week to keep your son talking.
3. Give your son other actions for working out his grief in private.

# YOUTH GROUP

*We go to church every Sunday, but my son has no interest in youth group activities. We don't want to make him go if he hates it, but maybe he just has a bad attitude. What should we do?*

Attitude and spirituality seldom have much to do with a teenager's interest in youth group activities. From my years of youth work, I've learned that friendship and habit are the main factors that determine involvement. Even the most spiritual and confident teenager will hesitate to attend a youth group function if he has no close friends there.

Start by asking your son to be specific about his disinterest in the group. If he says he doesn't have any friends there, encourage him to invite a good friend to go with him. If he's more vague or won't give a specific reason, find out what it would take for him to get interested. Most likely, it will be a problem you can solve with a little effort.

If your son's never been involved with youth group events, unfamiliarity may keep him from wanting to try. Explain that anything new is uncomfortable at first, even for adults. Then insist that he pick one youth event a month to try. Do this for about six months to let a habit of attendance grow.

Let's say, though, that the problem has something to do with the way this particular youth group relates with your teen. For instance: Is he being teased by other students? Is the Bible study over his head? Do the games seem too competitive or too childish? If he doesn't seem to be clicking with the group, talk with the youth pastor. Let him or her know your concerns. Brainstorm strategies that will help both your son and the group.

If patient trouble-shooting doesn't seem to help, you and your son might check out youth groups at other churches. Involvement in a Christian peer group is important, but that group need not be the one that happens to meet at your current church.

**ACTION STEPS:**

1. **Help your son identify his reasons for not wanting to attend the group.**

2. **Encourage your son to try one youth group event a month for six months.**

3. **Work with your pastor or youth leader to solve any problems that might exist within the group.**

# NEW YOUTH PASTOR

*Our son has always enjoyed youth group. But our church recently hired a new youth pastor whom our son just doesn't like. The youth pastor seems OK to us, but for whatever reason, he and our son just don't click. We'd like our son to stick with the group, but we don't want him to be miserable. What should we do?*

The new youth pastor probably is OK, but he's not the former minister. One thing your son may be feeling is grief. He misses the youth pastor he loved. He misses the jokes they shared, the trust they had developed. He misses the way the other leader did things. If that trusted leader left, what's to keep this new youth pastor from leaving also? Why grow close to someone he might lose? So your son keeps his distance.

Give it a little time and a lot of prayer. Talk honestly about grief and the way it plays into your son's feelings about youth group. Insist that he keep attending the group—he can't learn to like this new pastor if he doesn't go.

Help your son figure out a reason to attend that's beyond what meets his own needs. Maybe he can play guitar with the worship team, lead a small group, or help set up activities. Remind him that he can have a positive impact on other group members.

Finally, help your son see that youth group is about growing closer to God, and his attitude about the youth pastor shouldn't get in the way of that (see Heb. 10:25).

One last note: Check in with your son on this issue from time to time. If his concerns about the new youth pastor don't fade after several months, talk to a few other parents of group members to find out how their kids are feeling. If there are problems with the youth pastor, do what you can to help solve them.

**ACTION STEPS:**

1. **Recognize that your son might be grieving the loss of a youth pastor he felt close to.**

2. **Help your son find other reasons for attending the group.**

3. **Check in with your son regularly to see if things improve.**

# GIVING ADVICE

*How much advice should we give our teenagers? We want them to learn from their mistakes, but we also want to protect them. How "hands-off" should we be right now?*

To figure out the right balance of protection and freedom, look at the way God guides you—does he leave you on your own as you grow in your faith? Of course not. He continues his guidance, as you reach new levels of understanding and commitment. Give your teenagers this same guidance. They still need you to help them know how and why to do right.

Following God's example, use action, not just words, to guide your teenagers. And don't assume your teenagers know the reasons behind your values. If you're establishing new rules to reflect your teens' growing independence, help them see why you want them home at 9, or why they can't date until they're 16. Be an active presence in their lives, not just an enforcer of rules. Then, when your teens are looking for advice, they'll be much more likely to come to you.

**ACTION STEPS:**

1. **Look to God as your example of of continuing love and guidance.**
2. **Back up your advice with actions that show your teens how and why to carry out that advice.**
3. **Help your kids find joy in choosing right over wrong.**

"When I was younger, my parents really lectured me about how when people come over and see your room messy, they're going to think you're a disgusting pig. So I've gotten to the point where I like to keep my room really neat, even under the bed. I think all their lectures really paid off, because I just like having a clean room so much better." — Bethany C., 13

# DISCIPLINE

*My son is 14. Can we still discipline him, or should we let him make it on his own?*

Discipline, which means "training," is one of a parent's primary jobs, no matter how old the child. In many ways, discipline is more critical for young teenagers than any other age group. Young teens are eager to explore their growing independence. They're beginning to make more decisions for themselves and, more than ever, need to be reminded what's right and wrong.

Obviously, you don't discipline a 14-year-old the way you would a 4-year-old. Because your son is now mature enough to think things through, you can give him more than just rules. You can show how and why certain choices lead to long-lasting good (or bad) outcomes. Then when he's an adult and ready for life on his own, he'll know what to do and why. Imitate the way God disciplines: provide positive consequences for good choices and negative consequences for bad choices. Here are a few ideas for age-appropriate discipline:

- Set a consistent curfew with rewards for meeting it and penalties for missing it.

- Insist that your son complete homework before anything else. Some say you can't make anyone study, but if you sit with your son and make study a prerequisite for other activities, he will study.

- Expect common courtesy with family members and friends. If he says ugly words to his sister, he loses phone time with friends. When he speaks kindly to his friends, they can come over more often.

- Allow and encourage your son to speak about any subject, but insist he do so kindly and appropriately.

- Make church attendance a priority. Sports and other activities can't cut into time with God and other Christians.

Your son still needs your guidance as he matures. He needs you to help him learn how to live out his faith. Use boundaries and consequences to train your son "in the way he should go, and when he is old he will not turn from it" (Prov. 22:6).

**ACTION STEPS:**

1. Keep in mind that discipline is crucial at this stage.

2. Guide your teen by setting clear consequences—both positive and negative—for his actions.

3. Set age-appropriate rules, and explain the rationale behind them.

"My room is always a mess, and I get grounded a lot. I always say, 'It's my room, so I should be able to keep it the way I want.' My parents say, 'But it's our house.' It's not fair."

— Bethany M., 13

A CURFEW WAS NOT SOMETHING TO BE TAKEN LIGHTLY IN THE MILLIGAN HOUSEHOLD.

# TRUST

*We want our son to know we trust him, but we also want to monitor his activities. How can we keep track of him without making him think we don't trust him?*

You've described one of parenting's greatest tensions—the one between deciding for them and letting them decide. The best advice is to look at God's example and go from there.

God parents us with a watchful eye. He never abandons us to live by our own wits, nor does he control our every move. God is a permanent presence who watches over us. He's always there when we need him, and even when we think we don't. That's what your son needs from you.

Having worked with teenagers for over 20 years, I've discovered something that surprises most parents: Teenagers want their parents' interest, instruction, and protection. They sometimes contradict this in practice, but in their hearts they treasure parental involvement.

If your son dislikes your interest in his comings and goings, remind him that trust is something he must earn, and that you want to give him plenty of opportunities to show you how trustworthy he is. Explain that the move toward independence is gradual, not an instant rite of passage. The more communication he gives you about his activities, his friends and his plans, the more freedom you'll likely give him.

"My parents pretty much trust me with music. I listen to secular radio sometimes, but what I mostly listen to is my CDs. My mom goes through a few of them to make sure they're not dirty. But they basically trust me—I know which stations and songs not to listen to." — Shauna, 13

**ACTION STEPS:**

1. Look to God as the ultimate example of caring, involved parenting.
2. Know that deep down, your son treasures your involvement.
3. Remind your son that trust is something he can earn by keeping you informed of his comings and goings.

# NOTHING IN COMMON

*My son and I have completely different personalities and have very little in common. Naturally, I love him and always will, but I don't enjoy spending time with him. I'm pretty sure he feels the same. Is it normal to not connect with your own child?*

It's normal to feel aggravated by your child or to feel occasionally confused about how to relate to him. It's normal to not like some of the things he does. But to say you don't enjoy being with your child is to say you're not willing to build bridges, to find what you do have in common.

I urge you to work on bridge building before you do irreparable damage to your son. Young teens need their parents, and they consistently name parents as the people they most want to be close to. If your son acts like he doesn't want to be with you, it's probably because he senses you don't want to be with him. Choose to love your son by taking time to know him.

Begin with the little in common you do have. Perhaps it's something as ordinary as, say, tacos. Go to a taco restaurant and order your favorites. Sit down and invite your son to tell you about his day. What did he like about it? What did he hate about it? Really listen. Hear his passions and fears. If tacos won't do, play some catch, watch a ballgame, paint the house—whatever you can do together, do it.

He may not talk much your first time out, but accept even one-word answers with interest and appreciation. Remember that you haven't enjoyed him much recently; he realizes that. He'll wonder what your motive is for taking him out. It will take time for him to believe you really do just want to be with him. Give him that time.

# Thanks...

As a teenager, I thought I must be the most entertaining company in the world because my folks loved to be with me--and with each of my siblings. It didn't occur to me until years later that they chose to spend time with us. Since my parents believed in me and in what God could do through me, it never occurred to me that I couldn't follow whatever dream God placed in my heart. My parents always answered my question, "Can I do it?" with "Of course you can." Because of that belief, I've been resilient.

Twila Paris—recording artist

Spend time with your son again next week and the week after that and so on. As you spend time together, the two of you should begin to form bonds. Don't stop. Firmly keep the commitment to do something together once a week. You might be surprised at how much you'll grow to like him.

ACTION STEPS:

1. Be willing to figure out what you do have in common.

2. Use what you have in common as a starting point for learning more about your son.

3. Commit to spending time together once a week.

# TIRED OF TALKING

*Are there alternatives to lectures? It seems like my wife and I constantly talk to our kids about the same issues. Clearly, talking isn't working. They tune us out, and we get tired of harping on them. How can we get them to talk through issues with us?*

Like most parents, you don't really want your kids to just talk through issues with you; you want them to act on those truths. You want them to think before they make decisions and then deliberately choose what is right and good. You want them to honor Jesus with every word and friendship. And you're right—lectures aren't the best way to accomplish those goals.

What you need to do is start fresh. Explain to your teenagers that you will stop lecturing. Instead you will communicate what is expected and why. You'll tell them clearly what positive results will come from doing what you ask of them and what negative results will come from doing otherwise.

Then, put your words into action. Together as a family, set up ground rules for behavior, rewards, and consequences. Maybe you'll decide that anyone who gets to bed on time on school nights gets to stay up later on the weekends. At the same time, you can decide to deduct 30 minutes from Friday night's bedtime for every 10 minutes they're up past bedtime during the week. Once a teenager has to go to bed at a humiliating 8:00 on Friday night, he'll become more serious about getting enough sleep during the week.

There's one small catch to this plan: You'll have to enforce it. If they could monitor their behavior without you, they would have been hatched from eggs or pushed out on their own as 12-year-olds. Instead God gave you to them and promised you the power to raise them (2 Tim. 1:7). When you access this power and put action behind your words, your teenagers will trust your words, listen more attentively, and eventually monitor their own good behavior.

**ACTION STEPS:**

1. **Start putting your words into action.**
2. **As a family, determine a code of behavior, rewards, and consequences.**
3. **Remember that God has equipped you with the tools you need to raise your children.**

"My parents have a rule that if I want to buy non-Christian music, I have to make sure it's OK with them and I have to pay for it myself. And I'm not allowed to listen to the dance/hip-hop station on the radio."

— Jennie, 12

# FAMILY FUN

*We need some ideas for having fun with our kids, who are 12 and 14. They obviously don't want to do the same things we did when they were little. What are some things we can do to have a good time and bond as a family?*

One of the biggest mistakes parents of young teens make is to stop spending time with them. This is understandable when you consider teens' self-consciousness and total embarrassment over the way their parents act in public. But you're attempting to move past all this to meet your teenagers' need for family fun. I applaud you!

Your best bet is to take your teens' lead. Pay attention to what they like to do and create family time based on that. If your daughter likes having plants in her room, take her to the garden center and let her help you plant the family garden. If your son loves to read, plan a family outing to a local bookstore that offers live music or poetry readings.

Of course, you can also just ask them what they want to do. Get them involved in planning your family vacation, a weekend away, or just a Saturday outing.

In addition, don't be afraid to stretch your teens a little. Present new ideas that your teens are now mature enough to try. Communicate a sense of adventure, of privilege, and of responsibility. You might say, "Now that you're older, we're going to try something new—a twilight canoe ride down the river. We'll need you to help with the paddling." Your teens may be a bit reluctant at first, but once they're there, you'll build bonds like you never expected. Use every outing as a way to affirm your teens' emerging maturity, to train them in a new life skill— teamwork, an appreciation for nature, the delight of discovery, and more.

Classic family activities for teenagers include going out to eat, working on a car together, cooking and baking together, and having birthday dinners. Longer trips could include touring historical sites or camping.

One caution: It can be tempting to lure teenagers into family time by plying them with gifts or activities that cost a lot of money, such as theme parks. While it's OK to do those things on occasion, do your best to focus your family time on being together, not on feeding into the materialism that's so rampant among teens.

**ACTION STEPS:**

**1. Center family activities around your teenagers' interests.**

**2. Get their input when planning family trips or events.**

**3. Encourage your teenagers to try new things.**

# EMBARRASSED BY PARENTS

*Our daughter is embarrassed by us. When we see her friends at the grocery store or the mall, she won't even acknowledge our presence. Who does she think she is?*

She doesn't know who she is yet. That's exactly the reason she's embarrassed. Her not wanting to be seen with you is an indication that she wants people to know her as herself, not an extension of you. And she fears they may not like her if they don't like you. Also, she wants to be seen as a mature person, not someone who needs Mommy and Daddy along. Even with all this, she still wants and needs you. Those conflicting feelings are expressed as embarrassment in public places.

Of course, you have feelings and needs too—the need to know where she is, to keep her safe, and to spend time with her. So talk to your daughter about ways you can both get your needs met. Start by telling your daughter you're willing to give her a little more space in public places. Then, ask her to request her space in a respectful way. You might even want to create a code of conduct that will help you both know exactly what the other needs and wants. Here are a few "rules" you might want to include in your code:

1. We (Mom and Dad) will back off and follow you secret-service-style when you give us a signal to leave you alone.

2. We will not hug or kiss you when you're around your friends or other teens.

3. We will watch your excellent social skills from afar and tell you the good we see, after we get home.

4. We will allow you to walk away from us for a while if you allow us to know where you're going and who you're going with.

LORRAINE'S WORST NIGHTMARE COMES TRUE.

5. We will give you the honor of being known as yourself; you will give us the honor of sharing your feelings and dreams when we're alone.

Feel free to surprise your daughter by backing off even before she gives you the signal.

**ACTION STEPS:**

1. **Recognize that your daughter is trying to establish her identity as a teenager.**

2. **Create a code of conduct that helps all of you know what to expect from each other in public.**

3. **Start giving her more space in public places.**

# SHOWING RESPECT

*How can we help our kids learn to express their own opinions without being disrespectful?*

Start by letting them know you want to hear their opinions and you expect them to express themselves in a respectful way. Remind them that whenever two people are close, they will disagree and have varying ideas. That's OK, even good. But the way people disagree will either bring them together or tear them apart.

Then show them how. Do this in a way that invites their ideas, too—it will become your first exercise in mutual respect. Invite them to help you list some ways to disagree agreeably, and some ways that aren't appropriate expressions of disagreement. You might make a case for no raised voices, your daughter might ask for no interruptions when a person is talking, and your son might recommend voting on issues that can't be resolved.

Once you agree on the rules, work together to come up with consequences for breaking them. Maybe anyone who interrupts has to wash the dishes for a week, or yelling results in a loss of TV privileges for the night. Make sure you as parents follow the rules and experience the consequences, too.

To really drive the point home, you'll have to be willing to be affected by their opinions. If you're deciding where to eat dinner, let the kids choose once in a while. If they want a higher allowance, hear them out and work together to figure out how they can earn that privilege. Naturally, there will be times when what you say goes. But knowing you take their opinions seriously will go a long way toward helping them be respectful.

**ACTION STEPS:**

1. Let your teenagers know you value their opinions.

2. Work together to create a list of acceptable and unacceptable ways to express an opinion.

3. Take your teenagers' opinions seriously.

# FINANCIAL WORRIES

*My husband and I are going through a difficult time right now. He's in danger of losing his job, so we're stressed out and worried about our financial future. I'm sure our kids have sensed the tension. How much should we tell them about this situation?*

What kids don't know is always worse than what they do know. Parents hide things to save children pain, but children imagine things much more horrible than the real problem. So be honest with your teenagers and work through this difficult time together.

I don't think you need to tell every last detail, but do give the basics. You might say, "You've probably noticed that Dad and I have been tense recently. There's reorganization going on where he works, and that means he may lose his job. That's a scary possibility, and it may not even happen, but if it does we'll find a way to earn money. It's hard to figure it all out, so for a while we kept it to ourselves. Now we're telling you. Families face tough times and happy times together, and this is one of the tough times. We can face this together."

Then, let your kids ask anything, even things that don't seem related to the problem. Answer directly and simply. For instance, if they ask, "Can we still have pizza on Friday nights?" you can reply, "Probably not for a while. But we'll still watch our special shows together. If we give up pizzas, we can have money for ice cream." They might even be upset that you've told them, but in the long run, they'll feel better knowing the truth rather than imagining something worse.

In the coming days and weeks, reassure your kids, both through words and your own attitude, that God will provide for your family, no matter what happens. In Philippians 4:11-13 the apostle Paul reminds us that it is God who gives us what we need and he will never fail us. That's a message you, your husband, and your children need right now.

**ACTION STEPS:**

1. Be honest with your teens about what's going on.

2. Give your teens a chance to ask any questions they have, no matter how silly they seem.

3. Show your teens that you trust God to provide for you, and encourage them to do the same.

# SCHOOL CHOICE

*Should we send our children to a Christian school? I'm concerned about the influences in our public school, but the kids don't want to be separated from their friends.*

A solid group of friends and a quality education are both important to your child's well-being, so sacrificing one for the other isn't the best option. Hopefully, the two don't have to be mutually exclusive. If your children are getting a good education and have established some healthy friendships, I'd hesitate to move them.

There are plenty of good reasons to send your children to a Christian school. But trying to protect them from negative influences isn't one of them. We live in a fallen world, and that means there are negative influences all around us, even in the halls of a Christian school.

So let God and the specifics of your particular situation guide you. Here are three principles to help the process:

- While many Christian schools have excellent academic programs, putting the name "Christian" on a school doesn't guarantee an educational experience that's better than the public school. Talk to parents, students, and teachers at both your children's public school and the private school you're considering. Probe for the pluses and the minuses of each school.

- Peer groups do not grow easily. It takes at least a year to feel even partly at home in a new group of friends. Think carefully about your kids' current friends. Are they friends you feel good about? Are they friendships that could be maintained no matter which school your teenagers attend? Are your kids the types who make friends quickly or could this be a traumatic change for them?

- The dangers of public schools are often overstated. Before giving up on public education, find out as much as you can about your local public school. Attend school board meetings, talk to other parents and meet with teachers.

Whichever way you go, work in partnership with your school to provide quality education.

ACTION STEPS:

1. Resist the assumption that all Christian schools are good and all public schools are bad.
2. Assess the quality of each school you're considering by talking to parents, teachers, and students.
3. Consider your teenagers' ability and interest in making new friends.

"At our school dances, everybody just dances or talks. Nothing bad happens— maybe kissing at the most." — Scott, 13

# AFTER-SCHOOL ACTIVITIES

*In the last year, our daughter has been involved in soccer, ballet, volleyball, softball, tennis, piano, and violin. We love that she's excited about so many things, but her ever-changing interests are exhausting, not to mention expensive! How can we encourage her to explore her interests while narrowing her involvement to just a few activities?*

I'm a firm believer in one after-school activity at a time. If your daughter does soccer, she doesn't do volleyball, unless the seasons are totally different. This is not to limit her fun, but to preserve enough energy to have fun. It also allows energy for her to spend time with God and your family—two essentials in her development. Offer Ecclesiastes 3:1 as a promise—there is a time for everything, but everything has its time.

While it sounds like your daughter is genuinely excited about all these activities, she might also simply have a hard time saying no to commitments. Teaching her that skill will not only help her cut down on her activity list now, but it will be a valuable life skill as she enters adulthood.

Give your daughter a few phrases she can use to say no to others, such as:

- "I'd love to, but I already have a commitment."
- "I'm a person who needs some time to myself."
- "I try to do one sport a season and I've already chosen this season's sport. Maybe next year."
- "My parents won't let me. They say it's too much."
  (Volunteer to be the bad guy whenever she needs you to be.)

I also recommend she finish the entire season in any activity she starts. Talk through this issue at the beginning of the school year, or before the start of the next sports season. Then let your daughter make her choices. To help with this, ask her to write down every activity that she's interested in. Then pray about these things together. Using the wisdom God gives in those prayers, rank the activities, prioritize them, and jot down their pros and cons. Then pray again. Wait a few days to let it all settle. Then choose that year's (or season's) activities. Prayer, wisdom, and time will help you make choices you can all live with.

**ACTION STEPS:**

1. **Limit the number of activities in which your daughter can be involved at one time.**
2. **Help your daughter learn to say no to commitments.**
3. **Pray with your daughter and seek God's guidance as she chooses activities for the year.**

> "My parents don't have a reward system for good grades, but I wish they did. They just motivate me by saying I'm not going to get a very good job when I'm older if I don't get good grades."
>
> — Taylor, 14

# GRADES

*Should we set up a reward system for earning good grades? We'd like our kids to work hard for learning's sake, but many of their friends earn rewards for good grades. We're not against the idea, but it seems hard to find the balance between acknowledging good work and bribing them to study. Any suggestions?*

You're right on both counts—working for learning's sake is the best motivation, but there's no problem with providing some rewards.

Observe two cautions: Don't give rewards just because friends get them. Give rewards if they help motivate your teenagers. Second, only use rewards as part of a total plan to help your kids take their studies seriously.

Rewards imply that teens don't already want good grades. Most teens do, but sometimes they give up somewhere along the way. So before you make any changes, talk to your teenagers about their current grades. Find out which ones they're happy with and where they think they could do better. Then, talk about your expectations and the teacher's grading standards. You might find out that a B in math is excellent with that particular teacher. If that's the case, try to compromise on a reasonable grade expectation.

"I start off with $15 for each report card. Every time I bring up a grade it's $5 more and every time I bring down a grade it's minus $5. I think it works for me because when I feel like not doing my homework, I'll think about the money and do it." — Kent, 13

AS PUNISHMENT FOR HIS LOW GRADES,
WAYNE'S MOTHER FORCED HIM TO WATCH
12 HOURS OF HEE HAW RERUNS.

This is where you need a total plan, not just monetary rewards. For instance, offer to check your teens' homework, or answer any of their questions about it. Know when their tests are and make yourself available to help them study. When they do well, reward them with verbal praise, a special meal or, if you've decided it's appropriate, money—whatever helps them feel good about their progress. If they don't do so well, acknowledge their hard work just the same.

No matter what grades your kids are earning, go out as a family each time they bring home their report cards. Invite your teenagers to talk about what they learned during this grading period, what teachers they like and which ones aggravate them, and what goals they'd like to set for the next grading period.

**ACTION STEPS:**

1. **Consider rewards as part of an overall plan to motivate your teens.**

2. **Help them discover ways to live up to their abilities.**

3. **Make learning a family activity and celebrate each step of progress.**

"I don't have a reward system, and I don't think I really need one because I'm self-motivated. My parents just expect me to get good grades, and I just want to keep them happy." — Kevin, 14

# PERFECTIONISM

*I think my son is a perfectionist. He's very concerned about grades—so much so that he can't relax and have fun. How do I get him to loosen up?*

A surprising number of teens deal with this issue. And while many parents treat it as simply a personality issue, I tend to think it's a spiritual and theological issue. God took a day to rest from his work (Gen. 2:2) and Jesus took time out of his hard-working days to rest and pray (Matt. 14:23). God has made us with the need for hard work and solid rest. Show your son how to honor God in both.

It's important to understand that perfectionism comes primarily from three places—teenage drive, parental expectations, and peer competition. Just as some teens choose to prove themselves through popularity or sports, others prove themselves through grades. This internal drive is tough to change directly, but it can be eased or intensified by the way parents respond.

So start with your own expectations. Have you unconsciously communicated that only A's are acceptable? Or that your son will need perfect grades to attend the "right" college someday? If you realize you're contributing to the problem, do what you can to convince yourself, and your son, that learning is more important than perfect grades. Even if you're not putting any pressure on your son, he might have some misperceptions about your expectations. So tell him what you really do expect. Let him know that, while strong grades are good, shooting for the absolute top can produce anxiety rather than knowledge.

Also invite your son to talk about what the pressures are like at school. Ask him about the level of competition among his classmates. Talk to some of his teachers to find out if all his work is necessary or if he truly is overdoing it.

Help your son find a relaxing activity or two he really enjoys. Maybe he can go for a run with you after dinner. He can join a school club that's simply for fun, not for competition.

Most of all, remind your son of God's love for him—love that isn't based on how well he performs or how many honors he wins. God accepts him, no matter what.

## ACTION STEPS:

1. Help your son see that rest and hard work are both part of God's design for us.

2. Think about the parental expectations you might be communicating.

3. Find one relaxing activity your son can enjoy regularly.

# HATING PARENTS

*I think my son hates me. He's told me so a number of times because I won't let him do everything he wants to do. Can't he see I'm trying to protect him, not ruin his life?*

Young teenagers can be very emotional and use extreme language to express those intense emotions. Your son probably does hate some of the things you demand of him, but he likely doesn't hate you. Testing your authority is your son's job. Continuing to raise him well is yours.

Still, it's painful for a parent to be rejected like this. My first suggestion is to find a time when you and your son can talk. Go out for pizza or do something fun together first, then have a good heart-to-heart. Start by telling your son how much it hurts you when he tells you he hates you. Explain that you know it's hard for him to follow your rules but that you've set them up because you love him. Read Hebrews 12:5-6 to help him see that this is how God demonstrates his love for us as well.

Then, calmly tell your son you won't tolerate his saying he hates you. He can say he's mad, he hates the rule, he feels picked on. But there will be consequences for showing disrespect to you.

Finally, help your son see the benefit of the rules you have in place. If there are some you need to reevaluate now that he's older, be willing to do that. But always remember that your son won't be in this stage forever. No matter how much he claims to hate you, deep down, he wants and needs your unconditional love and consistent rules to carry him through to the next stage.

**ACTION STEPS:**

1. **Recognize that testing parental authority is something teenagers need to do.**
2. **Talk about the effect your teenager's words have on you, and determine the consequence for disrespect.**
3. **Keep expressing your love by enforcing caring, consistent rules.**

# RESPECT FOR OTHERS' PROPERTY

*Last week a neighbor called to tell us our son had emptied her trash can into the street. We talked to him about it, but he acted like it was no big deal. Yesterday, that same neighbor called to say our son had dumped her trash again, and this time he had also dented her trash can. How can we get through to our son and teach him to respect other people's property?*

Words won't do it. Actions will.

Start by walking your son over to your neighbor's house and supervising him while he picks up every scrap of trash. Picking up trash with his own hands lets him experience what his action did to his neighbor. Then, walk with him to the door of that neighbor and witness his apology and his vow to replace the trash can. Finally, drive him to the store where he can buy a new trash can with his own money.

He won't like this, and he'll take his anger out on you. But you show him deep love when you make him do it anyway. Tell him you'll stand with him as he picks up trash. Offer to help him word his apology before he goes over there. Give him extra jobs around the house if he needs to earn money to buy a new trash can. And insist that he go ahead and do all this even if he's embarrassed to have people watch him.

If your son still doesn't get the message, firmly but kindly say, "Son, we respect people and their property. This is a way to love others as we love ourselves. Until you demonstrate that you can treat people with respect on your own, I'll insist you do it with me."

That will hopefully help you resolve this particular problem. But I think it's important you also get to the feelings behind his actions. Such blatant disregard for others is not only an issue of respect, but also one of anger. Your son may be dealing with a great deal of rage that he's expressing through these acts of vandalism. Ask him again, privately and in a non-threatening tone, why he's acted destructively toward your neighbor's property. If he won't talk to you, consider getting the help of your son's youth pastor or a Christian counselor. Whatever is causing this anger in your son needs to be dealt with before his acts of disrespect turn into something much more destructive.

ACTION STEPS:

1. Supervise your son as he cleans up the mess he's made and apologizes to the neighbor.

2. Help him understand that respecting people and property is a way to show love for God.

3. Do what you can to find out what's behind your son's actions.

# RESPECT FOR AUTHORITY

*I was surprised to learn recently that my daughter has a "problem with authority" at school. I didn't see this coming. I always thought she respected her leaders.*

Because problems with authority impact the way your teen reacts to God, deal with this immediately. This isn't something you can let slide. If you do, it will only get worse.

Start by meeting with your daughter, the teachers with whom she's having problems, and a neutral party who has authority over both, such as the school principal. Leave any suspicions, objections, pride, or fears outside, and do your best to really listen to what the teachers have to say. Since your daughter may have her own version of things, make sure she has a chance to talk as well. As you listen, try to hear both sides objectively. Together, decide where you should go from here. I'd suggest setting clear expectations for your daughter and making sure she understands which actions are acceptable and which ones aren't. Then, ask her teachers to work with you to affirm her when she shows them respect and establish fair consequences when she's disrespectful.

There's always a chance your daughter doesn't have a problem with authority, but she simply has a teacher or two with unreasonable expectations. If you feel that's the case, use this as an opportunity to teach your daughter a valuable life skill—getting along with people she doesn't like.

Encourage your daughter to do all she can to be polite to teachers who might consider her disrespectful. If you feel a certain teacher truly is picking on your daughter, talk to the principal.

In any case, make sure you're consistent about encouraging your daughter to show respect. Listen to the way she talks to her grandparents, store clerks, and other adults. Praise her when she's respectful and follow through on consequences when she isn't.

**ACTION STEPS:**

1. Take this issue seriously. Problems with authority can translate to a bad attitude toward God.

2. Meet with school officials to come up with a plan of action.

3. Encourage your daughter to show respect to all adults, whether she likes them or not.

# DISRESPECT

*My once-polite son has started to openly challenge our authority. He is routinely disrespectful and rude. I don't want to get into a power struggle with him, so how can I handle these expressions of disrespect in a calm, productive manner?*

This is already a power struggle, and one you need not fear. Your son is begging you to win. He wants to find a secure source of authority he can depend on as he explores his growing freedom and independence.

Calmly but firmly say, "Son, lately, you've been disrespectful and rude. It's come on so gradually that I haven't acted on it as quickly as I should have. But now, each time you're disrespectful, you'll lose an hour of your free time that day. Instead of free time, you'll stay home and help me out with projects around the house. You'll also stay home Friday night that week." You can adjust the consequences to fit what he hates losing most, but let him know ahead of time exactly what the consequence for disrespectful behavior will be. Then consistently carry it out.

Your son will not embrace you and say, "Oh, thank you for giving me security." In fact, you may even need to punish him for his disrespectful response to this new rule. If he does respond rudely, you will calmly, and much to his surprise, find a project that you'll work on together. You'll also stay in with him Friday, no matter how many plans either of you has already made.

This will be intense and agonizing. It will take time that you'd much rather give to other pursuits. But only by insisting on respect for you and other family members can your son respect God, himself, and other people. Remember that he's begging for you to hold him accountable. Let him discover that respect earns privileges, while rudeness takes away fun.

**ACTION STEPS:**

1. Recognize that your teenager needs, and wants, distinct boundaries.

2. Set up clear consequences for showing you disrespect.

3. Be prepared to carry out the consequences, even when it's inconvenient.

# NEGATIVE INFLUENCES

*I can see signs that our daughter is starting down a bad path. She's been swearing and becoming more secretive. I think some new friends are influencing her. When she was young, I could simply pick her up and carry her away from a dangerous situation. But now I'm not sure how to pull her away from these negative influences.*

You're wise to pay close attention to changes in your daughter's behavior. The best approach is to be both direct and subtle. Say, "I'm concerned about some behaviors I see developing. You've been swearing and seem secretive. Let's work together to solve this problem." She may deny it. She may break down in tears of relief. She may argue that those words are no big deal. But whatever the reaction, you should continue: "Honey, this is emotional for me too. But it's important because you're important. I love you. Please spend a few minutes listening to my ideas for solving this problem. I'll do the same for you."

If she's not willing to talk right away, offer to meet with her later in the week. But have her make a list of things that are bothering her and what she thinks the solutions might be. Make your own list as well. When you meet again, share your lists. The conversation may get intense, but try your best to remain calm. If your words turn into a scolding, she will simply shut down. Also, really listen to her. If she's like most teenagers, she craves your attention and wants you to know and understand her. Throughout the conversation, remind her, and yourself, that you're in this together. Repeat this often, and show it in your actions. End this talk by praying out loud for your daughter. Let her hear you bring her before God in a way that shows unconditional love.

Finally, do everything you can to guide your daughter down another path. If that means driving her across town to a youth group meeting, do it. If it means opening your house to her and her friends every day after school, do it. If it means making her check in with you before she goes anywhere, do it. Helping our children choose good instead of bad takes more attention and energy than letting them run their own lives, but it's effort well spent.

**ACTION STEPS:**

1. **Keep paying close attention to warning signs.**
2. **Talk to your daughter about the problems you see and ask her to help you find solutions.**
3. **Do everything you can to help her make better choices.**

"My parents say if a CD has any swears or a parental advisory, it's not allowed in the house. They're pretty strict. I have two older brothers, and they have some music they shouldn't listen to and our parents wouldn't like, but most of my CDs are OK." — Wade, 14

# MUSIC

*Our son is starting to listen to some really trashy music. We've always allowed our kids to listen to secular music, and they've made pretty wise choices. But now our son seems to be making poor decisions about music, including wanting to go to some secular rock concerts. Where should we draw the line?*

While your son might try to convince you otherwise, music is a big deal. Teenagers often listen to more than 20 hours of music each week. The lyrics of this music influence them for good or bad.

Since it can be hard to know which secular music is acceptable, I suggest sticking with Christian music, at least until you feel confident your son can make better decisions on his own.

Set up a test period—maybe three to six months—where your son can choose any music he likes as long as the artist is a Christian and the words and the music reflect Christian values. There is such a wide variety of Christian music—hard rock, alternative, r&b, urban—that he should be able to find several groups he likes. Magazines like *Campus Life, Group,* and Focus on the Family's *Plugged In* offer charts to help your son know which Christian groups fit into which categories. Take your son to a Christian music store and offer to buy him one or two CDs to get him started. Take him and a few friends to a Christian music concert where they can see that music doesn't have to be vulgar to be entertaining.

After the test period, talk to your son about what he's been listening to. Compare the messages he's getting in Christian music to those found in secular music. Hopefully, he'll find that he doesn't really miss secular music. However, he might feel like an "outsider" in his peer group if he can't listen to what everyone else likes. If secular music is still a big deal to your son after a few months, consider an arrangement where he is allowed to purchase and listen to music by non-Christian artists if, and only if, (1) you are allowed to read all the lyrics first and retain veto power on anything you don't approve of and (2) he pays for the CDs with his own money.

I'd also suggest looking closely at your own listening habits. Even nice, mellow adult contemporary music can celebrate sex outside of marriage and other values that contradict those you're trying to teach your kids. Consider getting into the Christian music habit yourself, and it will be much easier to pass that habit on to your kids.

**ACTION STEPS:**
1. Strongly consider limiting your son's choices to only Christian music.
2. Encourage your son to evaluate the music he listens to so he can learn to make good choices.
3. Evaluate your own listening habits.

"My parents check a Christian magazine to make sure the music I want to buy is OK. Sometimes I listen to stuff they don't like, at school or with friends, but not that much. And I don't listen to anything evil. I don't take what the music says to heart, so I don't see why it's a big deal."  — Chris, 13

# LYING

*Our son has been lying to us constantly. We haven't snooped or invaded his privacy, but we've still caught him in several lies. How can we stress that lying is a sin and not just a way to get around the rules?*

Your son, like many people, probably agrees in principle that lies are wrong, but he lies anyway. So make his lies less rewarding. Once lies deliver more pain than pleasure, he'll hopefully stop deceiving you. Give very stiff punishments for lies, punishments that fit the crime.

For example, if your son lies about his whereabouts, saying he was at the library studying when he was actually at the movie theatre, take away all movie and television privileges for a month. Increase library time for that same month and accompany him there. Explain that lies bring reduced privileges, not greater freedom. If your son said he did a chore when he didn't, then he must stop whatever he is doing and complete the chore. If he's at a friend's house, go get him. If he has a house full of friends, pull him aside and quietly inform him that he must do the chore before he returns to his guests.

Your son also needs to understand that lying will have consequences down the road. Tell him that by lying to you now, he's made it harder for you to trust him in the future. When he's 16 and wants to borrow the car, it will be hard for you to just toss him the keys. When he wants more freedom, he'll have a hard time getting it from parents who don't trust him.

Lying can easily become a habit—one your son needs your help to break. Carrying out these punishments is a lot of work. But doing this now may prevent greater trouble and heartache later.

**ACTION STEPS:**

1. Let your son know there will be consequences for lying.

2. Carry out those consequences, no matter how inconvenient.

3. Explain that by lying, he's losing your trust.

"When my parents lecture me about my room, I pretend like I'm listening, but I'm really not. That way, when they ask me about it later, I can say I didn't hear them. But when they eventually catch me, I will clean my room.

If I don't, after a while, I can't see
the top of the desk, the floor, the
bed..."
— Kyle, 14

# INVADING PRIVACY

*I was cleaning my daughter's room, and I came across her open journal. I couldn't help myself, and I read a few pages. Well, my daughter caught me and was understandably furious. I feel awful and have apologized to her over and over again, but she's still angry. How can I possibly regain her trust?*

Do with your daughter what you ask her to do when she breaks your trust—offer an honest confession and demonstrate a change of behavior.

You have begun well by apologizing. But review what you said. Did you tell your daughter you couldn't help yourself? If so, you've given her the impression that you have no control over temptation. Instead, think of 1 Corinthians 10:13 where Paul explains that God will provide a way out of every temptation. Humbly tell your daughter there's no excuse for what you did and ask for her forgiveness.

While there might not be an excuse for your actions, there probably is an explanation. Many parents have sneaked a peek at their teenager's diary in hopes they'll gain some insight to their child's thoughts and feelings. If this is what's behind your actions, tell your daughter you feel distant from her and want to know more about what's going on in her life.

Then, give her time to talk. She needs to tell you, in a respectful way, how she feels and why it bothers her that you read her journal. Listen to her and show respect for her feelings. Knowing you understand her feelings will go a long way toward defusing her anger.

Once both of you have your feelings on the table, take a day or two to digest them. Then, talk again and try to resolve any lingering resentment she might have.

There are times, very carefully considered times, when you might need to read your teenager's diary. If you have reason to believe your daughter is in trouble—harmful friendships, drug use, sexual activity, violent behavior—you have good reason to read her journal. During emotional, physical, or spiritual dangers, the responsibilities of good parenting take priority over privacy. Sometimes kids are faced with bigger problems than they know how to voice. While she may be angry that you've invaded her privacy, she might eventually grow relieved when you help her manage a problem that's overwhelming.

**ACTION STEPS:**

1. **Offer your daughter a sincere apology.**

2. **Ask your daughter to respectfully tell you how she feels.**

3. **Take a few days to decide what to do and then talk again.**

# PRIVACY

*My son wants his bedroom door closed all the time. He won't let anyone go into his room, even when he's not there. I know he needs his privacy, but isn't this a little extreme?*

Yes. There's a fine line between privacy and hiding. Your son may be perfectly innocent or he may be hiding something. There's a greater chance he's doing nothing wrong, but for some reason he wants to isolate himself. Both have their dangers.

Take your son out for pizza and talk about this issue. Explain to your son that this isn't just an issue of privacy (he'll try to convince you it is), but that it's also about his well-being. Help him see that you want to help him deal with times of sadness and celebrate his times of joy. Explain that by withdrawing from the family, he adds to any feelings of loneliness and isolation he might be experiencing. If he makes this an issue of trust, remind him that an open door gives you the opportunity to catch him doing the right things, like studying, enjoying friends, reading good books. Seeing him do those things actually helps you trust him more.

After you've talked, set up some ground rules you can both live with.

Here are a few suggestions:

- His door must be open more than it is closed, and when it's closed you have the right to knock and walk in within 20 seconds.

- When he goes to his room, the family will take that as a signal that he wants less company. He is still expected to come to meals and other family times.

- You understand his need for privacy and will not allow his siblings to go into his room or touch his stuff without permission. But as parents, you will keep an eye on what he does and what possessions he has. This keeps him from the temptation to hide wrong actions or bad stuff.

> "It's my room, so I should decide how I want it. I should only have to clean it when guests are coming over, because that's important—to make it neat for them."
> — Kevin, 14

Even if your son argues, stand firm. Teenagers need the security of knowing that when they do wrong they will get caught, and when they do right they will be rewarded. An open door and open room gives this security.

**ACTION STEPS:**

1. **Invite your son out for pizza to talk about closed doors.**
2. **Help your son understand that too much privacy is unhealthy and lonely.**
3. **Set up some ground rules to clarify when he can close his door and when he needs to leave it open.**

# COMPETITION

*My two teenage daughters are extremely competitive with each other. They're gifted in different areas, but that doesn't stop them from competing in school, sports, and even dating. How can I stop this?*

You can lay it on the table with compassion and care. Siblings compete—it's in their nature. But the competition must be monitored to keep it from becoming ugly and destructive. When everyone's in a good mood and getting along well, ask for a few minutes of your daughters' time. Tell them you're concerned about the competitiveness between them. Then, ask them for ideas for how they can keep their competitive spirits in check.

Let both of your daughters speak with honesty and sensitivity, and encourage them to listen to each other. Then, work together to set up a "sisters contract" that encourages them to use their competitive spirits to spur each other on and support each other. The contract might include "rules" like:

- We will push aside jealousy or competitiveness, not comparing each others' victories. We'll work hard because it's the right and good thing, not to top each other's accomplishments.

- We will keep our successes in perspective by thanking God, win or lose.

- We will live by Ephesians 4:29, which says, "Do not let any unwholesome talk come out of your mouths, but only what is helpful for building others up according to their needs, that it may benefit those who listen."

You can even add a few rules for parents that help you give your daughters equal attention.

**ACTION STEPS:**

1. Understand that some competition between siblings is normal.

2. Talk to your daughters about your concerns, and hear their concerns.

3. Create a contract both siblings can agree to.

# ADULT FRIENDSHIPS (1)

*My daughter has become close to one of her male teachers at school. Do I need to be concerned, or is this acceptable?*

This can be very healthy or a cause for great concern. Her teacher may be an adult who is deliberately serving as an honorable role model for teenagers. Or he may be an adult who is letting his own needs interfere with hers. Invite your daughter to tell you about her teacher, what she likes about him, how he helps her. Together you can help keep this relationship healthy, at least from your daughter's side.

Most teenagers get a crush on an opposite-sex teacher during their middle school years. This usually healthy development gives them a safe adult with whom to practice relating to someone of the opposite sex. Because this adult has no romantic interest in the teen, they do not have to worry about acceptance or rejection. They can talk to, listen to, and model their lives after this mentor. But if the adult feels or shows romantic interest in this teen, the only result is big trouble. The teenager's emotional development takes a tailspin. Both teacher and student get hurt.

So pray this adult will be the good example your teenager needs. At the same time, teach your teenager to be wise and cautious. No matter how innocent and healthy the situation, instruct your daughter not to be alone with this teacher. Direct her to make sure a door is open whenever they are together or that a third person is with them. She must avoid even the appearance of sin for both her sake and his (1 Thess. 5:22).

If the teacher does act inappropriately, talk to the principal immediately. He or she should handle the situation from there, but be sure disciplinary action is taken.

## ACTION STEPS:

1. **Talk with your daughter to find out what she likes about this teacher and how he's helping her with school.**

2. **Recognize that teens often develop crushes on teachers. As long as the teacher is handling the situation in a healthy way, this can actually be a good thing.**

3. Give your daughter some guidelines for appropriate interaction with any opposite-sex teacher.

# ADULT FRIENDSHIPS (2)

*My son has been spending a lot of time with his male youth leader. My husband thinks the youth leader is a little strange and doesn't feel comfortable with our son being alone with him. How can we make sure our son is safe without scaring him or falsely suspecting the youth leader?*

Begin by taking your husband's suspicions seriously. This doesn't mean you blab them all over the church, but that you talk directly and confidentially with your son. In the fairy tale *Sleeping Beauty*, the princess would have been much safer if her guardians had told her about spinning wheels rather than try to hide them from her. Similarly, educating your son will help protect him even when you're not there to shield him from every bad influence (Matt. 10:16).

Sadly, persons who use or abuse teenagers sometimes volunteer at churches. A built-in tendency to trust and an unhealthy hesitation for church folk to "judge" people give potential abusers a protected place to perpetrate cruelty. Ask your pastor what kind of background research they do for potential youth staff. If your church doesn't run background checks on people who work with children and youth, it should.

Even if you don't think there's immediate danger, say, "There are some people who touch teenagers in a sexual way. There are other people who abuse teenagers emotionally, perhaps urging you to listen only to them and prompting you to pull away from other adults. If you see hints of anything like this, talk to us about it. Together we'll figure out how to deal with it. If someone says or does something that makes you uncomfortable, don't wait to talk to us— get away from that person immediately. No matter how embarrassed you feel, find someone to help you."

Urge your husband to go ahead and share his concerns about the current youth leader with your son. He could say, "I've been concerned about some behaviors of our current youth leader. When he ___ I wonder if ___." Have him follow it with, "My feelings might be right or they may be totally off base. What's your take on this?"

Encourage your son to set healthy boundaries with his youth leader. Encourage him to bring a buddy with him when he and the youth leader do something together. Make sure your son is developing plenty of peer relationships in the youth group, and make sure he feels free to say no to his youth leader's requests to spend time together. Any adult with pure motivations will respect these boundaries.

**ACTION STEPS:**

1. **Discuss your concerns with your son in a calm, confidential way.**

2. **Help your son understand the difference between appropriate and inappropriate adult behavior.**

3. **Encourage your son to establish healthy boundaries with adults.**

# SCHOOL DANCES

*My daughter likes to go to dances, but they're not chaperoned very well. I know from experience what can go on at those events. We trust her, but peer pressure is so strong. Are we doing the right thing by letting her go?*

Only you can know what's right for your child. And to do that, you need some facts, not just suspicions. To find out what really goes on at these events, talk to a parent who has chaperoned in the past.

"My parents let me go to dances. Sometimes there's bad stuff going on, and there's a lot of pressure to get into it, but I never do anything because I know most of it is wrong. I just go to have a good time with my friends." — Caitlin, 13

If you have good reason to suspect improper activities going on at these dances, don't let your daughter go, at least not alone. Volunteer to chaperone or plan another fun activity. Though your daughter might think otherwise, you're not a mean parent; you are a caring and wise parent.

If your daughter insists on going, help her understand your reasons for saying no. Explain, "Honey, I know you want to go but the event is not a good one because of __ and __. I'd be happy to help you plan a party here, or I can volunteer to chaperone the next dance. I won't hang around you, but I will help the dance be fun rather than dangerous. You deserve a truly good time, not just something that looks fun on the surface."

Your daughter probably won't hug your neck and thank you for caring. She'll likely accuse you of spoiling all her fun and treating her like a baby. But way down deep inside, she may be just a tiny bit relieved that she can blame you for not having to attend an event she's uneasy about.

## ACTION STEPS:

1. **Separate fact from rumor by talking to parents who've chaperoned in the past.**
2. **Explain to your daughter the reasons for your decision.**
3. **Help your daughter plan alternative events for her friends.**

"I don't even want to go to dances anymore because they're so boring. But I've been to a lot of other parties this year that got out of control. I've seen some things I know were wrong. But my parents are pretty lenient and I'm pretty responsible. I know what's right and wrong." — Brandon, 14

# SCHOOL VIOLENCE

*With all the school violence, we can't help but feel concerned for our kids. How can we help our teenagers feel safe and secure in a world where violence seems to touch everyone?*

Your concern is well warranted. But as Matthew 6:27 reminds us, worry is a waste of energy. So rather than worry, take action.

Start by talking to your teenagers. Ask them what scares them. You might be surprised by what they say. Many teens are less concerned about the random acts of violence we see in the news and more concerned about getting beaten up or teased.

Still, the school shootings of the last few years have raised the question of how kids can possibly feel safe at school. In the wake of these tragedies, talk to your teens about specific ways their school is dealing with the issue of safety (if you don't know, talk to the principal). Give them specific actions they can take such as hitting the ground when they hear popping sounds. That response will offer both reality and reassurance.

Reassure your teens that no matter what happens, God will be there (Ps. 119:150-151). Remind them of this promise each morning by starting the day with a prayer for guidance and protection. It will make all of you feel better.

Then go even deeper. Ask your teens, "Why do you think students shoot people? How can we solve that problem?" Many of the violent students we've heard about in the news were kids who were teased and left out of popular circles. Being ignored or slammed day after day can build up a rage so explosive it kills. Middle school students are especially prone to making ugly comments and rejecting all but those considered "cool." So challenge your teens to think about the power of their words and attitude. Help them live by Ephesians 4:29, which tells us to use our words only for building people up. Remind them that by choosing to build up people, rather than put them down, they'll build a much safer school.

**ACTION STEPS:**

**1. Talk to your teenagers to get a real idea of any fears they have.**

2. Assure them that God will be with them, and show them what to do, even in the face of violence.

3. Encourage them to prevent violence by building others up consistently.

# FIGHTING

*My son seems to be getting into a lot of fights at school. He says kids call him names. How can we teach him to turn the other cheek without feeling like a wimp?*

Explain to your son that a person of real power doesn't give in to verbal taunts. He shows himself to be much stronger than his attackers when he lets the words roll right off his back and into the dirt.

Of course, that's much easier said than done. The only way your son will actually take the biblical mandate to turn the other cheek to heart is to discover for himself that it's the best option. So invite your son to tell you a dozen ways he could respond when people call him names. He could punch them, call names back, walk away, say it takes one to know one, smile and be silent, respond with kind words, change the subject, respond in a witty way, and more. Then invite your son to name the pros and cons of each approach. Ask your son to name someone who handles verbal taunts well, and how he does it.

As you talk, explain that to turn the other cheek in the biblical sense means to do whatever it takes to stop the evil, to break the cycle of retaliation (Matt. 5:38-39). Suggest he respond in ways that take the sting out of the taunts. "It's good to see you too!" or "How are you doing today?" take the wind out of ugly words.

Having power over our emotions takes much more strength of character than putting up fists. Support your son as he does his best to ignore cruel words. Then let him rant and rave at home about how unfair it is to have to take it rather than fight—because it is. But remind him that as he follows God's command, he stores up energy for managing tomorrow's taunts.

**ACTION STEPS:**

1. Help your son think of all the ways he could respond and list the pros and cons of each.

2. Explain that it takes real power to turn the other cheek.

3. Talk about ways your son can break the cycle of retaliation.

# PREMARITAL SEX

*My daughter's had sex, and she's only 14. I'm shocked and grieved. We've always taught her that premarital sex is wrong. Where did we mess up?*

I don't want to add to the guilt that I'm sure you're already feeling, but you seem to want to know how to prevent this from happening again, so I'll be direct. I suspect that your daughter was allowed to be alone with boys before she was ready.

When it comes to sex, parental warnings usually aren't enough to overcome the strong pull of hormones. It takes action and parental supervision to keep teenagers from having sex. No young teenage girl should be alone with any boy long enough to have sex.

Now is the time to establish a few never-to-be-bent rules. Make it clear to your daughter that any time a boy is in your home, or she is at the home of a boy, an adult must be present. She is never to go into boys' quarters at camps and youth events unless an adult is present. Boys are not allowed in her room, nor is she allowed in a boy's room.

Your daughter might think you're being too strict. Help her understand that she has broken your trust and shown that she isn't responsible enough to be left alone with a boy. The loss of that privilege is just one of the consequences of her action.

As you talk to your daughter, stay calm and assure her that you are acting out of love. Explain that even adults give in to sexual pressures when no one is watching. We all need people to keep an eye on us and to know what we are doing. Assure your daughter that you love her, that you know sexual temptation is powerful, and that you will help her establish habits that keep the pressure from overtaking her.

If your daughter feels bad about what she's done, be sure to pray with her as she confesses and asks for forgiveness. Then, give her the attention she needs to stay away from future temptation.

**ACTION STEPS:**

1. **Recognize that most young teens are not mature enough to fight temptation on their own. They need parental boundaries to make good choices.**

2. **Set boundaries by establishing clear rules about the time she spends with boys.**

3. **Pray with your daughter as she confesses her sin and asks for God's forgiveness.**

"We don't really have chaperones at our dances—they sell the tickets and then go off to a corner where you don't see them. So boys and girls will go to the back hallways, and you don't see them for a while, so you can only imagine what they're doing. But there's no pressure to go back there because you can always say you don't want to get caught. Who would actually catch you, I don't know." — Lauren, 13

# SEX JOKES

*I overheard my son and a buddy telling jokes with sexual innuendoes. Sex is a gift from God, and he's treating it so lightly. How do I correct him?*

Your son wasn't born knowing how to talk about sex. It's all new and strange to him. So he imitates what he hears. The joking is more an indication of his uneasiness with the subject than of his disrespect of sex. But because his words are disrespectful and possibly offensive, he needs to correct them.

After your son's friend goes home, say something like, "Son, I heard you and your friend joking around about sex. I know you didn't mean it this way, but the jokes you were making throw mud in God's face. He created sex to be good, not a gross joke."

Help your son learn acceptable ways to talk about his emerging feelings about sex. Make sure your son knows he can talk to you about his questions and confusions. Let him know it's all right to admire a girl's beauty, but he needs to see her as a creation of God, not as a sex object.

Also, think about the influences that might be at work in your son's growing understanding of sex. Is he watching TV or movies that have strong, or even subtle, sexual overtones? Is he hanging around boys who are dating and talking about girls in a vulgar way? What about the adults in his life? Does he see a healthy respect for sex in his parents, aunts and uncles, or family friends? While you can't keep your son away from all bad influences, you can avoid some influences and help him learn to discern what's appropriate and what isn't.

Genesis 2:22-25 paints a clear picture of God's design for sex. Read it with your son and ask him what he thinks God is getting at. When your son sees that God values sex, he'll be more likely to take it seriously.

**ACTION STEPS:**

1. **Help your son understand that his words are inappropriate and dishonoring to God and to girls.**

2. **Take a look at the things that could be influencing your son's views of sex and help him learn to discern the good messages from the bad.**

3. Read Genesis 2:22-25 and talk about God's reasons for creating us as sexual beings.

# MASTURBATION

*We recently discovered our 13-year-old son masturbating. How should we address this with him? What does the Bible say about it?*

The Bible does not address masturbation directly, possibly because young people back then married about the time they reached sexual awareness. Still, the topic is emotion-packed, and few parents have a clear answer on what to do about it. No matter what you say to your son, do your best not to shame him or make him feel dirty for what he's been doing. Those emotions will only confuse him and cause more anguish.

Instead, tell your son that curiosity about one's own body is good and right. Suggest your son invite God to teach him about his body, about his sexuality, and about how God wants it expressed. He can do that by reading the Bible with you and talking about sexuality with you and other Christian adults he trusts. As he learns to see God as guiding his sexual maturity, he'll develop a relationship that will make him a better individual, a better boyfriend, and a better husband. As he recognizes his sexuality as a gift from God, he will more likely express that gift appropriately.

Remind your son that God himself lived on earth in the person of Jesus. He was a young teenager and had all the same sexual feelings your son has, and yet did not sin (Heb. 4:14-16). Invite your son to ask Jesus to help him avoid sexual immorality, such as lust and sex outside of marriage, and learn to control his yearning (1 Thess. 4:3-4).

ACTION STEPS:

1. Share your own feelings about masturbation without shaming your son.
2. Encourage your son to keep asking questions about sex and sexuality.
3. Help your son turn to God for help and answers about sexuality.

# PORNOGRAPHY

*Recently I discovered pornographic magazines in my son's bedroom. How do I confront him about this?*

First remind yourself that interest in the opposite sex is normal and healthy. It's a longing God gave to your son (Gen. 2:18). But there are appropriate and inappropriate ways to express this longing, and your son has found an inappropriate way.

You're right to confront him about this, but as you do, try not to condemn him. Instead, send him to godly sources of information: the Bible and Christian books like *Getting Ready for the Guy/Girl Thing* (Focus on the Family).

To start this conversation, ask your son to meet you in his room. Close the door and make sure no one is listening in. Show your son the magazines and invite him to tell you where he got them. Hear him out, and then explain, "Many guys go to these magazines to understand girls. But I want to let you in on a secret. These magazines tell lies. They say girls are toys to play with, rather than people to know. It's simply dishonoring to girls and to God to look at these images." Then, look at what the Bible has to say about sex, especially in the first two chapters of Genesis and the Song of Songs. Affirm that God created sex, and he knows just how girls are to be treated. Explain that you're happy your son is interested in girls, and invite him to ask you questions anytime. Then insist that he never look at a pornographic magazine again. Explain that you take this seriously and that there will be consequences—loss of allowance or other privileges—if he does this again.

This will undoubtedly be an embarrassing conversation for your son. But if you handle it in an honest, straightforward way, his momentary discomfort will lead to lifelong good. When he finds out that God knows all there is to know about girls, he'll be on his way to treasuring both God and the girls God brings into his life.

## ACTION STEPS:

1. Confront your son with what you found and tell him why you're concerned about it.
2. Explain the false view of women found in pornography.
3. Guide your son toward God's teachings on women and sex.

## Thanks...

"Son," my mother said firmly one morning, "when you came home from Dicky's yesterday, I had a very strange feeling go through me." She paused, thoughtfully. "At first, I didn't know what to do about it; then, I prayed last night, and I believe the Lord showed me simply to do what I'm doing right now.

"Jack, I want to ask you what happened at Dicky's house yesterday. And I'm asking this in front of Jesus."

I was frozen to the floor. The moment was one of those crystalline ones that seem like they could be shattered by a whisper. On the one hand, I knew what happened at Dicky's house and knew I didn't want anyone else to know. And on the other hand, the throne of my Living Savior, Jesus Christ, was suddenly as real to me as though I were in heaven itself.

I began slowly ... awkwardly ... guiltily.

"Well, Mama," I said rather quietly and with hesitation, "when I was at Dicky's, after we'd been playing in the living room for a long time, he said to me, `C'mon into my room for a minute.'

"When he said that, he kinda laughed, and looked around to see if his mom or dad were anywhere they could hear. Right then I felt something bad was about to happen, but I went with him anyway.

"When we got to his room, he closed the door and then opened one of the drawers of the chest there. He reached way back and brought out a little tiny telescope."

I hesitated all the more, feeling the embarrassment of the confession I was about to make.

"But, Mama, it wasn't a telescope." I paused again. "Instead, Mama, when you

looked into it, there was ... a naked woman."
My eyes were moist. I looked into the face of
my mother, feeling ashamed.

"What did you do, son?" she inquired.

"We laughed," I admitted.

"How did you feel then?"

"Mama," I said with sincerity, "I felt bad."

"Then, son, what do you want to do now?"

I walked toward my mother, whose arms
opened to me as I did, as I said, "I want to
pray, Mama."

I'll always be grateful to my mother
for what she said to me that morning. Her
sensitivity to God's Spirit, coupled with her
willingness to lovingly confront me, helped
open my eyes to this reality: I am always
living my life in front of Jesus.

Jack Hayford—pastor, speaker and author

# COMPUTERS

*Our son has always been a computer whiz, and he loves surfing the Internet and taking part in chat rooms. The problem is, he never gets out of the house to interact with people face-to-face. He says all of his best friends are online. What can we do? We're afraid that if we take his computer away he might do something rash.*

Proceed gradually. Let your son know you're extremely proud of his computer skills. Then, try saying, "I'm happy you're finding so many friends online. Since you're so good at online chats, I know you can use the same skills to get to know some of your classmates. To give you more time to develop these friendships, we're going to limit your computer time. It's not that your computer is bad, but that other things are important also."

Don't push him to go cold turkey at first, but do consistently limit his computer time to 60 minutes a day. He'll probably have trouble filling his extra time at first. But little by little he'll take up other pursuits. If he doesn't, help him out. Encourage him to invite friends to come to your house or to a local bowling alley or ice rink for some fun. Together, you can generate even more ideas.

Friendships are tenuous and difficult to build, especially in the middle school years. Let him know that you know it's hard, and that it's very tempting to retreat. Show him specific skills such as how to keep a conversation (or a game) going. Explain that the more time he spends with people, the better sense he'll have about what it takes to build a solid friendship. Stress the importance of real, live friends who will care for him and support him (Eccles. 4:10-12). Most importantly, offer the whole process to God through prayer so you'll know how to equip, when to push, and when to wait.

## ACTION STEPS:

1. Limit your son's computer time to give him time for face-to-face friendships.

2. Show him how to meet new people and try new activities.

3. Stress the value of God's gift of friendship.

# LONER

*I think our son is a social misfit. He spends all his time reading and drawing, watching TV, or just being bored. What's wrong with him?*

No one is born knowing how to make friends. You've got to show your son how to initiate fun and encourage him to use your home to practice his social skills. It might be tempting to throw a party where he can invite a bunch of kids over and you can send them to the basement to have fun. But he'll have more fun, and more success, if he begins by getting to know one person at a time.

Encourage your son to invite one acquaintance to come over after school for a couple of hours, maybe on a Friday, so homework won't be an issue. In the days before his friend comes over, help your son think about things they can do. Try to get him to think beyond videos or television, which do little to build friendships. As he thinks about activities, encourage him to think about the other person's interests. Once he chooses activities, offer to help in any way you can. For instance, if his friend also likes to draw, maybe you can provide new pencils and fine drawing paper.

When the day arrives, peek in on the boys every now and then to see how they're doing. After his friend goes home, talk to him about the high—and low—points of the day. This will help him begin to pinpoint what he looks for in a friend and figure out who he'd like to spend more time with.

As your son gets more comfortable with making friends, he might be ready to have a few friends over together. They can play card games, mystery games, and board games. Move in and out with food and new games to keep the interaction going.

Even though your son might feel more comfortable keeping to himself for the rest of junior high, this is a good time for you to challenge him a little. The skills he learns now will serve him well as he moves from these initial friendships to the kinds of relationships that last for years. So be deliberate about helping your son relate to people. Like many young teens, he could use some gentle assistance.

**ACTION STEPS:**

**1. Encourage your son to invite a friend over after school.**

**2. Help your son plan activities he and his friend will enjoy.**

**3. Continue building your son's social skills.**

# SHYNESS

*Our 13-year-old daughter is so quiet that she hardly talks to us or anyone else. Should we force conversation or let her set the pace? And how can we create a conversation-friendly environment in our home?*

Definitely encourage conversation. Nobody is born knowing how to converse. So show your teen how to share her thoughts and how to treasure the thoughts of others. It matters in your present family, in friendships, in church work, in dating, and in establishing a family of her own.

Start by establishing times when your daughter can count on you to listen to her. When she comes home from school, take a break, grab some snacks, and give her your full attention. Ask questions that need elaboration, such as, "What was the best part of your day?" She might not say much at first, but as this becomes a routine, she'll talk more.

Play talking games at supper. Choose a topic from the news, school, church, or whatever. Keep a jar on the table for family members to add their topics. One family member names (or pulls from the jar) a topic. The others each say two sentences about it. Questions could be: How much television should a person watch? What should Bible studies be like? How much allowance does a teenager need? What kind of chores should teenagers have? You'll be amazed at the things your kids are thinking.

Whether talking by topics or not, ask family members to always add "I like that because" before moving on to their comments—"Annie, I like it that you said teenagers should pick one fun chore and one not-so-fun chore because it shows you want all family members to share both the yuck and the fun. I think ..."

You may get some eye rolling, but the games will grow into habits of listening, cherishing, and understanding. Shy or not, teens long for these.

**ACTION STEPS:**

1. **Help your daughter understand the importance of communication.**

2. **Set up a regular conversation time where your daughter can talk about her day.**

3. **Play conversation games at dinner to get everyone talking.**

# MAKING FRIENDS

*We recently moved to a small town and are attending a small church. Our 13-year-old is desperate to find some Christian friends, but isn't having much luck. He's one of only five teenagers in our church and hasn't found any other Christians at his school. How can we help him find solid Christian friendships?*

The best thing you can do is help your son recognize that building friendships takes time. Assure him that friendships grow with deliberate kindness and considerate persistence. The more he shows genuine interest in the other teenagers at church, the more quickly they will learn to trust and accept him. Even then, it will probably take up to a year or more for him to build good friendships.

New kids often make the mistake of waiting for new friends to come to them. A better approach is to get to know others by asking questions like: How much homework do you have this weekend? What kinds of things do you like to do after school?

As your son is openly kind to people, suggest he watch for those who are nice back. At least some of those students will be Christians. He can spend more time with these people talking about homework, activities at their churches, school functions, and more.

Even though your church has only a few teens, your son can still find valuable friendships there. After all, every student there has other friends and contacts, too. To help your son build friendships with the students from church, invite them over to your house. Don't just bring them in and supply food. Plan activities and games. Close with a Bible study led by one of the youth leaders.

If your son's still struggling after a month, talk to the youth leader at your church. He or she can probably tell you about Christian clubs or other fellowship opportunities in town.

**ACTION STEPS:**

1. **Understand that building new friendships takes time and persistence.**

2. **Encourage your son to take the initiative in talking to people.**

3. **Invite the other teens from your church to your house for a night of fun and food.**

# CHRISTIAN FRIENDS

*Our son wants to make good Christian friends, but says they don't accept him. Unfortunately, the kids who do accept him are part of a bad crowd. How can we help him?*

Sadly, your son is right—some Christians are unaccepting. Even Christian teens who are leaders in their youth groups can be smug or self-righteous around other believers in the church and school halls. Other Christians can unintentionally form a clique that's built on inside jokes and shared experiences. These groups can say they're accepting, but they still make it hard for outsiders to feel like part of the group.

Invite your son to give you specific examples of the rejection he's experienced. Together, devise some strategies for managing the specifics. Then explain that those Christians aren't the only Christians and, without rejecting those kids, encourage your son not to give up his search for faith-based friendships.

As your son looks, give him the tools to build relationships with other Christians. Remind him to be open-minded—a person who initially looks unaccepting may just be shy. A few friendly hellos from your son might solve the problem. The person who appears to have it all together may be lonely. A smile from your son might invite this fellow to let down his guard. The guy who works passionately on the computer in technology class at school might be delighted to discover your son likes computers, too. An invitation for an afternoon at your house could build a friendship.

Consider that your son may have behaved in ways that cause well-meaning Christians to back away. Maybe his language is ugly or critical. Maybe he thinks skipping class is funny. Perhaps he dresses in clothes that communicate anger or a desire to be left alone. Guide your son to evaluate and improve his own actions in the same way he expects others to.

## ACTIONS:

1. Acknowledge your son's experience—rejection does happen.
2. Give your son tools to take the initiative in building solid friendships.
3. Help your son evaluate the messages he might be sending by his attitude and appearance.

# POSSESSIVE FRIEND

*Our daughter has a friend who is extremely possessive. This friend gets angry when our daughter does things with other girls or even talks to them in the halls at school. Our daughter is very caring and doesn't want to hurt her friend, but the stress of always trying to make her friend happy is starting to wear on her. How can we help?*

Your daughter's friend, we'll call her Beth, is possessive because she's probably not getting enough emotional encouragement from other sources—parents, teachers, other adults, peers. Beth has probably sensed kindness and strength in your daughter, and she's drawing on it. And, since your daughter seems to be her only source of encouragement, Beth has drained her dry.

What to do? Encourage your daughter to gather a group of friends to help care for Beth. Suggest your daughter ask at least two more friends to make an effort to get to know Beth. Have her invite Beth to her youth group, where she can meet other kind, caring people. These simple acts of friendship could give Beth enough encouragement to drop her possessiveness.

But that might not be the case. It could be that Beth has a history of being possessive and getting rewarded for it. Kind people, like your daughter, have allowed Beth to have her way. Now Beth is emotionally crippled. She'll have to practice a long time before she's ready to establish friendships without clinging so tightly.

As Beth practices, encourage your daughter to let Beth's jealousy roll off her back. Your daughter has done nothing wrong, so she doesn't need to feel bad about spending time with other girls. It won't be easy; even experienced adults have trouble managing possessive friends. But each little effort your daughter makes can help. Let her rant and rave to you, and then continue to show kindness to Beth and her other friends. Encourage your daughter to draw on God's promise "I can do everything through him who gives me strength." (Phil. 4:13).

## ACTION STEPS:

1. Recognize that your daughter can't handle this on her own.

2. Encourage your daughter to help this girl make more friends.

3. Help your daughter manage her feelings by sharing them with you.

# SELF-ESTEEM

*Our daughter has a prominent birthmark on her face. It didn't used to bother her, but now she's becoming so self-conscious that she doesn't even want to go to school. How can we help her get over these feelings and get on with her life?*

Your daughter must discover that people really will like her and accept her, birthmark and all. Because she must have contact with other people for this to happen, send her to school no matter how fiercely she resists. But rather than send her like a defenseless lamb among wolves, show her what to do.

Agree with her that, yes, some people will make fun of her birthmark, especially during the middle school years. But others will look past it to see the wonderful person she is.

Don't minimize the struggle or make light of her self-consciousness. Instead build her up so she can manage it. Highlight what's beautiful about her—inside and out. Remind her to show genuine care to each person. Hear the good and bad of her day, insisting she give a plus for every minus. Encourage her to build one or two solid friendships with girls she trusts. Teach her to ask questions that invite others to be comfortable: "What's your favorite class?" "What do you like and not like about today?" "How was the test you took yesterday?"

Assure your daughter that every middle schooler on the planet has something she hates about her appearance. Each teenager must discover ways to move past what she doesn't like to what she does. This slow but steady path takes months, even years, but it can't start at all without a few baby steps toward that goal.

You'll feel brutal forcing your daughter to go to school every day— my family has been there—but do it anyway. Explain that you do this because you trust in the fact that character always triumphs (Col. 3:12-14).

**ACTION STEPS:**
1. Acknowledge that some people her age can be cruel, but most people will learn to look past her appearance.
2. Help your daughter focus on the positive parts of her personality.
3. Remind your daughter that most people are unhappy with some part of their appearance.

Thanks...

I cannot remember a day my mother didn't tell me she loved me—even when I was a teenager and mad and wanting to borrow the car. I cannot remember a day I did not know my mother adored me. The confidence that gives a kid!

Chonda Pierce—comedian and speaker

# LACK OF COMMUNICATION

*My 14-year-old brings friends over quite often. I have really enjoyed getting to know these boys. One day it struck me that I know more about my son's friends than I know about him. Why will my son's friends talk to me but my own son hardly says hello?*

Congratulations for building a home where friends feel welcomed. You're giving your son a wonderful chance to build solid friendships.

The reason his friends talk more easily to you is because you're not their parent. They likely think their own parents are embarrassing, but you are cool. Friends may even do chores cheerfully at your house. It's simply the fun of newness and not-my-houseness.

Use your good standing to connect with your son. You can start by privately affirming your son—something parents should do every chance they get. Say, "You certainly do pick good friends. What do you like about them?" Simple affirmations like these can assure your son of your interest in him and spur him to talk. If he still stays quiet, don't despair. There's more you can do.

It doesn't hurt to explain the you're-not-my-parent-so-you're-OK phenomenon. You can say, "Your friends like talking to me because I'm not their parent; you may like talking to their parents because they're not yours. But even though I'm your uncool parent, I still enjoy hearing your thoughts and ideas. You're my favorite teenager. What's been on your mind lately?"

As nice as it is to get along with your son's friends, there is one caution: Some teens really believe their parents like their friends better than them. Debunk this by talking about it directly: "I like your friends because they like you." Give him specific affirmations every day, and as you voice what you like in your son, he'll give you even more reasons to know and like him.

**ACTION STEPS:**

1. Keep making your household a place where your son and his friends feel welcome.

2. Let your son know you're interested in his thoughts and feelings.

3. Find ways to praise and affirm your son every day.

# CALLS FROM GIRLS

*In recent months, our son has started getting phone calls from girls. I don't think it's appropriate for girls to call boys. How can I communicate that to these girls without embarrassing my son?*

You don't communicate it to the girls. You communicate it to your son. If you don't want girls to call because it precludes your son taking the lead in relationships, now is a good time to let him practice that lead role. Tell him exactly what you've told me: "I don't think it's appropriate for girls to call guys because ___. To keep from embarrassing you by telling the girls this, I'm telling you."

Invite your son to tell you how he feels about girls calling him. He might be as uncomfortable about it as you are. Then, get his ideas for what he can do about it. You can offer some ideas, too. You could decide that if a girl is calling to talk about a homework assignment or a question about school, he can talk for a few minutes. But if she doesn't have a real reason for calling, encourage him to politely get off the phone. He could say something like, "Thanks for calling. I'll call you next time we need to talk about something." If he isn't interested in calling her back, a simple "See you at school" could nip it in the bud.

This would also be a good time to help your son learn how to talk to girls and how to get to know a girl he might be interested in. Let him know that he should talk to girls just like he would any other person —ask questions, listen well, and show interest in what she's interested in. Doing these things doesn't mean he has to start dating. But he is at a good age for learning how to develop friendships with girls that could someday lead to dating relationships. And when that time comes, he'll be ready to make his own phone calls.

**ACTION STEPS:**

1. Talk to your son about the phone-calling situation.
2. Help your son find a solution by suggesting ways he can politely tell the girls not to call.
3. Use this as a springboard to helping your son build healthy friendships with girls.

# PHONE USE

*My daughter is constantly on the phone, to the point that urgent calls and family can't get through. Aside from call waiting, which we find rude, is there anything we can do?*

Phone calls are important to teenagers—it helps them feel connected to friends. (I once heard about a teen who called her friend while they did homework. They didn't talk; they would just breathe together.) But overcoming selfishness is also important for teenagers. So explain to your daughter that you want her to talk to her friends, and you also want her to show respect to others by sharing the phone.

To help her do both, set up a schedule that seems reasonable to you. Maybe you can allow her 10 minutes on the phone for every hour between the end of school and bedtime. Or if she prefers, tell her she can save up her 10-minute conversations for a 30-minute call every three hours. Obviously, you can negotiate a little with your daughter. Maybe you can give her 15 minutes during the hour after school, then 10 minutes each hour for the rest of her day. Work with her, and she may be more willing to work with you. Even if she's unwilling, the plan remains in effect.

Of course, for this plan to have any sticking power, you'll have to monitor phone time. Use a timer, refuse to give in to the pitiful "just-one-more-thing-to-say!" pleas, and make certain she doesn't sneak extra phone calls. This process may be tense at first, but keep the end in mind: Your daughter will make the most of her phone calls and will have time to pursue other projects: reading, writing letters, and of course, completing homework.

## ACTION STEPS:

1. Help your daughter see that she can both talk on the phone and show respect to her family by freeing up the phone.
2. Set up a calling plan.
3. Monitor her phone use as she adapts to the new system.

# MESSINESS

*Our son is such a slob! He leaves half-eaten food in his room, dumps his books and jacket in the middle of the living room, and throws his dirty clothes on the floor with the clean clothes he hasn't bothered to put away. We've talked to him about the importance of cleanliness and showing respect for other people in the house, but he tunes us out and doesn't change a thing.*

If a picture is worth a thousand words, parental action is worth ten thousand words. Every teenager, child, and adult knows how to tune out words they don't want to hear. So forget words. Your son will pick up his stuff when you make it happen. If you won't do it for yourself, do it for the wife he will someday live with.

> "My parents don't check up on my room all the time—it's just up to me to clean it. But every three months we weed out my closet and under my bed, throwing out stuff I don't need so there's space for new stuff. It's a pretty good system." — Kent, 13

You can start by saying, "I have deprived you by not insisting you pick up your food, books, and clothes." (He'll likely disagree that this is deprivation, but continue anyway.) "I have failed to show you how to be a caring family member. So things will change. As soon as you get home from school, and before you do anything else, you will pick up clothes, food, and books. On Saturdays, you'll go nowhere and do nothing until dirty clothes are in the laundry, clean clothes are put away, food is out of your room, and books are on your desk. If you do this before going to bed, you can sleep in the next day. Otherwise you'll be up at 7:00 a.m. to do it."

"Yeah, whatever," your son will agree. He assumes you don't mean this any more than the other words you've said about cleanliness. But the next time he asks, "Mom, can I go to Jeff's house?" check his room and see how things look. If the mess is still there, calmly say, "Sure. As soon as you pick up your stuff." Then, follow him to his room and watch him until he's finished.

For those times he refuses to do what you've asked, make sure he experiences the consequences—like not going to Jeff's house. You can also use natural consequences—if he doesn't get his clothes in the laundry room, let him run out of clean clothes. Or refuse to buy him any new clothes until he demonstrates he can take care of his current wardrobe.

If this is going to work, you'll need to make sure your expectations are reasonable. Will his room be spotless? No. But if he puts a good-faith effort into picking up after himself, let him know how much you appreciate it.

ACTION STEPS:

1. Use action, not words, to get your point across.
2. Make cleaning up after himself a prerequisite to doing something fun.
3. Make sure you have reasonable expectations for what "clean" means.

"I have to clean my room once a week, and I keep it somewhat clean during the week, so my parents don't really lecture me about it. When they do, I just ignore them. I think that as long as it's 'somewhat' clean, it should be fine."
— Chris, 13

# LISTENING IN:

*Here's what 13- to 14-year-olds have to say...*

### ... about being rewarded for good grades:

"My parents don't have a reward system for good grades, but I wish they did. They just motivate me by saying I'm not going to get a very good job when I'm older if I don't get good grades." — *Taylor, 14*

"We have a reward system: For an A I get $5, nothing for a B, and if I get a C I have to pay $10. So I really try not to get bad grades. I've never gotten a C." — *Caitlin, 13*

"I don't have a reward system, and I don't think I really need one because I'm self-motivated. My parents just expect me to get good grades, and I just want to keep them happy." — *Kevin, 14*

"One of my friends has a reward system, but he doesn't do too well in school—he gets B's, C's, and D's. I don't have a reward system, but I get A's and B's. My parents just keep telling me to hit the books and encourage me to do my homework. The minute I come in, if I'm just watching TV, they tell me to get to work." — *Mez, 14*

"Every time I get an A on my report card I get $2, and it's $1 for each B. But the money doesn't really motivate me because I want to do good anyway." — *Kim, 13*

"I start off with $15 for each report card. Every time I bring up a grade it's $5 more and every time I bring down a grade it's minus $5. I think it works for me because when I feel like not doing my homework, I'll think about the money and do it." — *Kent, 13*

*... about cleaning their rooms:*

"I have to clean my room once a week, and I keep it somewhat clean during the week, so my parents don't really lecture me about it. When they do, I just ignore them. I think that as long as it's 'somewhat' clean, it should be fine." — *Chris, 13*

"My room is always a mess, and I get grounded a lot. I always say, 'It's my room, so I should be able to keep it the way I want.' My parents say, 'But it's our house.' It's not fair." — *Bethany M., 13*

"When my parents lecture me about my room, I pretend like I'm listening, but I'm really not. That way, when they ask me about it later, I can say I didn't hear them. But when they eventually catch me, I will clean my room. If I don't, after a while, I can't see the top of the desk, the floor, the bed..." — *Kyle, 14*

"My parents don't check up on my room all the time—it's just up to me to clean it. But every three months we weed out my closet and under my bed, throwing out stuff I don't need so there's space for new stuff. It's a pretty good system." — *Kent, 13*

"When I was younger, my parents really lectured me about how when people come over and see your room messy, they're going to think you're a disgusting pig. So I've gotten to the point where I like to keep my room really neat, even under the bed. I think all their lectures really paid off, because I just like having a clean room so much better." — *Bethany C., 13*

"It's my room, so I should decide how I want it. I should only have to clean it when guests are coming over, because that's important— to make it neat for them." — *Kevin, 14*

## ... about choosing their own music:

"My parents have a rule that if I want to buy non-Christian music, I have to make sure it's OK with them and I have to pay for it myself. And I'm not allowed to listen to the dance/hip-hop station on the radio." — *Jennie, 12*

"My parents check a Christian magazine to make sure the music I want to buy is OK. Sometimes I listen to stuff they don't like, at school or with friends, but not that much. And I don't listen to anything evil. I don't take what the music says to heart, so I don't see why it's a big deal." — *Chris, 13*

"My parents have always wanted me to listen to Christian music, and I didn't really think that was different from anyone else. Now it's just a habit to listen to Christian music. But if I ever want to get something that isn't Christian, my mom will go through the words to make sure they're clean, and if they aren't, I can't listen to it." — *Kim, 13*

"My parents say if a CD has any swears or a parental advisory, it's not allowed in the house. They're pretty strict. I have two older brothers, and they have some music they shouldn't listen to and our parents wouldn't like, but most of my CDs are OK." — *Wade, 14*

"My parents pretty much trust me with music. I listen to secular radio sometimes, but what I mostly listen to is my CDs. My mom goes through a few of them to make sure they're not dirty. But they basically trust me—I know which stations and songs not to listen to."
— *Shauna, 13*

"I just caught my mom looking through the liner notes on one of my CDs, so I've started looking at the backs of CDs before I buy them to make sure that if my mom ever does that again, there won't be anything in there that she won't approve of." — *Kyle, 14*

## ... about school dances:

"My parents let me go to dances. Sometimes there's bad stuff going on, and there's a lot of pressure to get into it, but I never do anything because I know most of it is wrong. I just go to have a good time with my friends." — *Caitlin, 13*

"I've been to some dances, but I didn't tell my parents that boys and girls danced together, because then they probably wouldn't let me go. Still, I think my mom and dad trust me and know I wouldn't do something like that." — *Laurel, 13*

"At our school dances, everybody just dances or talks. Nothing bad happens—maybe kissing at the most." — *Scott, 13*

"I don't think the chaperones at school dances are really paying attention. People these days think they can do anything. The worst stuff goes on outside, where there aren't any parents watching. The adults just don't have any idea what's going on." — *Bethany C., 13*

"I don't even want to go to dances anymore because they're so boring. But I've been to a lot of other parties this year that got out of control. I've seen some things I know were wrong. But my parents are pretty lenient and I'm pretty responsible. I know what's right and wrong." — *Brandon, 14*

"We don't really have chaperones at our dances—they sell the tickets and then go off to a corner where you don't see them. So boys and girls will go to the back hallways, and you don't see them for a while, so you can only imagine what they're doing. But there's no pressure to go back there because you can always say you don't want to get caught. Who would actually catch you, I don't know."
— *Lauren, 13*

# The Middle TEEN

## Ages 15-17

by Jim Burns

# The Middle TEEN
## Ages 15-17

The teenage years are not easy for parents, or for our children, who are rapidly moving from dependence on us toward independence. This weaning process rarely comes without a few bumps along the road. I've heard the years between age 12 and age 20 referred to as the "unplaced years." Our teenagers aren't children, but they aren't adults either. Most are not sure of their role in society and this leads to a great deal of confusion, which often gets expressed through sullenness, rudeness, rebellion, or anger. And just when you finally think you have it figured out, something happens to stir life up again.

If you're one of those parents having a hard time doing the teenage thing, you're in good company. Most of us struggle with more conflict, more fears, more frustration, and more worries than we ever anticipated. And yet the world is full of parents who've made it through those years and are still breathing. There is hope!

I believe that understanding what's happening inside your teenager is one of the most important factors in surviving these years. Knowing why your child is acting a certain way can go a long way toward helping you handle the situation in a loving, productive way. While every family faces its own challenges during the teenage years, most teenagers share some common characteristics. Teenagers tend to be:

*Self-absorbed:* There are just too many transformations going on in their lives for them not to be focused on self. They are self-conscious of everything from pimples and breasts to mustaches and armpit hair. The same child who just a few years ago was kind and sweet and other centered might now make a statement like, "Why would Grandpa die on a Saturday and ruin my weekend." Keep in mind that your teenager isn't acting this way just to bother you. In his mind, his experiences are absolute reality. You can help him return to a caring, compassionate, respectful human being by modeling those traits as you make your way through these years.

*Experimental*: Statistics tell us that the teenage years are when kids will try their first drink and possibly drug. A majority of the kids will have sexual intercourse before they get to adulthood. That doesn't mean your child will experiment, but don't be surprised if she does. You probably experimented when you were a teenager, too. While your child's curiosity can certainly lead to tremendous trouble, remember that not all experimental behavior leads to a crisis. This is a time of exploration and freedom and a great deal of learning. That is why your teen needs your calm, consistent presence more than ever.

*Searching for a sense of self:* This is the season where kids are establishing more lasting relationships with peers, experiencing a changing relationship with their parents, and hopefully solidifying a relationship with God. All of these relationships are shaping your child into the adult he will become. He needs your guidance to develop the social skills to find friends who will build him up, not tear him down. He needs your unconditional love and grace to keep the lines of communication open between you. He needs your example of a vibrant, relevant faith to deepen his own understanding of how God is at work in his life. Most of all, he needs your patience as he jumps from soccer player to poet to swimmer to rap artist. At this stage, teenagers will try on all kinds of different hats in an effort to find one that fits. Give them the freedom to explore with the knowledge that you will remain their safety net.

*Emotional!:* Need I say more. With the onslaught of puberty also comes a rise in emotions. Guilt, passion, anxiety, fear, and anger are just a few of the many intense emotions in your child's body and on her mind. Again, your patience and understanding are crucial. As you help your child find healthy and appropriate ways to express her emotions, you'll be equipping her with an invaluable life skill.

In my work with teenagers, I often see parents take a backseat. They figure they got the kids through childhood and now it's time to coast. My guess is that you don't believe this philosophy or you wouldn't pick up this book. I want to affirm your committment to continue being an active part of your child's life. While your role will change over the next few years, it is no less important to your child's destiny. So take a deep breath or a nap, maybe even a trip away from the kids, and get ready to push on toward the home stretch. And remember, once you get them through the teenage years, you can relax and spoil your grandkids!

—*Jim Burns*

# LIKING YOUR KIDS

*I want so much to feel good about my kids, but it's not easy. There are days, sometimes weeks, when they drive me crazy! How can I have a positive attitude about my kids?*

Parenting isn't easy. If you know someone who says they have no conflicts with their family, then they simply aren't telling you the truth. For me, parenting is both the greatest and the most difficult part of my life. When we first had children, I expected the highs but I completely underestimated the lows, the difficult moments. In other words, your feelings are completely normal.

I believe parenting is one of God's highest callings. God's Word is quite clear: When he entrusts us with a family, we are to do our best to serve him by serving our family. Sometimes, when my children are wearing me down, I try to remember that eternal perspective.

Practically speaking, make sure you're finding time to enjoy your kids. Our family takes regular trips to the beach because we all enjoy that activity. We try to have a "family fun day" once a month and let our girls have a say in how we spend that time. I also have regular dates with each of my kids. These times all remind me of the positive side of raising teenagers.

Take time away from your kids once in a while, too. Get away with your spouse, some good friends, or even by yourself. Spend time doing something you enjoy. Take time to pray and renew your spirit. Share your struggles with someone who can encourage you and support you on your rough days.

As difficult as they can be sometimes, teenagers really are terrific, often fascinating people. They see the world in interesting ways, can be incredibly inspiring when they talk about their dreams, and are really a lot of fun. Do what you can to start seeing your teenagers through fresh eyes, and I think you'll find your attitude changing, too.

**ACTION STEPS:**

1. **Realize it's normal to feel frustrated by your teenagers.**
2. **Remember that you serve God as you serve your family.**
3. **Make time to have fun with your teenagers and get to know them as people.**

"I choose to go on vacation with my family because I lead such a busy life that not only is it great to get away, it's also good to spend time with my family. Vacations are good because you get to spend time together without having to worry about things like work and stress." — Sandy, 17

# FAMILY VACATIONS

*Our children, ages 15 and 17, each want to bring a friend along on our family vacation. We don't really mind, but we can't help but feel that adding two more people will make for a crowded, not to mention expensive, vacation. Any suggestions?*

At the risk of sounding a little prudish, I'm not for taking friends on a family vacation. I see vacations as a time to get away from the pace of life most of us live and bring the family closer together. It's difficult to have close family experiences when others are always with you.

We recently went on a family camping trip—our first in 15 years! One reason it worked so well was because our girls actually hung out with each other. If their friends had been along, the three girls would have wandered off with their friends and not spent time with their sisters. Cathy and I were able to have quality time with our daughters because we, and not their friends, were their social circle for a few days.

However, if you decide to say no to your kids' requests, be prepared to put more energy into doing what your kids want to do and possibly hear a few more phrases like, "I'm bored." Give your kids some say in where you go and what you do. If they have a part in planning the trip, they'll be much more inclined to enjoy themselves and their family.

Obviously, there will be times when you'll want your kids to bring their friends along. And allowing friends to join you on occasion will give you a bit more negotiating power when you want to limit a trip to family only. But for the most part, I would guard the family vacation as an important time of family interaction and recreation, as well as a time for building each other up.

**ACTION STEPS:**

1. **Help your kids think of a family vacation as a chance to spend time together without any distractions.**
2. **Let your kids help plan the family trip and include plenty of activities they'll enjoy.**
3. **Be willing to include friends on occasional trips.**

"My parents have never given me a choice of whether or not to go on a family vacation. I've always wanted to go. However, by the end of the vacation, I can't wait to get home. My brother and I always end up fighting, which makes my dad mad, and no one is in a good mood." — Megan, 17

# Thanks...

I grew up in a very poor family in West Philadelphia. My parents' stories are quite dramatic. Let me just say they endured the usual suffering immigrant people in the early part of the 20th century had to endure, came to know Christ, and brought me up as a Christian.

We were so poor that we never went on vacation anywhere. But once a year, my father would pack up the family and we would go from Philadelphia down to Atlantic City, which was some 60 miles away, to spend the day at the shore. That was our vacation, and it was a big day.

I remember during World War II when it was very, very difficult to get automobile tires, that we had bald tires. But my father was determined to get us to the shore.

The tires were so horrible. Going to Atlantic City and back, which was 120 miles, we had a total of 13 flat tires. And in those days, when you changed a tire, you took the innertube out, blew up the innertube, found the leak, put a patch on the leak, put the whole thing together. But my mom and dad made it a fun time of laughing and joking instead of a time of despair. We would sing and joke as we changed the tire. It was almost as though every time we had a flat, we greeted it with "Yay!"

I've always thought, Wasn't that great. They could take something that obviously would have driven most people up a wall and turned it into something fun.

Tony Campolo—sociologist, author, speaker

# TEEN CULTURE

*My husband and I are clueless about teen culture. It's hard for us to connect with our 15-year-old daughter, much less help her make good decisions, when we don't know what her world is like. How can we learn to understand teen culture?*

By recognizing that today's teen culture is different from the one you grew up in, you're off to a good start. As parents, we must become students of the culture. Even if we don't like what's going on, we must study the latest trends. I find three ways to keep up with the culture most helpful.

*1. Ask lots of questions.* Constantly ask the teenagers in your life about their music, heroes, and media. For example, yesterday I took my seventh-grade daughter out to breakfast, and I asked her who were the latest popular music groups at her school. She told me the names of a few groups. I told her I wanted to listen to some of the music with her. Even though I didn't like what I was hearing, it helped me understand what's popular among her peers.

*2. Read magazines written for teenagers.* I find that the latest teen magazines available at the library give parents a great cultural lesson. To be honest, some of the articles geared toward teens scare me because of the high degree of sexual innuendoes. However, teen magazines will immediately place you in their culture.

*3. Listen to their music.* More than any other medium, music is the language of youth culture. Today, because there are so many different styles of music, make sure you know what kind of music is influencing your teenager. A 15-minute look at MTV or VH1 will possibly disgust you, but it also will give you insight into the culture that is influencing your kids. I'd advise doing the same with the TV shows and movies your daughter sees.

One last piece of advice: Don't always react too negatively to the teen culture. Spend time really trying to understand what your kids are going through. They need understanding, wisdom, and insight, not horror or dismay.

**ACTION STEPS:**

1. Talk to your teenager about what's popular with her friends and at her school.
2. Read teen magazines to get an insight into teen issues.
3. Keep up with the media trends that pervade youth culture.

"We are going on a vacation soon, and I don't want to go. My mom isn't giving me a choice about going, and we fight about it every day. She doesn't care what I want or say." — Ryan, 15

# NAGGING

*My teenagers hardly talk to me. My husband says it's because I nag them too much and I'm too critical. I suspect he's right—my mother was the same way. How can I stop being a nag and be the kind of mother my kids want to talk to?*

Bad habits are difficult to break, especially when it comes to parenting. If you truly are quick to criticize and nag, your husband probably has a point.

But there is a way to break out of the nagging habit. The more clearly you express your expectations and boundaries in a positive and loving manner, the less you'll have to nag. Let me give you an example from my own not-so-perfect home. We drive our three girls to school in the morning, and they are almost always late. My wife, Cathy, and I used to spend the hour before school nagging, bribing, and threatening them. By the time we got in the car, nobody liked anyone else in the family.

One day I announced that it was a "no nag day." The kids cheered. Cathy wrote out the morning responsibilities and put the list on message central—our refrigerator. Our parental role was to give two time warnings at 20 and 10 minutes before it was time to leave. Any delinquent daughter would get fined an agreed-upon amount from her allowance.

The first week, we made money on the deal, accompanied by a few tears and arguments. Since then, the girls are seldom late, and my blood pressure is back to normal. Now I actually like mornings with our family!

In addition to setting up clear expectations and consequences, think about the words you use with your teens. Phrases like *"you idiot"* or *"that's the dumbest thing I have ever heard"* tend to kill a conversation. And remember, even if your words don't keep your kids from wanting to talk, your attitude might. Do your best to be open, resist confrontation unless it's absolutely necessary, and listen more than you speak. Your teens will pick up on the change.

## ACTION STEPS:

1. Express your expectations clearly and in a positive way.
2. Establish consequences for not following through on expectations.
3. Think about the words and attitude you use when you talk to your teens.

"I am way too busy! My parents, however, do play an active part in helping me prioritize my life. They encourage me to participate only in activities that are important to me and to not get so involved that I never have free time. They also do the most important thing any parent can do: They are my cheerleaders!"
— Lauren, 17

# MARRIAGE PROBLEMS

*My wife and I are really struggling in our marriage. Our 16-year-old son hears us fighting, but we haven't told him how badly we're doing. How much should we share about our relationship?*

I bet your son already knows that your marriage is on rocky ground, and I bet he would appreciate some communication on the subject. It might be difficult for you, but it's important that he hear the truth from you, rather than imagining something even worse.

If you don't know what to say, try something like this: "As you know, your mom and I don't always see eye to eye. This has been a difficult season for our marriage, and we are struggling. However, we want to assure you we are truly working on our marriage, and we need your prayers. If you have any questions about our relationship, don't hesitate to ask. We'll do our best to be open with you." While it's not essential to give your son every detail of the conflict, I would encourage you to tell him—and show him—what you're doing to help heal your marriage: counseling, time away together, re-prioritizing your relationship, or whatever else you're trying. A healthy family includes each other in the difficult times as well as the good times.

**ACTION STEPS:**

1. Be honest with your son. He's probably already aware of the problems.

2. Assure your son that you're working to improve your marriage.

3. Let your son see you working on your relationship.

# FAMILY MEALS

*Our family has gotten away from eating dinner together. With three active teenagers and our own busy schedules, we tend to eat on the run. It doesn't seem to bother my kids or my husband, but I really miss sitting down as a family. Is it realistic to think we can have a family meal?*

It's realistic, but it's not easy. To make it happen, start with one night a week when you can all sit together for at least half an hour.

If that means eating early to make it to your daughter's soccer game, that's OK. If it means Mom picks up a pizza on her way home, that's OK. Do what it takes to make sure this doesn't become an event that simply leads to more stress for the family.

Is it possible to have dinner together every night? Probably not. But with a little sacrifice and forward planning, it's possible to make family meals more than a chance happening. If you just can't arrange a family dinner, try sitting down together for breakfast, bedtime snacks, or any other time you can spend as a family. Quality family time and communication are not optional for healthy families; they are a necessity!

**ACTION STEPS:**

1. Realize that family meals are a crucial element of building a healthy family.

2. Start by planning one low-key family meal each week.

3. Be flexible about when and where you spend your family time.

"My family eats dinner together every night. After that we don't see much of each other, unless one of us needs to talk. I think I spend enough time with my parents, though I know I will realize when I'm older that I probably took them for granted." — Stephen, 16

# ' DEVOTIONS

*agers think our family devotions are dull. Any suggestions*
*for livening things up a bit?*

I want to commend you for the fact that you have family devotions together. You are further along than most. And you're also experiencing something very common. As children grow into teenagers, it gets more challenging to keep them interested in family time, much less family time that involves reading, studying, or listening to Mom and Dad talk.

Now is a great time to expand your idea of what "devotions" can be. Jim Rayburn, the founder of Young Life, was fond of saying, "It's a sin to bore a kid with the gospel." So rather than stick with the model of reading a few verses of the Bible and discussing them, try really bringing faith to life for your teens. My wife and I know a family who took a week-long vacation to Yosemite National Park. Each day, they hiked the waterfalls, swam the rivers, and looked for deer. Every night around the campfire they played a game they called "I Spy." Each person had to share 20 ways he or she saw God working that day. As they talked about their discoveries, a fun vacation turned into a meaningful spiritual time.

You don't have to head to the woods to break out of a devotions rut. Act out a Bible story as a family. Take a current event and turn it into a Bible discussion. Listen to one of your teens' favorite songs and base a devotional on that. Include your teenagers as you plan. They probably have some great ideas. Don't forget to have a supportive time of prayer together. Create a family devotion time with an emphasis on love, encouragement, and fun. It will be a positive spiritual memory that will last a lifetime.

ACTION STEPS:

1. Stick with your efforts to have regular family devotions.

2. Stretch your idea of what constitutes a devotion.

3. Let your teenagers help come up with ideas for family devotions.

"OH, LOOK AT THAT! FIRST A LAWN MOWER AND NOW A SNOW SHOVEL! HOW ABOUT A BIG 'THANK YOU' FOR YOUR FATHER, MARTY?"

# FAMILY ACTIVITIES

*Our 15-year-old son refuses to participate in family activities. He won't go out for dinner, visit relatives, or even join us at his little sister's soccer games. I know he needs some independence, but he's still part of this family, and we'd like him to realize that, too. Any suggestions?*

Your son is moving rapidly from the dependence of a child toward the independence of an adult. You're right that he needs some autonomy to move through that process and that he also still needs to be connected with his family. My advice is to work with him to create a plan where he is part of most family experiences and on rare occasions given the freedom to not participate.

Part of what might be happening with your son is that he feels he has no choice about these family activities. Or he feels like outings and events are sprung on him without notice or consideration for his schedule. I find one of the keys to successful communication is to clearly express your expectations. How many family dinners would you like him to attend each week? How many soccer games can he realistically go to? What do you expect from him when the relatives come to town or your family visits them? I suggest holding a family meeting once a week where everyone can talk about the upcoming week. Then, decide as a family who will attend what. Be willing to let your son bow out of an activity or two on the condition that he joins you for others.

Believe me, I've learned this lesson the hard way. Every time I expect one of my daughters to fall in line with my plans without talking to her about my expectations, we all end up frustrated. Be clear with your son, give him the chance to do his own thing now and then, and I think he'll become more inclined to spend time with the rest of the family.

**ACTION STEPS:**

1. **Make your expectations about family activities clear to your son.**

2. **Plan a family meeting to let everyone know what's happening each week.**

3. **Negotiate with your son about which family events he needs to attend and which ones he can miss.**

"We always go somewhere during the summer, whether I like it or not ... usually not. I'd rather stay home and have time alone with God and my friends than be away somewhere I'd never choose to go. I'm at the age when I should be able to make my own decisions. I want my freedom." — Tammy, 17

# TROUBLED CHILD

*Our 17-year-old son has had some emotional problems in the last year. We've spent a great deal of time and effort on him. But we're concerned that our two other teenagers are being left out. How do we balance the needs of each of our children?*

This is a surprisingly common problem. I think the answer has two parts: boundaries and seasons of life.

It's essential that your "needy" child not consume the whole family. To keep that from happening, you need to set some boundaries. You need to be able to say, "I can't talk with you right now. I need to spend some time with your brother." Saying "no," or at least "wait," to your son might not be easy, but it will communicate to him that he's not the only one in the family with needs.

I suggest you and your spouse set up regular "date nights" with each of your children. Go out for a quick meal, take a walk, or just hang out. Don't talk about homework, curfew, or the other issues. Literally make your agenda the relationship, and save lectures or correction for another conversation. Make a commitment to keep these dates, no matter what.

Thinking in terms of seasons can also help you keep this difficult period in perspective. While it's true your problems might not end soon, most struggles have intense and not-so-intense times. Encourage your other children to think about this time as a season, too. Understanding that your family is going through a certain season that will eventually end can help them be more patient.

One last thought: For the sake of your other children, your marriage, and your own well-being, make sure you find the best support you can to help you through this time. The Scripture clearly states, "Make plans by seeking advice" (Prov. 20:18a). Your problems won't magically go away when you seek advice and counsel, but you'll gain strength from sharing your burden with others.

**ACTION STEPS:**

1. **Establish clear boundaries so that you can meet the needs of each of your children.**

2. Remember this is a season of your family life that will eventually pass.
3. Find people who can offer you help and support.

# GRIEF (1)

*We recently lost our 14-year-old son in an accident. While we know our son followed Jesus, there's a hole in our family now that will never be filled. How can we help our 17-year-old son cope with this loss in the midst of our own pain?*

Your tragedy is one of the most difficult burdens I can imagine. You have my deep condolences. To answer your question simply, if you want to help your son through his grief, you'll need to deal with your own grief in a healthy way. Your son will follow your lead, so don't be afraid to let him see your pain.

Most people who grieve go through five stages: anger, denial, depression, bargaining with God, and after some time, acceptance. Still, every person grieves differently. When my mother died, I didn't experience a great deal of anger. My brother on the other hand experienced intense anger. If one of my children died, I know I'd grieve in a completely different manner than I did for my mother.

It's part of the parental instinct to want to protect our children from pain and sadness. But in the case of grief, it's essential your son knows he is free to feel and express the emotions he experiences. Try to be open to his expressions of anger and doubt. Do what you can to show him you can accept his anger, sadness, and pain. Talk openly about your own feelings and encourage him to do the same.

Also, keep looking to God for help, comfort, and an eternal perspective. As painful as your loss is, you can find some peace knowing your son is with God and he is whole and healthy. Even as you draw on the power and strength of God to get you through your grief, gather people around you who can support you and your son through the early weeks and months of your loss. It would be good to locate a support group for grieving families. I would also strongly encourage family counseling. Ask your pastor to help you find the support and psychological assistance you need.

As awful as this situation is, help your son remember that God never promised he would free us from all pain and tragedy, but rather that he would give us the strength to live one day at a time under the care of his love. Hold tight to that promise.

**ACTION STEPS:**

1. Allow your teenager to see you grieve.
2. Let him know he is free to express any emotions he feels as he grieves.
3. Cling to God's promise to comfort and heal your family and seek support to help you through your pain.

# GRIEF (2)

*One of our daughter's good friends from church recently died in a car accident. How can we help her cope with this horrible crisis?*

The death of a friend is one of the hardest issues a person can face—and that's especially true of teens. You can see your daughter through this time by helping her understand she's going to feel a wide range of emotions pain, sorrow, doubt, anger, bitterness. It's essential to help your daughter understand that all of these emotions are OK.

Encourage your daughter to find a way to say goodbye to her friend. She could write a letter to her friend, read a poem or Scripture passage at the memorial service, or if it's too late for that, place a copy of the poem or verse at the gravesite. For one young woman I know, it helped to put one of her prized possessions, her Bible, in her friend's casket.

It's important to remind grieving teens of the eternal perspective. As your daughter grieves, use God's Word to reassure her. Emphasize that God prepares an eternal home in heaven for all who believe in him—including her friend. Our time on earth is only the beginning of life with God. I love how Jesus comforted his disciples before he went to the cross: "Do not let your heart be troubled. Trust in God; trust also in me. In my Father's house are many rooms; if it were not so,

I would have told you. I am going there to prepare a place for you. And if I go and prepare a place for you, I will come back and take you to be with me that you also may be where I am." (John. 14:1-3).

Your daughter may have all kinds of questions about God and his sovereignty right now. If her friend wasn't a Christian, she might be feeling tremendous guilt over not doing more to lead her friend to Christ. These are difficult spiritual issues. You might want to consider having your daughter meet with your pastor, a Christian counselor, or another Christian adult she trusts to talk over her concerns and questions.

## ACTION STEPS:

1. **Help your daughter work through the broad range of emotions grief can bring.**

2. **Encourage your daughter to find a way to say goodbye to her friend.**

3. **Access other resources to help her deal with both the psychological and spiritual aspects of her grief.**

# BEING EXCITED ABOUT FAITH

*Our 15-year-old doesn't seem to have much interest in the spiritual side of life. We attend an excellent church with a great youth group, but our son just isn't excited about his faith. What can we do to help him feel the "fire of faith" in his life?*

There are a hundred different ways I could answer your question, but for the sake of space, I want to focus on you. When it comes to keeping the faith fires burning in the lives of your children, you set the pace. One of our primary jobs as Christian parents is to place spiritual deposits into the lives of our children. You are fortunate to have a good church and excellent youth group to reinforce those spiritual values, but the primary source of Christian education tends to be the home.

I've learned from experience that I can't be a good "spiritual depositor" if I'm too busy to spend quality spiritual time with my kids. And I know I can't help my kids grow in their faith if I'm not working on my own relationship with God.

If you feel like there's more you could do to make spiritual deposits in your son, try some of these ideas:

- Read a Christian youth devotional together once a week (keep your session under 10 minutes).

- Give your son a new Christian music CD or cassette. Make sure it's his style of music, not necessarily your style. Listen to it together and talk about the message behind the music.

- Offer to pay for your son and a friend to go on the church youth group's next outing.

- Invite some of the kids from the youth group over for a party. Don't forget, positive peer influence is just as powerful as negative peer pressure.

- Be vulnerable with your children. Share a personal need or struggle and then ask for prayer.

Let your son see a consistent "fire of faith" in your life and, in time, you'll start to see a spark in him as well.

## ACTION STEPS:

1. Recognize that you can set the pace for your son's spiritual growth.

2. Identify any hurdles that might be keeping you from being a strong example of vibrant faith.

3. Find creative ways to get involved in your son's spiritual development.

"I want to go to a different church, but my parents won't let me leave. I'm not getting anything from my church spiritually, and I need something more. If I were a parent, I would be proud

to let my child grow strong in the Lord even if it meant letting them go to another church. I'd back them 110 percent."
— Nancy, 16

"I switched churches a few years ago because the youth group at my parents' church fell apart. My parents were kind of disappointed that I didn't want to go to church with them, but they understood that I needed to do something different. I'm still attending the new church, and it's been great for me. Plus, when I leave for college and need to find a new church, I'll know how to find one that's right for me."
— Meredith, 17

# Thanks...

I remember talking with my mother the night I became a Christian at a youth meeting at church. I'd felt God calling me to commit my whole life to him. I went home afterward, sat on my bed with my mom, and cried. She wrote in her journal that I said, "It makes me cry when I realize how much Jesus loves me." She put her arms around me and talked to me about the sacrifice Jesus made when he gave his life for us. It was a beautiful moment.

Rebecca St. James—recording artist

# YOUTH GROUP ACTIVITIES

*Our daughter isn't interested in going to the youth group camps or retreats offered by our church. We think these experiences would be a great opportunity for her to grow in her faith. Should we force her to go?*

I've never had a student come to me at church and say, "Jim, I'm considering going on the church retreat and I was wondering what biblical passages you'll be using when you speak?" I've had hundreds ask, "Who else is going on the retreat?" In other words, relationships are the key. The difference between forcing your daughter to go and her being at least mildly excited will be the presence of at least one friend on the same retreat.

So help your daughter find a friend to go with her to camp or on a retreat. Once they are on the retreat, chances are good they'll have a great time, make new friends, and even learn a thing or two about God.

If your daughter still seems reluctant to go, ask her why. It might be that she hates the idea of sleeping in a cabin, or she doesn't like hiking or canoeing. Whatever her concerns, listen to her and do what you can to allay any fears. If she's just not ready for this experience, don't force her. But do encourage her to think about going on the next retreat.

I like retreats and camps a lot. It seems like when you get people out of their routine they open up to spiritual issues much more easily. In a recent survey from *Group* magazine and Youth For Christ, students placed a retreat or camp as their number one source of spiritual growth. That's why I hope you'll do everything you possibly can to get your daughter interested in at least trying out that retreat experience. When she returns, she'll most likely thank you.

**ACTION STEPS:**

1. **Encourage your daughter to bring a friend with her.**

2. **Talk to your daughter about any fears or concerns she has.**

3. **Continue to give her opportunities to experience this great chance for spiritual growth.**

"At my parents' church, the youth
group is really small, and I felt like an
outcast. Now I go to a different
church, where there's a wider range of
people I can relate to. My parents were
totally against me going to another
church at first. But they've seen how
much I've grown up in Christ since
then, and they're cool with it now."

— Katelyn, 16

# YOUTH GROUP

*We just moved to a new city and are searching for a church. We want one with a strong youth program. What should we look for in a youth ministry?*

Since spiritual development is a vital part of your teenagers' faith, you're wise to consider youth programs as you look for a new church.

As you visit churches in your area, get your teenagers' impressions. If they like a church, even a little, arrange to meet with the youth leader. Ask about the theology of the staff, the program, activities, camps and retreats, size of the group, and the school or schools from which it draws students. You may want to take a look at the teaching curriculum. If you and your teens feel good about what you learn, ask to meet the volunteers who work with the youth group. Ask these volunteers why they're involved in the group and find out about their experience working with teenagers.

You'll never find "the perfect group." However, by investing time in getting to know the leadership team, you'll be much happier and understand more about what your kids are experiencing. Remember: the bottom line in youth ministry is not how many kids are coming to the meetings, but rather what's happening with the kids who are there. If kids feel connected to the church, they will stay with it well beyond their teen years.

One last comment: Keep in mind that the primary responsibility for a child's Christian formation is placed on parents and the church as a whole, not the youth group. Don't expect any youth group to take the place of your God-given responsibility to "train a child in the way he should go" (Prov. 22:6).

**ACTION STEPS:**

1. **Get your teenagers' reactions to churches you visit.**

2. **Meet with the youth leader and adult volunteers to get a feel for the group.**

3. **Remember that youth ministry is a supplement to, not a replacement for, your own efforts to help your teens grow in their faith.**

# PRAYER

*Our 16-year-old came to me in tears the other night saying she didn't know how to pray anymore. She feels like God isn't listening to her and that she doesn't know how to talk to him. I need some suggestions to help her.*

It sounds like your daughter has a tender heart for God. I don't know anyone who feels God's presence in prayer at all moments. Make sure you reassure her of God's unfailing faithfulness and love for her.

Help your daughter consider adding other spiritual disciplines to her life, such as occasional 10-12 hour fasting or discipleship by a more mature Christian whom she trusts. There are some smaller changes that can help too. If she's been praying by herself, offer to pray with her. If she prays sitting on her bed, suggest she get on her knees. She could sing praise and prayer songs, read a devotional book or try special prayers like the Lord's Prayer, The Serenity Prayer, or The Prayer of St. Francis of Assisi. She can pray the Psalms.

You might want to introduce her to other types of prayer. For example, if she is primarily praying prayers of supplication (asking), encourage her to spend some time in praise, thanksgiving, confession, and listening.

When I feel like my prayers are going nowhere, I often take an extended time of praise and thanksgiving with God. Praise and thanksgiving put life in proper perspective. Praise is the purest form of worship. When we begin to have an attitude of praise, we free our spirits to live for God. There is nothing more exciting or fulfilling than lifting our hearts to God in praise. The Bible even reminds us, "They who seek the Lord will praise him" (Ps. 22:26). When I'm feeling low or far from God, thanksgiving helps remind me of all the ways God is present in my life. Hopefully, it will do the same for your daughter.

ACTION STEPS:
1. Help your daughter find additional spiritual disciplines to add a spark to her prayer life.
2. Introduce her to other types of prayer.
3. Encourage her to praise God and offer thanks for all the ways he is present in her life.

# CHURCH

*Our daughter's bad attitude about church is starting to rub off on her little brother and sister. We've been pretty understanding about her desire to be away from the church right now, but we don't like the idea of her taking the other two kids with her. Should we say something to her about this?*

Yes. As parents, one of our jobs is to guard our children from destructive influences that can hurt their faith. Unfortunately, your older daughter has become that influence in the lives of your

189

younger children. When you talk with her, help her see that one of your deepest desires is for all of your children to thrive in their faith and experience God's presence through the body of Christ, the church. Remind her that you've been willing to let her make some of her own decisions about church and that she needs to let her siblings do the same. It's not her place to tell them what they should and shouldn't think about church.

Since I don't know the particulars of your daughter's feelings about church, let me make a couple of general comments. It's normal for teenagers to rebel and go through a time of doubting God or the church. She may have some very good reasons for disliking church but nevertheless, the church is still God's vehicle for showing the world that Jesus Christ is Lord.

Despite your daughter's feelings about church, it's essential that you continue to nurture her spiritual development (Deut. 6:6-7). Have a regular family devotional time, pray with her, take her to a Christian bookstore to find a book that addresses some of the issues she's facing. Encourage her to get involved with a solid parachurch organization like Young Life or Youth for Christ. Maybe she'd thrive in a youth group at a bigger—or smaller—church. Where do her friends go to church? Who could be positive role models in her life?

I know it can be very disturbing when a child strays from the church. But rest assured that teens often return to faith when they are from a home where Christ is honored. So stay committed to your own church involvement and spiritual disciplines and pray like crazy that God will protect your daughter and draw her back to his church.

ACTION STEPS:

1. Ask your daughter to watch her words and attitude around her younger siblings.

2. Continue to nurture your daughter's spiritual growth through other methods.

3. Model a faithful relationship with God through your own church involvement and spiritual growth.

"When I got to high school, I began to feel like I'd seen everything my parents' church had to offer. I had the whole church service memorized; I repeated the words without thinking about what they meant. So I started seeking God more, and that meant finding a new church. My family was shocked. My mom cried for days, saying I'd betrayed my family and my heritage. But eventually, she noticed a change in my life. Now she's seeking God more, too." — Wally, 17

# SEPARATE CHURCHES

*We've been going to our church for 23 years, and raised our kids there. They've always loved it. Now all of a sudden, our 15-year-old daughter says she wants to go to church with her best friend. She visited their youth group a few weeks ago and came back telling us, "I've found a church that's really alive and on fire for God. I'd like to go there from now on." Should we let her go or is it more important for us to worship as a family?*

I don't have an easy answer for you. I love the idea of young people worshiping with their families, and I love that you've been at the same church for 23 years. That speaks volumes about your commitment. It's important that your daughter understand that commitment. She needs to realize that just because a new youth group comes along, that's not a good enough reason to drop her commitment to her own church. Sometimes the best learning experience for an adolescent happens when she perseveres in a situation that's less than perfect.

But if you feel like letting her try something new, my advice is to make sure she knows this change is a very serious one. Many young people go through a period of rebellion toward the church as they move from following their parents' faith to owning their own. Talk to your daughter about the importance of her commitment to a body of believers and involvement in the ministry of your church. Church is not about entertainment; it's about worshiping God and growing with other believers. If your daughter's choice is based on a desire to grow closer to God, then let her explore this other youth group on a temporary basis.

After a few months, talk again and see what she's thinking. Is her friend's church helping her grow? Has she learned things she could bring back to the youth group at your church to help them get that "fire" she sees at the other church? Can you come to an agreement where she attends church with you and youth group with her friend?

This is a serious decision for you and your daughter. Please pray about it, talk about it, and think carefully about where your daughter can best build a solid relationship with God.

## ACTION STEPS:

1. **Recognize that your daughter might gain the most from staying at your church.**

2. **Consider allowing your daughter to try out the other youth group on a temporary basis.**

3. **Pray about this decision.**

# TITHING

*Our son just got his first job. It doesn't pay much, but we'd like him to start tithing. Is that too much to expect?*

One of the best things we can do for our children is teach them about responsible stewardship of their money. I would encourage him to tithe. It will help him gain an eternal perspective on money and possessions.

I would also recommend that you take him through one of the many outstanding books available on teenagers and money. Look for Christian books that focus on tithing and other stewardship issues.

This is a great time to teach your son the practical principles of saving, delayed gratification, and debt. When our children were very young and they first began to receive their allowance, we encouraged them to save at least 10 percent and give at least 10 percent. I'm amazed how It still carries over today.

Christian stewardship is based on the principles Jesus taught in the Sermon on the Mount, "For where your treasure is, there your heart will be also (Matt. 6:21). He went on to say, "No one can serve two masters. Either he will hate one and love the other, or he will be devoted to the one and despise the other. You cannot serve both God and Money" (Matt. 6:24).

To drive these lessons home even more, talk to your teen about your money management practices. Not only do we need to teach and train our children, we also need to demonstrate these important values in our own lives.

ACTION STEPS:

1. Help your son gain an eternal perspective on money through tithing.
2. Guide him through a book on teens and money.
3. Serve as a strong example of responsible stewardship.

# SCIENCE AND FAITH

*Our son is in an advanced science class in school. His teacher is very much an agnostic and is teaching things that contradict our family's faith. How can we help our son hold on to his beliefs when he's being taught things that go against Scripture?*

All of us learn and grow by being challenged. Your son's current situation might be just what he needs to investigate his own beliefs and strengthen his faith. Frankly, we can't expect the public schools or the government to teach our children Christian education and morals. That's the job of parents (Deut. 6:6-7). Still, it can be troubling when you feel as though the school is contradicting what you've worked so hard to teach.

In my years of working with teenagers, I've found that they sometimes learn a great deal by digging into difficult issues themselves. If you want your son to really understand the biblical view of Creation, then help him systematically study what the secular world teaches about Creation. Then have him look at what knowledgeable Christian scholars believe. If you don't know where to find a solid Christian perspective on Creation, talk to your pastor or a science professor at a Christian college.

Your son will undoubtedly face this tension again and again, especially if he continues in a science field when he heads off to college. You'll do him a great service by dealing with these issues in the sanctuary of a loving home and supportive church. One of our most important jobs as parents is teaching our children to be critical and discerning thinkers. Instead of shying away from this responsibility, we need to train our children to know *why* they believe.

As your son deals with this class, and any other challenges to his faith he might face in the future, remind him of the Bible's advice for handling these debates: "Always be prepared to give an answer to everyone who asks you to give a reason for the hope that you have. But do this with gentleness and respect" (1 Pet. 3:15).

ACTION STEPS:

1. Stay active in your son's schooling and his spiritual growth.

2. Help your son learn more about the secular and Christian views of Creation.

3. Encourage your son to deepen his understanding of his faith and learn to express his beliefs with respect.

# JUDGMENTAL ATTITUDE

*My daughter went on a short-term mission trip last summer and came back a different person. After seeing people who live in abject poverty, she seems to be very judgmental about our middle-class lifestyle, our somewhat wealthy church, and even the "shallow" Christian kids in her school. I'm glad she feels a strong need to minister to the poor, but she's become so self-righteous about it. How can we help her readjust her attitude without squelching her passion for the poor?*

When teenagers (and even some adults) have a life-changing experience, they often come back with incredible zeal and some rough edges as they try to process what happened to them. You can help your daughter by supporting her newfound passion and encouraging her to show love and compassion to all people, rich or poor, just like Jesus did. It's true that throughout the Gospels Jesus is adamant about the need to care for the poor and oppressed. But he is just as intense about a judgmental attitude. "Do not judge, or you too will be judged. For in the same way you judge others, you will be judged, and with the measure you use, it will be measured to you." (Matt. 7:1-2).

I would also suggest that you help your daughter find a Christian organization that works with the poor in your area. Encourage her to ask the adults who work there how they deal with the tension of ministering to the poor and oppressed and yet living in relative comfort themselves. People often learn best when faced with tension, so talk to your daughter often as she processes all she's learning.

This is a great opportunity for you to help your daughter explore her faith and start making plans for her future. What a privilege for you as a parent to help her find her place in the world of ministry. Walk with her through this process, and it will be an experience that helps your family draw closer together and closer to God.

**ACTION STEPS:**

1. Tell your daughter you admire her new passion for the poor.

2. Remind her of Jesus' words on judging others.

3. Help her find ways she can put her passion into action.

# FLIRTING WITH ADULTS

*I caught my 16-year-old daughter flirting with one of the single adult leaders of her youth group. He didn't seem to mind, and he actually flirted back. My husband thinks it's pretty harmless, but I'm not so sure. What should we do?*

Even if it is harmless, I wouldn't let it slide. It's very natural for a 16-year-old to flirt and even get a crush on an adult who has some positive authority in her life. And although flirting can be innocent on your daughter's part, an adult, especially one who is working with young people, ought to be cautious about flirting back.

I suggest talking to the youth leader or whoever supervises adult volunteers. You don't have to make it a big deal, just express your concern. Any healthy youth group should have a policy in place that forbids flirting, dating, or inappropriate relationships between adults and students. If your church doesn't have such a policy, talk to your pastor and develop one immediately. Far too often what starts as innocent flirting can lead to misunderstanding, inappropriate relationships or, at the least, hurt feelings.

You might also want to talk to your daughter. You don't have to embarrass her by talking about specifics, but it wouldn't hurt to remind her that she should be cautious about the message her flirting might send.

We parents are in the "protection business." If you have concerns about something in your daughter's life, it's right for you to act on them.

**ACTION STEPS:**

1. Let your youth leader know about your concerns.

2. Check with the pastor to find out what kind of policy the church has on adult/student relationships.

3. Talk with your daughter about the message her flirting might be sending.

# ROLE MODELS

*My son idolizes his football coach. The trouble is, I know the man's not a good role model—he doesn't mind when the guys on the team drink, and he brags about his exploits with women. How can I gently knock this coach off the pedestal my son has put him on?*

Some people would suggest that you confront the coach and the school administration. That's one option, but it won't help your son learn to develop positive values and discern effective role models.

Sometimes the best way to put good thoughts and sound thinking into the lives of our children is to approach a situation not with power but with clear, thought-out questions. That helps kids come to their own conclusions.

So I'd deal with this situation with logic and wisdom. Without putting the coach down for his lifestyle, look for a casual way to have a serious conversation with your son about the coach. You might want to ask your son, "What qualities in your coach's life draw you to him? What do you see in him that you'd like to imitate? What aspects of his life do you not want to follow? What would make him a more effective leader?"

I think your son is more likely to see this coach for who he is if he can do so with his own eyes. With just a few simple questions you may learn a great deal about what your son thinks and help him discern the negative influence the coach may have on his players.

Although playing the comparison game can sometimes be dangerous, you may want to ask your son about someone he knows who's a strong role model. Perhaps there's a youth worker in your church or another coach in his life who lives in a more exemplary way. Ask the same type of questions about that person.

The bottom line is, you'll help yourself and your son best by having him evaluate his coach as a role model, rather than trying to censor the coach yourself. These kinds of situations can provide some of the finest opportunities to help our kids grow, discern, and decide what kind of people they want to become as they enter adulthood.

**ACTION STEPS:**

1. Ask your son questions about the coach to get him thinking about the kind of role model he makes.

2. Help your son think about other people he knows who'd make strong role models.

3. Use this as an opportunity to help your son start thinking about the kind of person he wants to be.

"I think it's very important that my parents are involved in my dating life. God gave me my parents as a source of guidance. They're wrong sometimes, but through the years I've learned to trust them and let them teach me things, especially about guys and dating."

— Jennifer, 16

### Thanks...

My mother was a saint. She loved the Lord with all of her heart.

On the ranch we got up early, long before the break of day, and went to bed long after dark. My mother would awaken to read her Bible and pray before the rest of us got up, and then, after we all went to bed, she would spend time with the Lord, praying and reading her Bible. And all day long she would hum hymns of praise and worship to the Lord. She always demonstrated her faith by her actions and her conduct.

I remember in particular, when I was in school, I was involved in athletics and drama and various other school activities, which meant that I would stay out long after dark. And on occasion, I would have to walk the five miles home to our ranch. But I always knew that somewhere, in the last mile or two, my mother would be there to meet me. We would talk, and it was very, very meaningful. Her love was demonstrated in a thousand ways by her actions. I would say she was the greatest influence in my life.

Bill Bright—President, Campus Crusade for Christ

# EXTRACURRICULARS

*Our older kids were into every kind of extracurricular activity you can imagine. But our 15-year-old isn't interested in anything besides school. In fact, if he didn't have to go to school, he'd probably just stay in his room all day and listen to music. Is this normal or should we be concerned?*

There are actually two parts to your question. The first involves extracurriculars. They are important. extracurricular activities often form your child's relationship patterns. It's a proven fact that active teens with positive friendships are much less apt to fall into "at risk" behaviors like drugs, gangs, and sexual promiscuity. However, busy for busy's sake is not always better.

Your son may be one who doesn't thrive on lots of activity the way your other children did. If he has friends and gets along well with you and other adults, then I wouldn't worry too much about it. He may just be reacting against overly busy siblings. However, if he sees himself as someone who just doesn't fit into the world of social activity, then consider helping him find his place. If his personality is quite different from those of his siblings, you may have to look into activities besides the ones they enjoyed. Help your son think about his interests, then talk to a counselor at school to find some clubs or groups that he might enjoy.

The second part of your question concerns your son's tendency to isolate himself. If you believe he is in a major state of withdrawal and/or depression, think about having him meet with a Christian counselor and talk with his school's social worker or school psychologist. There might be nothing wrong, but trained professionals can help you stop a potential downward spiral while it's in its early stages.

On the other hand, your son might simply be more of an introvert who gets energized by being alone. Even so, I encourage you to help him get out of his room and into one or two activities that will be meaningful to him.

**ACTION STEPS:**

1. Keep in mind that while extracurriculars are important, they aren't necessarily for everyone.

2. If your son wants a social outlet, help him identify a few activities that might interest him.

3. Look for signs of serious withdrawal and/or depression. If you suspect either one, help your son get professional help.

"I'm involved in tons of clubs, sports, musicals, and volunteer work. My parents think it's good for me to be as busy as I am, but it has taken a toll on my health. I also don't get much family time at all. Either I'm busy, or they're busy. I really wish I got to spend more time with them, but even if I wasn't as busy, they would probably be too busy to do something with me."

— Brooke, 17

# MAKING FRIENDS

*Our son is starting high school this year and will be with all kinds of new kids. How can we help him cultivate good friendships and weed out the bad ones?*

I'm a big supporter of church-based youth ministry for hundreds of reasons, but at the top of my list is positive peer influence. Church youth groups, although not perfect, tend to be made up of kids who are growing in their faith. In the best groups, you also find kids who are holding each other accountable to live godly lives.

I hope your church has a good youth group with students who are actively living their faith. It's difficult for a teenager to walk into the group alone, so if your son isn't currently attending the youth group, encourage him to bring a friend along.

If you want to help your son develop strong friendships outside of church as well, keep these principles in mind:

- Know your son's friends and their families. Ever since our children were young, my wife and I have made a point of calling the friend's parents before any party or gathering. I simply ask if they're going to be around, and I offer to help in any way I can. In our experience, the other parents have been thrilled we called.

- Invite your son's friends to your house and to occasional family outings. I've learned more about my kids' friends than I ever imagined by driving them to and from events.

- Talk with your son about his friends. Find out what he likes and dislikes about them and the things they like to do together. Remind him you're willing to lend an ear if he ever needs to talk about his relationships.

- Pay attention to where he goes and who he's with. More than anything else, this can help you encourage healthy friendships and nip unhealthy ones in the bud.

Now is a good time to talk with your son about the person he's becoming. Ask about his goals, hopes and dreams. Remind him that his choice of friends can help or hurt him as he matures. With your guidance and continued attention, your son can eventually learn the fine art of building strong friendships.

ACTION STEPS:

1. Encourage your son to get involved in your church youth group.

2. Meet your son's friends and make them welcome in your home.

3. Talk with your son about the importance of having friends who help him be the person God made him to be.

"If I'm good friends with a guy, my mom gets all uptight and wants to know everything about him—if he's a good Christian, if he has a criminal record, if the mole on his left hand is cancerous ... well, maybe I'm getting carried away, but she is very picky. It drives me nuts, but I have to remember that she loves me and just wants to protect me."    — Cambria, 15

# BEING JUDGMENTAL

*My son seems so judgmental. He's quick to label other kids things like "jock" and "preppie." He doesn't mean these as compliments. What can I do to get him to stop labeling people?*

As teenagers search for their own identity, they tend to label people. It's a way of defining themselves based on who they aren't, rather than who they are. But as natural as it is for teenagers to label each other, it certainly isn't right, especially when those labels become an excuse for treating others badly.

There are two ways you should approach this problem with your son. The first is based on Ephesians 4:29, which says, ""Do not let any unwholesome talk come out of your mouths, but only what is helpful for building others up according to their needs, that it may benefit those who listen." It's possible that your son has had bad experiences with some jocks and preppies. Maybe he's even been called names himself. If so, talk with him about his feelings and help him see that labeling others is not a healthy way for him to deal with his hurt or anger.

Your son might not be ready to give up his bad attitude, but you can start him in a good direction by helping him stop saying hurtful things about others. Consider instituting a "No Put-Down" rule in your home. Some families even enforce this rule by fining anyone, including Mom and Dad, a quarter any time an unwholesome word comes out of their mouth. Eventually, your son can break this habit of badmouthing others.

The second way you can address your son's judgmental attitude is by urging him to examine his own heart. Yes, rules can help your son improve his behavior, but until he has the will to change and the motivation to ask God for a better outlook, the rules can only go so far. You can help him move toward a change of heart by reminding him that all people are created in God's image. Explain to your son that since all people are part of God's creation, insulting them is also an insult to God. God loves the "preppies" and the "jocks" and has called your son to do the same (John 13:34-35).

Finally, help your son find positive ways to define himself. Encourage him to explore his interests and talents. Help him figure out what he likes doing and give him opportunities to do it. Talk to your son about the unique person God created him to be and remind him that he is fearfully and wonderfully made by a Creator who loves him.

## ACTION STEPS:

1. **Help your son use words to build others up, not tear them down.**

2. **Remind your son to see others as people created by God.**

3. **Encourage your son to learn more about the person God made him to be.**

# DISRESPECTFUL FRIENDS

*My son is a good kid, but some of his friends aren't. They're rude and disrespectful, and I really don't like having them in our house. Still, I'd rather have my son here than out with them somewhere else. Should I talk to my son about his friends and risk him getting angry or just be happy he's around?*

I'd do both. As your son enters the second half of adolescence, he can become more responsible for the actions of his friends when they're in your house. Sit down with him when things are calm and talk with him about what's acceptable and what isn't. Try to do this in a way that tells your son you trust him and believe he's mature enough to help you solve this problem. If he feels like you're trying to work with him, he's more likely to see your point and make an effort to help. Then, ask him to share these expectations with his friends.

At the same time, continue to let your son's friends spend time at your house. As you talk with your son, make sure he knows you want him and his friends to feel welcome and will do what you can to make sure they feel that way.

My wife, Cathy, and I have tried to make our house as friendly as possible because we want our children to invite their friends to our home. Sure it can get to be a bit much. There are times when we have to slow the traffic flow or remind our teenagers what is appropriate in our home and what isn't. We've made it clear to our daughters and their friends that our house rules are the same for everyone in the house, family or not.

One last note: I'm a bit concerned that you're worried about talking to your son because you don't want him getting angry. Nobody ever said being a good parent would put us in first place for a popularity contest. But Scripture is very clear that discipline helps produce kids who will thrive. Please keep these verses in mind as you prepare to talk to your son:

* "He who spares the rod hates his son, but he who loves him is careful to discipline him" (Prov. 13:24).
* "Discipline your son, for in that there is hope..." (Prov. 19:18a).
* "Discipline your son, and he will give you peace; he will bring delight to your soul" (Prov. 29:17).

ACTION STEPS:

1. Talk to your son about his friends and enlist his help in solving the problem.

2. Continue to make your home a place your son feels he can bring his friends.

3. Remember that your son needs your discipline as well as your friendship.

# TOUGH LOVE

*We feel like our daughter is starting to take advantage of us—staying out late, talking back, ignoring our rules. A friend suggested we try a "tough love" approach. What does that mean and does it really work?*

Staying out late, talking back, and ignoring rules are all signs of rebellion. To some degree, they are normal behaviors for teenagers who are moving from dependence toward independence. But if your daughter is acting this way more often than not, then tough love is an appropriate way of handling the situation.

Tough love means establishing very clear expectations, then consistently carrying out specific consequences when the expectations are broken. For instance, talk with your daughter about her curfew. Set up a curfew that seems reasonable to both of you. Tell her ahead of time what her reward will be for keeping her curfew (maybe you'll add on an extra half hour if she makes it home on time for six months straight) and the consequences for breaking it (maybe she's not allowed to go out the next weekend). Do the same thing for talking back and any other rebellion issues you're facing. If your daughter continues to break your rules despite your consistent efforts to administer consequences, you might want to consider setting up a family meeting with a Christian counselor. A counselor can give you more ideas targeted specifically at your situation.

As difficult as it is to take a strong stance with your children, you need to take a firm but loving approach with your daughter. The teenage years can be very rocky for many young girls, and they need parents who will set consistent, loving boundaries.

**ACTION STEPS:**

1. Establish clear expectations for your daughter's behavior.
2. Set up rewards and consequences to encourage your daughter to follow the family rules.
3. If the problems persist, seek help from a Christian counselor.

**"And here are the keys to the car."**

# ANGER

*Our 15-year-old son has an explosive temper. Whenever he gets upset, he yells, swears, and even throws things. I'm afraid he'll eventually hurt himself or someone else. How can we help him learn to control his rage?*

An explosive temper is not appropriate for a person of any age. It's true that people express their anger in many different ways and that some will struggle with a temper much more than others. However, uncontrolled rage cannot be tolerated, and it often indicates serious problems.

One of the greatest gifts you can give your son is the ability to deal with his anger in a positive, less destructive manner. The best way to do that is to find a counselor who can teach your son proper ways to cope with stress and manage his anger. The counselor can determine if your son is dangerous to himself or anyone else. He or she will also be able to assess whether your son's anger is tied to depression, a learning disability, or other emotional or physical problems.

No matter what its cause, your son's behavior is inappropriate. Work with his counselor to establish ways to hold your son accountable for his actions. Avoid fueling his anger by keeping your own dealings with him calm and even-keeled. None of this will be easy, but remember that your efforts can save him from a life of misery and broken relationships.

**ACTION STEPS:**

1. Find a counselor who can get to the root of your son's rage.
2. Work with the counselor to find ways to hold your son accountable for his actions.
3. Think long-term, knowing that your actions now will help your son in the future.

# ALCOHOL

*My husband comes home from work every night and heads straight to the fridge to grab a beer. He and I often have wine with our dinner. Neither of us has a drinking problem, and we have tried to be examples of responsible drinking. Now our 16-year-old son is starting to experiment with alcohol. We are concerned he won't drink as responsibly as the adults in our family. Should we talk to him about our fears?*

My wife tells me I can be a little too blunt sometimes, but here I go again! I wouldn't start with your son. I would begin with you and your husband. I'm concerned that you may be subtly, or not so subtly, teaching your children that the way to manage the stress of the day is to grab a beer after work or a glass of wine at dinner. The truth is, no matter what you've verbally communicated to your son, your actions have sent an even stronger message.

In my book *DrugProof Your Kids* (Gospel Light), the first step of our "drugproof plan" is self-examination. It's a proven fact that if parents drink, their children will typically follow their example. So I encourage you and your husband to take a hard look at your own alcohol use and consider the impression you could be making on your son.

I choose not to drink for three reasons: Christy Burns, Rebecca Burns, and Heidi Burns. Because there is alcoholism on both sides of our family, there is a greater chance that my three girls have a "biological predisposition" toward alcoholism. For me, that daily before-dinner drink is not worth the gamble of one of my daughters struggling with substance abuse.

Now to get to your question. Yes, I would talk with your son immediately. He is under the legal age to drink, and besides that, experts tell us that the younger a child begins to drink, the easier it is for him to move toward problem drinking as he gets older. In contrast, if a person avoids drinking during his teen years, he'll most likely never drink or will at least drink more responsibly.

**ACTION STEPS:**

1. **Consider the example your own alcohol use is setting.**

2. **Talk to your son about the legal and physical ramifications of using alcohol when he's underage.**

3. **Help your son understand that the patterns he develops now will affect him in the future.**

# SMOKING

*We have had a few difficult years with our 17-year-old son. He is a Christian who has struggled with drugs and sexual relationships. I told him he could not live in our home if he continued that behavior. To my knowledge he's quit doing drugs and says he is staying sexually pure. Our problem is he still wants to smoke in our home. I don't want him smoking, but I do want him living in our home with a Christian environment. Is this a battle I should just concede?*

My heart goes out to you. Thank you for sticking in there with your son. And you get an A-plus for setting boundaries on the drugs and sex issues. You're also right to be concerned about his smoking. Not only is nicotine one of the most addictive substances known to humankind, it is, simply put, a killer.

To be honest, you and your spouse are the only ones who can decide if this is an issue to do battle over. If he were my son, I don't think I'd throw him out of the house over the smoking issue. But I would want to establish some very clear-cut expectations and boundaries on the subject. I'd institute a "no smoking in the house or car" rule. I'd also insist that he and I talk to our family doctor to get information on the very best methods to quit a really crummy habit.

If your son is willing to abide by a few house rules on smoking and keep his commitment to abstaining from drugs and sex, then I think he's on the road to recovery.

ACTION STEPS:

1. Continue to show your son love by setting clear boundaries.

2. Establish some "house rules" about smoking.

3. Help your son look into ways to stop smoking.

# STRESS

*Our daughter is an exceptional young woman. She's an excellent student, captain of the basketball team, and a leader in her high school and youth group. Lately, she complains of headaches and gets angry over the littlest things. She often goes all day without eating and will stay up well after midnight to do her homework. We think she's under too much stress, but she won't talk to us about it. What can we do?*

I think you're right: She's overcommitted and stressed out. Her outbursts of anger may be coming from fatigue and from keeping her emotions to herself.

I want to play out a hunch with you. Your daughter sounds like one of those wonderful people we call perfectionists. Watch out, because perfectionism can be hazardous to her emotional, spiritual, and physical well-being. For many perfectionists, winning is everything, a "B" is unthinkable, and amassing an impressive list of accomplishments is more important than actually enjoying those activities. There is no tolerance for being less than the best—a mentality that's impossible to live by. The depth and breadth of their perfectionism overwhelm many. What once seemed like just another task eventually becomes a larger-than-life problem. Ironically, perfectionists often have so many plates spinning that they begin to procrastinate and those plates start to fall. And when that happens, stress sets in.

That's a possible explanation for what your daughter's going through. Now I'd like to offer a possible solution. Talk to your daughter about what you're seeing in her. She might resent the implication that she can't handle all her commitments, so simply talk about the behaviors you've seen. Then, ask her to help you understand why she's acting this way. As you talk, encourage her to think about all her commitments and decide which ones could go. As you talk, make sure you remind your daughter that you love her and will continue to do so no matter what she does or doesn't do.

One other thought. You mention that your daughter often goes without eating. This is a bad idea for anyone. In fact, one of the most common traits of young women with the eating disorders (anorexia or bulimia) is a tendency toward perfectionism. Just because your daughter misses a meal every once in a while doesn't mean she has an eating disorder, but make sure that missing a meal is the rare exception, not the rule.

ACTION STEPS:

1. Recognize that your daughter might be a perfectionist.
2. Talk with her about the changes you've seen and help her find a solution to her busy schedule.
3. Make sure your daughter takes care of her physical needs.

"My life is so hectic that the only time I have with my family is the moments we discuss the high stress level of my life. My parents suggest taking easier classes or quitting extracurricular activities, but I can't let go. Being busy has become a part of who I am. I would love more family time, but I just can't squeeze it in." — Amy, 16

# DEPRESSION

*Our 15-year-old daughter attempted suicide and was hospitalized for depression. Since then, she has been taking medication and going to therapy. Even with all of this help, we are seeing no progress or improvement. We know that she is special in God's eyes, but neither her doctors, her teachers, nor we have been able to instill that belief in her. We're beginning to think she needs to leave our family for a time and attend a residential school or treatment facility that will focus on her extremely low self-esteem and help her believe in herself. What do you think? Are there other steps we should take?*

I only wish I had an easy answer for you. First, let me say that I think you're going about handling the problem in the best way possible. When anyone attempts suicide and is hospitalized with severe depression, you must get advice from experts in the field of medicine.

I really cannot say whether or not your daughter should be placed in a residential facility. So I encourage you to pose this question to your daughter's current psychiatrist and other health-care officials involved in her life. But don't stop there. Get a second opinion, even a third.

I'd also encourage you to explore other options. Talk with a caseworker from your county's mental health department. Sometimes the county has programs that utilize community social services, keep your family intact, and avoid residential care.

You should also begin talking right now with the school's social worker and psychologist. Ask about possible educational alternatives available to your daughter. If they are unclear about alternatives, call your school district's special services director or supervisor. If that doesn't get you anywhere, contact the superintendent and ask for his or her help. Also, seek out local support and advocacy groups for parents of depressed children. These groups can be very helpful because these folks have been there. You can learn from their mistakes, glean from their current wisdom, and take advantage of their own network of contacts.

On the positive side, your story is not an uncommon story. There are thousands of teens and their parents who have made it through these difficult waters to live a very meaningful life. Keep praying and reminding your daughter that God's love and acceptance knows no limits. And help her find a good Christian friend who can show her God's love and mercy in action.

Also be aware that your daughter is not the only one who needs support right now. Please make sure that you and your spouse are spending time together outside of the pressures of home. I would also recommend Christian counseling for the two of you and any other family members. There are deep layers of pain in a situation like this, and you'll need the help of a professional to deal with them in a healthy, healing way.

**ACTION STEPS:**

1. Continue to consult with medical and mental health professionals.
2. Look into options that allow your family to remain intact.
3. Make sure to get the support you need to keep your marriage and your family healthy.

# SELF-ESTEEM

*Our 16-year-old daughter is a great kid but has a very low view of herself. Do you have any ideas on how we can help her feel better about herself?*

I read about an idea in a marriage magazine and then used it for my wife and my daughters. It was the hit of the year! I called it the "100 Reasons Why You Are Special" box.

I decorated a shoebox for each person. Then I wrote down 100 reasons why I thought she was special, each on a separate piece of paper. I put the notes in the box and added a bow. I asked them to read one note a day, but each one of them read through all her notes in one sitting. They talk about these notes more than I ever imagined. Yes, this took a lot of time and effort, but the results were, and are, well worth it.

Obviously, a gesture like this isn't a cure-all for a poor self-image, but don't underestimate the power of written or spoken affirmation. Mark Twain once said, "I can live two months on one good compliment." Even if you think you're communicating love to your daughter, you can do more. A person can never receive too much love.

As you express love for your daughter, be specific. Don't just tell her you're proud of her, tell her why. Don't just tell her she's terrific, tell her why. Your words will carry more weight and truth if you tie them to concrete examples of what makes her so great.

Our job as parents is to help our kids know they are loved by us and God with an unconditional love that knows no limit. Pray with your daughter daily and let her hear you thank God for her. Surround your daughter with love, support, boundaries, and a sanctuary of encouragement. The teenage years can be rough on self-image, but the teens who do best in the future are the ones who have a consistently positive environment in their lives.

**ACTION STEPS:**

1. **Make your love for your daughter crystal clear through your words and actions.**

2. **Be specific as you praise your daughter.**

3. **Remind your daughter daily of God's unconditional love for her.**

# EATING DISORDERS

*I hear a lot about anorexia. One of our daughters is pretty thin and can be a picky eater. Still, I don't know enough about eating disorders to know if I should be concerned. What exactly is anorexia and how will I know if my daughter has a problem?*

You're asking great questions. Anorexia is an intense fear of being or becoming obese which does not diminish as weight loss progresses. It's literally a distorted body image where some claim to "feel fat" even when they are emaciated. For more information, look at Les Parrott's book, *Helping the Struggling Adolescent* (Zondervan).

I'm glad you're paying attention to your daughter's eating habits. If your daughter does have an eating disorder, early detection is essential to getting her help. So how do you know? Here are just a few signs.

1. She's losing weight.

2. She has not experienced a physical illness that would account for continued weight loss.

3. She has ritualized her eating patterns. For example: carrots must be five inches long and cut at an angle; she can only eat a cracker after she's had three glasses of water.

4. She's involved in an excessive amount of strenuous exercise.

5. She's using laxatives unnecessarily.

If you see any of these signs in your daughter, have her evaluated by someone trained in the area of eating disorders. Your family doctor can help you locate someone in your area.

Keep in mind that eating disorders are not strictly physical ailments. They are deeply psychological. Anorexics are often perfectionists who set impossibly high standards yet have low self-esteem. Eating disorders aren't about weight loss or weight control as much as they are about emotions, control, and self-concept. If your daughter is struggling with an eating disorder, make sure any treatment plan involves professional Christian counseling.

**ACTION STEPS:**

1. **Continue paying attention to your daughter's eating habits.**

2. **Look for signs such as unexplained weight loss and ritualized eating patterns.**

3. **Consult with your family doctor to find professionals who have studied eating disorders.**

# RISQUÉ FASHION

*Our 15-year-old daughter is very caught up in fashion and appearance. Unfortunately, many of the styles that are "in"—like tiny tops and visible bra straps—are "out" in my book. We battle about her appearance nearly every day. How can we find a compromise?*

Wait three weeks and maybe the styles will change! Actually this is one of the most frequently asked questions I get when I teach parenting seminars. Let's face it, young adolescents have an incredible need to measure up to cultural norms, especially when it comes to appearance. As a result, parents end up walking a fine line between their own needs and the very powerful needs of their teens.

How can you find some balance? Here are a few ideas:

1. *Choose your battles wisely.* When an argument involves clothes, hair or make-up, compromise as often as possible. If you're willing to let a few things go, like goofy hair colors, you'll have more leverage on those things that really matter to you, like modesty. If you just can't resolve the issue, get a second opinion from someone you both love and trust.

2. *Set clear expectations.* Since you say you're fighting every day, your expectations are either not clear or are being ignored. Consider going through your daughter's wardrobe with her and together making

a list of what's acceptable and what isn't. This list will serve as a constant reminder of what she agreed to. Kids are more likely to live by something they help create.

3. *Listen carefully.* The way we dress is one of the many ways we express ourselves. Talk to your daughter about what she wants to communicate through her clothing choices.

4. *Emphasize inner beauty.* God does not place prime importance on physical appearance. I like the discussion God had with Samuel: "Do not consider his appearance or his height .... The Lord does not look at the things man looks at. Man looks at the outward appearance, but the Lord looks at the heart" (1 Sam. 16:7). Be sure to compliment your daughter on her beautiful inner qualities.

## ACTION STEPS:

1. **Be willing to compromise a bit.**

2. **Work with your daughter to establish clear guidelines for what's acceptable and what isn't.**

3. **Build up your daughter's self-esteem by praising her great inner beauty.**

"WALTER, WE WON'T HAVE TO BUY DOREEN A NEW PROM DRESS AFTER ALL. MY OLD PROM DRESS FITS HER PERFECTLY!"

"I think it's a parent's right to enforce reasonable standards of modesty— understanding that 'reasonable' is a very ambiguous word. But parental strictness can't change the underlying reasons why their children want to dress a certain way. If someone wants to wear certain kinds of clothes badly enough, they'll start wearing them behind their parents' backs, which can lead to worse things." — Sarah, 15

# DATING (1)

*Now that our 16-year-old is dating, we'd like to meet the boys she goes out with. What kinds of questions can we ask to make sure these boys are trustworthy?*

Wouldn't it be nice if there actually were questions we could ask the people our kids date that would insure their trustworthiness? I can't think of even one question that's foolproof. I have three lovely daughters, so believe me, I've tried! Although there aren't simple questions to ask, there are some basic principles to follow:

1. *Start with your daughter.* Parents need to be proactive in talking to their kids about sex, relationships, and dating. Make sure your daughter knows what kind of boys you'd like her to date and why, and that you'll take an active interest in her relationships.

2. *Get involved.* Be the first to offer to drive your daughter and her friends or dates to the movies, have kids over to watch a video, take them to the park—whatever will give you the opportunity to get better acquainted with her peer group. We've taken each of our 16-year-old daughter's guy friends out to dinner with us. While following our daughter's strict instructions about how to act and how not to be embarrassing, we've found we can really get to know these boys over a meal. This is a great time to ask general, non-threatening questions—what he likes to do for fun, what activities he's involved in at school, what church his family goes to.

3. *Narrow the field.* It seems like most every time I speak on the subject of relationships I get the question: Should Christians date non-Christians? My answer is simple. Although I believe we all need to have non-Christian friends, I'm afraid that when a Christian and non-Christian date it's like mixing apples and oranges. I don't believe in what some call "missionary dating"—that is dating a non-Christian to make him a Christian. Once in a while the plan works, but most often it leads to hurt, rejection, misunderstanding, and at times, a real falling away from God. So strongly encourage your daughter to avoid dating boys who don't share her faith.

But even Christians can act in some pretty ungodly ways when it comes to dating, so continue to talk with your daughter about her dates. Ask her why she likes a certain boy, help her think up safe, fun dates, and make your home a place where your daughter and her dates feel welcome.

## ACTION STEPS:

1. **Talk to your daughter about your expectations for her dates.**

2. **Take the time to get to know the boys she dates.**

3. **Help your daughter understand why it's important to date only Christian guys who are committed to their beliefs.**

"I think it's OK for parents to ask questions like where we're going and what time we'll be back, but not personal stuff like what grades he gets or what his life plans are. Parents don't need to know all that for the first date. And if the relationship continues, there will be plenty of time to get to know the guy better." — Rebecca, 17

# DATING (2)

*Our 17-year-old son really wants to date, but he says girls aren't interested in him. I can tell he's really starting to feel bad about himself because of this. What can we do to help him?*

In my experience, teenagers tend to have major misunderstandings about dating. These misunderstandings lead many of them to either date when they don't really want to, or, like your son, feel bad about themselves when they don't date. Let me tell you about two of the most prevalent dating myths among high school students:

*Myth 1: Almost everybody dates in high school.* Wrong! Statistics tell us that 50 percent of the girls and 40 percent of the guys graduating from high school have not been on one official date. Contrary to popular opinion, not everybody goes to the prom and not everybody has a date every Saturday night. Many students have perfectly healthy relationships with the opposite sex but are not romantically involved with anyone.

*Myth 2: If you want to be popular, you must be sexually active.* Again this is simply wrong. Of the students elected to *Who's Who Among America High School Students*, 73 percent had never had sexual relations. Everybody isn't doing it. And some of the best, brightest, and most popular students are choosing to wait to have sex until they're married.

Help your son understand that his self-worth isn't based on whether girls do or don't like him. While it might not seem to make a difference to him right away, help him remember that God loves him just the way he is and that God has great plans for him (Jer. 29:11).

You can also help your son by giving him some tips on talking to girls. If he's shy or gets nervous around girls, help him think up some general questions he can use to start a friendly conversation. Maybe he can get more involved in his youth group or a school club. Those activities will not only give him opportunities to build healthy friendships with girls, but they'll give him something to focus on besides his lack of dates.

**ACTION STEPS:**

**1. Help your son realize that not everyone dates in high school.**

**2. Remind your son that his worth comes from God, not from dating.**

**3. Encourage your son to build non-romantic friendships with girls.**

*"PSST! MAKE SURE YOU GET HER HOME BY TWELVE."*

# PUBLIC AFFECTION

*Our son and his girlfriend are all over each other. She practically sits in his lap when they're watching TV with us, and they always stand with their arms wrapped around each other, even during fellowship time at church. They make us uncomfortable, and I know their public affection draws looks from others. How can we talk about this with our son?*

When young people fall in love, we parents usually call it puppy love. But puppy love is real love to teens. So instead of just closing our eyes until it's over, we parents can help our teenagers sort out what is and what isn't appropriate in a relationship. And as his parents, you have every right to hold your son accountable to the standards you set for your home and at your church.

To have a successful conversation with your son about this sensitive subject, make sure you bring it up in private, not in front of his girlfriend. Throughout the conversation, stay calm and state your feelings without being argumentative or judgmental. You could say something like, "Son, I've noticed that you and Amy feel pretty free to express your affection for each other in front of other people. Have you ever thought about what's an appropriate display of affection and what isn't?" Then express your thoughts on the subject. In a perfect conversation, your son will say, "Gee, I never thought of it that way," and agree with everything you said. Everyone lives happily ever after.

That probably won't be the case. He's more likely to get defensive and tell you you're being old-fashioned. So try to express your opinion without wagging your finger at him. You might simply tell him that some of his actions make you uncomfortable, or that church isn't the place to be focusing his attention on his girlfriend. Also, use the conversation to discuss some positive guidelines for building healthy relationships with the opposite sex. Obviously you can't join your son on his dates, but a thoughtful piece of advice might help him make some better choices even when you're not around.

## ACTION STEPS:
1. Remember that when it comes to relationships, your son still needs your advice and guidance.
2. Express your feelings in a calm, non-judgmental way.
3. Set up clear standards for what's not appropriate and why.

"If you watch teenagers in a group, a guy's eyes will always be on scantily clad girls. As a girl, my focus should be on what Jesus wants me to do, and not on getting a guy's attention. We girls have a responsibility to help guys focus on the things of God and not on earthly things—including ourselves." — Alisha, 16

# CHRISTIAN VALUES

*We recently learned that our 16-year-old daughter is having sex with her 19-year-old boyfriend. She knows we are strongly against this and didn't want her dating him in the first place. He's not a Christian, and he's dragging her into drinking and occasional drug use. She says she has no use for her Christian upbringing. We're heartbroken. How should we handle this?*

Hang in there with your daughter. Yes, she is violating your value system and making some very unhealthy choices that may haunt her for the rest of her life. But the chances are good that this is a phase of rebellion that will turn around eventually. You can increase those chances by continually telling your daughter that while you dislike the things she's doing, you love her deeply and that will never change.

That said, I think it's essential for you to communicate the real risks of these behaviors to your daughter. She needs to see that the things she's doing are not only dangerous, but also illegal. In most states, her boyfriend could be charged with statutory rape and providing drugs and alcohol to a minor. They could both face additional drug charges.

And that doesn't even begin to cover the health and safety risks involved. Teenagers tend to ignore their mortality, so remind your daughter that all of these behaviors can and do lead to death. Let her know that her actions have very serious consequences and that her relationship with this boy needs to end now.

Work with your daughter to create a contract that clearly states the house rules and expectations. Include consequences for negative behavior and rewards for positive behavior. Carry out these consequences, no matter what.

You might also want to seek the help and advice of your pastor or youth worker. They might be able to bring her back to her faith and her convictions, or recommend other sources of help.

Please don't give up on your daughter. Yes, she has broken your heart, but with your love and commitment to seeing her through this phase, she will hopefully leave this negative relationship and return to the convictions of her faith.

### ACTION STEPS:
1. Let your daughter know that while you don't approve of her actions, your love for her will never change.
2. Take steps to make your daughter accountable for her actions.
3. Seek the help of professionals who can talk to your daughter or suggest more resources.

# PREMARITAL SEX

*We have reason to believe our son's girlfriend recently spent the night when my wife and I were out of town. Our son was sexually active in the past, but has promised us he's stopped. We want to believe him, but this has made us suspicious. How can we talk about this without accusing him of something he may not have done?*

I think you need to have a very serious, focused, loving conversation with your son right away. Calmly explain your reasons for suspicion and ask him to respond. Tell him you have concerns and frankly, some fears. Remember that a loving confrontation is not a sign of lack of trust but a signal of love and support. Stress that at this point you are not accusing him. You're simply looking for a straight answer.

Your next step depends on his response. If he won't answer you, or gives you an answer that doesn't add up, it's time to establish more defined boundaries for him. Clearly state your expectations: he is not to engage in any sexual activity, you must be present if he invites a girl to your house, and so on. Then determine the consequences for breaking these rules. Consequences might include more restricted behavior and regular accountability meetings with his youth pastor.

Even if your son gives you a reasonable explanation and you believe he's telling the truth, I'd suggest you still draw up guidelines in the area of his sexuality. Sex education doesn't end with the "birds and bees" discussion. As our children move through their teenage years, we can have some of our most meaningful conversations about sex and relationships. Take this opportunity to talk with your son about the importance of staying out of tempting situations and discuss the reasons you believe he should save sex for marriage.

I believe the best relationships between parents and teens are based on open and honest communication. Just like younger children, teens need parents to set limits and help them make decisions about what's right and wrong. In my experience, kids respond to honest confrontation and dialogue if the relationship is built on mutual respect and love.

**ACTION STEPS:**
1. Give your son a chance to explain the situation.
2. Set up clear expectations for your son's relationships with girls.
3. Keep talking with your son about sexuality and relationships.

"When I start dating someone, my parents ask lots of questions about his personal beliefs, his parents' beliefs, how far he thinks is too far, physically. I think it's very fair, because, come on, my parents are responsible for me.

And I can't imagine how parents would feel if their daughter got raped or something and they hadn't asked questions." — Jessica, 15

# PARENTS' PAST

*My wife and I both have rather dark pasts. We both experimented with drugs and we lived together before we were married. In fact, our oldest daughter was born before we decided to get married. After we became Christians, we grew to be leaders in our church. Our children have no idea about our past, nor does our church. We're starting to feel uncomfortable about our "secret." Should we tell our children the truth? Won't it be harder to tell them to stay away from sex and drugs when we didn't?*

You'd be surprised how often I'm asked questions like yours in my parenting seminars. So you're definitely not the only Christian parents who experimented with drugs or fell short with sexual purity.

Personally, I don't believe you need to tell your children, or the church for that matter, every dirty story from your past. However, I still think "honesty is the best policy." If you present your past as an object lesson of the pain and damage drugs and sex can cause, the truth could actually help them resist such things.

I'd say something like, "Your mom and I made many mistakes in the past that we deeply regret. When we were younger we lived less-than- perfect lives when it came to drug use and sexuality. We aren't proud of our past and, believe me, we still suffer some of the consequences of those actions, like guilt. However, the good news is that because of our Christian commitment we are new people who have been forgiven and restored by God. Our hope is that you'll make wise decisions and not have to live with so many of the negative consequences we've experienced. If we had it to do over again, we would have abstained from drug use and strived for sexual purity."

As far as your church goes, I don't think it's necessary to tell people anything unless the subject comes up. Naturally, you should be honest if and when you're asked about your past, but I don't think you need to bring up the subject unless it seems relevant.

One last thing. I'd find a moment to tell your oldest daughter when, how, and why you got married. The odds are if she doesn't know already she'll put the dates together one day. Wouldn't it be better to tell her the truth yourselves? As you talk with her, and after your conversation, give her constant reassurance that she is not a mistake. Assure her that God took what could have been a tragedy and turned it into one of your greatest blessings.

**ACTION STEPS:**

**1. Be honest with your teenagers about your past.**

**2. Make it clear that you suffered the consequences of your actions and want to keep your children from experiencing the same struggles.**

**3. Assure your oldest daughter that she is a blessing from God.**

# ABORTION

*Our 16-year-old daughter is pregnant, and her boyfriend and his family are pressuring her to get an abortion. But our family is against abortion. What should we do?*

I can only imagine the range of difficult emotions you must be experiencing. I hope I can offer some help.

Your daughter is still under your care, so you have every right to ask her to carry her baby to term. You're dealing with the life of your daughter's unborn child and with the future of your own child's physical, spiritual, and mental health. Yes, being pregnant at 16 is not what you or your daughter had hoped for, but the reality is that she is with child. An abortion will only complicate her future, not resolve the pain of an unwanted pregnancy.

My advice to you is this: Start by reassuring your daughter of your—and God's—unconditional love for her. Now more than ever she needs your love and care, not your wrath. There will be a time for you to talk about your anger and disappointment, but now is the time to show your commitment to her.

Next, help your daughter sort through all the messages about abortion that she's hearing right now. Her boyfriend and his family are probably telling her to think of herself and her future, not to consider the fetus as a baby, and to remember her freedom of choice. It's your job to gently remind her that, regardless of the circumstances of the pregnancy, the baby developing inside her is a person who deserves attention and protection. Also try to help her think about her options. If she isn't ready to become a mother, she could always give the baby up for adoption.

To help your daughter think through all of this, take her to a Christian-based crisis pregnancy center (your pastor can help you find one, or you can call 1-800-NEWLIFE). At a Christian crisis center she can talk with a counselor in private. The counselor will talk with her about issues like abortion, post-abortion syndrome, keeping the child, and adoption. The counselor will also work with you as you guide your daughter to a decision you can all live with.

Finally, look at a few Scripture passages that will remind you and your daughter of God's view of life, such as Genesis 1:27 and Psalm 139:13-16. This is the time to intervene with love and help your daughter make the right choice about her pregnancy. Take one step at a time. Don't panic (if at all possible), but rather give your anxiety to God in prayer. Ask your daughter to do the same.

## ACTION STEPS:

1. Assure your daughter of your—and God's—unconditional love and support for her.

2. Help your daughter get advice from a Christian pregnancy counselor.

3. Turn to God for guidance and assurance.

# RAPE

*We learned last night that our daughter was raped by her boyfriend. We are devastated and don't know how to help her. The incident took place several weeks ago, and she didn't report it to anyone, so I doubt we could take any legal action. What can we do to help her get through this awful ordeal?*

What your daughter needs more than anything right now is your love, understanding and prayer. There will be times she'll want to talk with you and other times when she won't. Be available for her, but don't smother her. During this period, your presence and support will often be more important than your words.

Your daughter also needs professional help to deal with her feelings about the rape, so I recommend finding her a Christian counselor as soon as possible. Your daughter might resist this, since it will mean telling the story to a stranger. However, a trauma has taken place in her life. She is the victim of a crime and the victim of a great offense against her precious body, mind, and soul.

Also, make sure she has no contact with the boy who raped her. If they attend the same school, you may need to consider changing schools, or even homeschooling her. Your daughter's counselor can help her deal with ending the relationship and making sure he doesn't work his way back into her life.

Even as your daughter gets counseling, there are some things you can say and do to help her begin the healing process. Assure your daughter that the rape is not her fault. Most people who have been sexually abused place much of the blame on themselves. We see this often in date rape situations, but the fault always lies with the abuser.

As devastating as this situation is, be sure to offer your daughter hope. Unfortunately, thousands of people have been raped on a date. Many of those people have gotten the help they needed and are able to get on with their lives. Your daughter can too.

Your daughter can find great hope in God's love as well. It's sometimes very difficult to understand that God cares about us as individuals, especially after a traumatic experience. Help your daughter remember that Jesus wept at the death of a friend. If we have a God who weeps at the news of his friend's death, then we have a God who weeps when he hears of injustice and abuse. The spiritual side to her healing is very important.

Your daughter isn't the only one who needs support right now. Make sure you get the right kind of help for yourself and for the entire family. And keep in mind that your daughter's counselor will need to report this crime to child protective services. Reporting the incident is a very good thing, though your daughter probably won't think so. Even if your daughter chooses not to prosecute, the name of her ex-boyfriend will be placed in the system in case he ever does it again. Sexual abusers often strike more than once.

ACTION STEPS:

1. **Find a Christian counselor who can help your daughter work through her pain.**

2. **Assure your daughter that she is not to blame.**

3. **Help your daughter find hope and comfort in God.**

# SEXUAL ABUSE

*We adopted our 16-year-old daughter when she was five. She had been removed from her home after being sexually abused by her biological father. She seemed to thrive on our love for many years, and she seemed to have a happy childhood. But now the effects of her abusive past are surfacing again. She's petrified of boys and says she never wants to date. And she won't let my husband come near her anymore, which breaks his heart. Any suggestions?*

As much as you might want to wish your daughter's painful past away, she will carry it with her all of her life. My experience in working with abuse victims is that the difficult issues will periodically surface and then go dormant for a while. Your daughter's current struggles could be the result of the emotional, physical, or even intellectual changes she's experienced during her teen years. While she found ways to cope with her pain as a child, she's having to find new ways to cope now that she's a growing teen with new thoughts and feelings. And because developmental changes can trigger the issue all over again, don't be surprised if she goes through a difficult time again in college, with marriage, and then again when she has her own children, which will bring more painful memories of her traumatic childhood.

You might have done this already, but I would recommend that as a family you make a decision to get family therapy. Seek a Christian counselor with expertise in trauma caused by sexual abuse. With the right kind of help you and your daughter can enter the next level of healing and wholeness.

It's possible that as your family works through this time of pain, your daughter will actually develop a better relationship with your husband. It will never be easy for her to trust men, especially as she becomes aware of her sexuality. She will likely even struggle with the image of God as a loving father. So encourage your husband to be patient. If he consistently shows her the love and support she needs, she will love him all the more as she heals.

**ACTION STEPS:**

1. **Understand that the pain of her past will likely erupt throughout her life.**

2. **Seek counseling as a family to determine the best ways to help her deal with the issues she's facing.**

3. **Continue to show her love, patience, and support.**

# HOMOSEXUALITY

*Our 16-year-old son shows absolutely no interest in girls. My wife says it's no big deal, but I'm concerned he might be gay. Am I paranoid, or do I have reason to be concerned?*

There could be a hundred reasons why your son shows no interest in girls, so the odds are very slim that it's because he's gay. Your son could be a "late bloomer." Some very healthy, normal kids just don't seem to be as interested in the opposite sex until later in their teen years. Some kids are just so involved with other activities that they literally don't have time for the opposite sex. Your son could be interested but he just isn't telling you. Or your son might be perfectly happy hanging out with both guys and girls and doesn't see a need to date. In fact, studies show that a large percentage of students have no serious dating relationships while in high school.

It's true that approximately 10 percent of today's adolescents struggle with sexual identity issues. This doesn't mean that they're homosexuals, but rather that they have some confusion about their sexual identity. When I counsel students, I use a simple list to help recognize early predictors of sexual identity issues. This list is by no means all-inclusive. Just because a child possesses one of these traits doesn't mean he or she is a homosexual. These questions are simply a way to begin thinking about possible sexual identity confusion.

1. Is your child a sensitive child who gets mocked and downgraded by others and forced to feel different?

2. Did your son "hang out" almost exclusively with girls when he was young? Did he have a history of almost exclusively playing with girls instead of guys prior to puberty?

3. Does your son have extremely effeminate behavior or appearance? (For girls the question would be do they have extreme mannish or "butch" posturing? This is not to be confused with simply being athletic.)

4. Does your son have a much older same-sex friend that causes you any concern?

5. Is your child frail or "slow"? Does he have a disability? Is your child an "outcast"? Is his physical appearance not socially acceptable? (Again, understand that just because a child has a disability, it does not mean he is homosexual.)

6. Does your child offer comments like, "I must be gay"?

7. Is your child an extreme loner and preoccupied with self?

8. Has there been any strong rejection by same-sex peers or a same-sex parent?

If after reading this list you have some concerns, then I suggest talking with a Christian counselor who deals with sexual identity confusion. Please remember this is not a checklist to find out if your son is gay. It's only meant to help you determine whether your son could benefit from talking with a professional about issues of gender and sexuality.

No matter what your son's reasons for not dating, it's essential that you let him know you love him and are there to talk with him whenever he needs you.

**ACTION STEPS:**

1. Keep in mind that plenty of teens don't date until after high school.
2. Determine if your son could benefit from counseling.
3. Let your son know you love him unconditionally.

# PIERCED EARS

*Our 16-year-old son wants to get his ear pierced. My husband is dead set against it. Our son is a good kid and has never given us trouble. I personally don't like earrings on boys, but I don't think it's an issue that should divide our family. What do you think about earrings?*

I wish I had an easy answer for you. I don't. But as you make your decision, think about the following:

1. Why does your son want to wear an earring?
2. Is he trying to make some sort of a statement? If so, what statement is he trying to make?
3. Who is influencing this decision?
4. Are any of you willing to put your relationship on the line for this battle? If you are, set your boundaries now. If you aren't, negotiate, compromise, and pray a lot.

Our thoughts on fashion and what's acceptable change quickly. In 1959 my father wouldn't let me wear blue sneakers. He said, "Only women wear blue tennis shoes." At the age of 76, he wears dark blue tennis shoes. Eventually, your husband might change his mind about the earring issue. But if this becomes a battle of wills, you'll never get to that point. Do what you can to help your son and husband resolve this issue calmly.

This question is really less about earrings and more about respect. Will your son respect his father's opinion? Will you and your husband respect your son enough to work out this issue together? Whatever you decide, make sure you're making the decision based on real convictions and not simply a desire to control your son.

**ACTION STEPS:**
1. Consider the reasons behind your son's request.
2. Determine if this is really an issue to do battle over.
3. Work out a compromise calmly.

"In my own opinion, it should be up to the teens what they wear as long as their values or beliefs do not change due to peer influence." — William, 17

# APPEARANCES

*Our son wants to dress any way he likes and do whatever he wants with his hair, but when someone says something about the way he looks, or his teachers make assumptions about his behavior, he gets deeply offended. How can we help our son understand that, right or wrong, the world judges by appearances?*

Actually, your son is learning that lesson right now. When I was 18, I had long hair and a scraggly beard. It amazed me how many people treated me poorly because I didn't have the clean-cut look. Some people assumed I was a drug dealer or dropout or something other than who I was—a Christian kid studying to be a minister at a Christian university. My parents didn't especially like the look, and I'm not sure I really liked it either. But for some reason I needed to look different.

I learned two lessons from my experience. First of all, my parents let me know they didn't approve of the new look, but at the same time, they told me they were proud I wasn't living up to the bad stereotype that often went with the image. Second, I learned that people will jump to conclusions based on appearance. I honestly don't think I could have learned that lesson any other way.

Your son is learning that there may be some negative consequences to his appearance decisions. If you're willing to accept his appearance, I recommend letting him decide for himself if looking a certain way is worth the stares and questions.

If your son's appearance bothers you, you have every right to say no to certain looks while your son still lives in your house. However, I advise including your son in the process of deciding what's acceptable. Be willing to negotiate and work with him to get your wishes, and his, met.

ACTION STEPS:

1. **Recognize that your son is discovering the consequences of his choice already.**
2. **Allow your son to decide if he's willing to pay the price for looking different.**
3. **Include your son in discussions about his appearance and be willing to negotiate.**

# STEALING

*When I was doing the laundry recently, I noticed a few unfamiliar items in my daughter's pile of clothes. When I asked her where they came from, she got very nervous and agitated. I think she may have stolen these clothes, either from friends or from stores. Should I confront her with my suspicions? And if she has been stealing, what should I do about it?*

Yes, I would confront her with your concerns, but there's a difference between confrontation and blame. When you first approach your daughter about this, try to hide your assumptions and simply say, "The other day when I found those clothes and saw your reaction, I started to get concerned. I'm not accusing you of anything or calling you a liar, but you seemed very agitated and nervous, and your answer didn't make sense." Then wait for her response.

My guess is you'll end up with one of three scenarios. The first is that she gives you a reasonable explanation and the case is closed. The second is that she confesses to stealing the clothes. In that case, take her and the stolen clothes back to the store (or the friend) as soon as possible. Then have your daughter confess to the manager and pay for the clothes. Determine what the consequences of this action will be, and make it clear that there will be more serious consequences if it happens again.

The third and most likely scenario is that your daughter won't have a great answer, she won't confess, and you can't actually prove anything. In that case, you could say something like, "I want to believe you. In fact, it's taking a bit of faith for me to trust you." Then, work with your daughter to set up a reasonable consequence if unfamiliar clothes ever appear again.

The key here is that parenting isn't about punishing our children but rather training them. When the Bible says "Train a child in the way he should go, and when he is old he will not turn from it" (Prov. 22:6), I think the emphasis is on the word "train." You don't want your daughter to steal or lie, but you also don't want to punish her without proof of wrongdoing. We've gone so far with our kids to say, "If you tell the truth, the consequence will be much lighter. But if we find out you're lying, the consequence will be twice as severe. This is your chance to 'fess up and admit your mistake."

Whatever you do, please keep talking to your daughter about this. Intimate relationships are built around honesty, confrontation, and affirmation.

**ACTION STEPS:**
1. Confront your daughter with your concerns without casting blame.
2. If she confesses, carry out consequences for her action.
3. Encourage your daughter to be honest about her actions.

# DRIVING RULES

*Now that our oldest son is driving, we want to set up some rules about using the family car. Can you give us some tips on what's reasonable and what isn't?*

You're wise to think pro-actively about this subject. Families tend to run more smoothly when there are established rules and clearly defined limits as well as consequences for unsatisfactory behavior. These rules and limits are especially important when you're dealing with a potentially lethal weapon, a car.

You could set up your rules in a number of ways, but I like a simple "who, what, where, when, why and how" approach. Use the following questions to set up clear rules and expectations for your son:

- Who ... will be in the car with you and who will you be visiting?
- What ... will you be doing?
- Where ... will you and the car be?
- When ... will you be needing the car, and when can we expect you back?
- Why ... do you need the car?
- How ... will the gas be paid for?

These questions cover the basics. But your son needs to understand that driving is a privilege and a responsibility. So ask for his input as you write down other questions regarding curfew, drinking and driving, insurance and other expenses, the amount of time he can have the car each week, the number of people he can have in the car, and the consequences if he breaks any of your rules or traffic laws.

At our house, we've found that it's easier to write out our expectations, rules, and limits. That way our daughters can't come back and say, "But I didn't know about that rule."

Keep track of how well your son follows the rules you set and be consistent about carrying out consequences when he breaks the rules. Raising a cautious, conscientious driver is one of the nicest gifts you can give to your community—and to your son.

**ACTION STEPS:**
1. Set up clear, firm expectations for using the car.
2. Work with your son to lay out ground rules you can both live with.
3. Write out your rules so there is no question about what's expected.

"Teens should expect to run errands and tote their siblings around sometimes, especially if they're driving Mom and Dad's car. It's the old cliché: With privilege comes responsibility. Not too many teens are crazy about that one, but it's true." — Desiree, 16

# Thanks...

Though unstated, my parents' rule of thumb could be put like this: "If you think you are mature enough to handle something, then prove it by accepting responsibility."

They didn't harp about homework; they simply expected me to get respectable grades. They would not tolerate pouting and expected me to be civil to them, my sisters, and strangers. My parents didn't make an issue of getting home at a specified time—they just insisted that I be up before 7 a.m. and get my assigned chores done before school. They didn't mind if I burned candles at both ends, but they would not allow sleeping during the day or complaining about being exhausted. If I appeared overloaded, they would simply tell me, "You'd better take a look at your priorities and act like an adult if you expect to be treated like one."

Yet they did cut me some slack for my youth and immaturity. I remember one time in particular. I was returning from a date in my dad's car around 1 a.m. I fell asleep at the wheel only to awaken to see a freight train about 50 yards away blocking the road. I hit the brakes, spun around twice on the dry pavement and stopped about four feet from the moving train cars. When I arrived home, my dad was in his chair reading. I tossed him the keys, shared my experience, and told him I never wanted to drive again. He tossed back the keys and said, "My guess is that you are more ready to drive now than you were an hour ago."

It was a brilliant move on my father's part. He knew I had learned my lesson; there was no need for further punishment.

Jay Kesler—president of Taylor University

"When I found a car I liked, I made a deal with my parents to pay half. They thought this was a good idea, because by paying for half I would learn responsibility. But when I told them what privileges I thought I should have, they thought my requests were way out of line. They said I'd have to take my brother and sister to school every day, and I wouldn't be able to drive much after school. This is ridiculous — I'm paying for half of a car I can't even drive where I want to go! It just isn't fair." — Neal, 16

## MOVIES

We've never allowed our son to watch R-rated movies, but he's 17 now, and he thinks that since he can legally watch an R movie, we should loosen up. But age isn't the point; it's the content. Should we keep holding the line?

Let me say right from the start that because your son still lives in your home, you have every right to set whatever standards you feel are healthy, positive, and godly. All parents must choose their battles, and since this one sounds important to you, then you have every right to stand firm.

Look at this problem as a learning experience. Too often, parents make rules but don't take the time or energy to teach their children the reasons behind those rules. I encourage you to talk with your son about your concerns regarding R movies. Remind him of Paul's words in Philippians 4:8-9: "Finally, brothers, whatever is true, whatever is noble, whatever is right, whatever is pure, whatever is lovely, whatever is admirable—if anything is excellent or praiseworthy—think about such things. Whatever you have learned or received or heard from me, or seen in me—put it into practice. And the God of peace will be with you." Help your son see that there are very few R-rated movies that fit the description of "pure" or "commendable."

You might also want to consider working with your son to decide which movies he can and can't see. We do this with our daughters, and it's worked well. We all discuss movies together, then decide which ones to see and which to avoid. Our teenagers have enjoyed being part of the decision, but they don't always enjoy the outcome. More than once, my wife, Cathy, and I have heard the phrase, "You are the strictest parents at our school ... church ... neighborhood ... " However, our daughters do understand why we don't allow them to watch every movie that comes along. And as they get older, we see them using that information to make good decisions of their own.

**ACTION STEPS:**

1. **Use this as an opportunity to help your son understand why you object to R-rated movies.**

2. **Remind your son of Paul's words on discernment.**

3. **Work with your son to create a movie review process where you decide together which movies he can see.**

# CHRISTIAN MUSIC

*My daughter is a Christian, but she won't listen to Christian music. She says Christian music is a rip-off of secular music and isn't any good. How can I convince her there's some excellent Christian music out there?*

Your daughter might be right about the Christian music scene of several years ago, but I don't think she's right today. Christian music has come a very long way in the last few years.

Since music is such an important part of most young people's lives, we parents must become students of the music culture. In a few weeks, my wife and I are taking our kids to a Christian music festival for a day. Our girls will love the experience, and they'll probably hear a great message at the same time.

You and your daughter may have to make a similar commitment of time or energy to find Christian music she'll enjoy, but I believe there's something out there for her. Ask for ideas from your youth pastor or someone who plays in a Christian worship band. Go to a Christian bookstore and ask the salespeople for some ideas. Many stores now have listening stations where you can "try before you buy."

The world of Christian music is only getting better, so encourage your daughter to keep an open mind. Recently I was checking out one of the groups my oldest daughter likes and found out that they were a crossover band, which means they are Christians who have been accepted in the secular music world. I was so excited to tell my daughter. She said, "I already knew that, Dad." Oh well, I tried.

## ACTION STEPS:

1. Let your daughter know that there's a wide variety of excellent Christian music.
2. Be willing to put some time and effort into finding Christian groups your daughter likes.
3. Help your daughter keep an open mind.

# LISTENING IN:

*Here's what 15- to 16-year-olds have to say...*

*... about parents wanting to know whom their children are dating:*

"I think it's very important that my parents are involved in my dating life. God gave me my parents as a source of guidance. They're wrong sometimes, but through the years I've learned to trust them and let them teach me things, especially about guys and dating." —*Jennifer, 16*

"When I start dating someone, my parents ask lots of questions, about his personal beliefs, his parents' beliefs, how far he thinks is too far, physically. I think it's very fair, because, come on, my parents are responsible for me. And I can't imagine how parents would feel if their daughter got raped or something and they hadn't asked questions." — *Jessica, 15*

"Parents should have the privilege of knowing who their teen is going out with. But it gets out of hand when the parents say their teen can't go out with someone because of what they think of him or her. Teens need to be able to make their own decisions and learn from their mistakes." — *Lauren, 16*

"If I'm good friends with a guy, my mom gets all uptight and wants to know everything about him—if he's a good Christian, if he has a criminal record, if the mole on his left hand is cancerous ... well, maybe I'm getting carried away, but she is very picky. It drives me nuts, but I have to remember that she loves me and just wants to protect me." — *Cambria, 15*

"I think it's OK for parents to ask questions like where we're going and what time we'll be back, but not personal stuff like what grades he gets or what his life plans are. Parents don't need to know all that for the first date. And if the relationship continues, there will be plenty of time to get to know the guy better." — *Rebecca, 17*

*... about driving responsibilities:*

"My parents sometimes ask me to run errands for them, but I don't think it's a big deal. It's so great to finally have some freedom, I don't mind that it comes with a few strings attached." — *Katelyn, 16*

"Teens should expect to run errands and tote their siblings around sometimes, especially if they're driving Mom and Dad's car. It's the old cliché: With privilege comes responsibility. Not too many teens are crazy about that one, but it's true." — *Desiree, 16*

"When I found a car I liked, I made a deal with my parents to pay half. They thought this was a good idea, because by paying for half I would learn responsibility. But when I told them what privileges I thought I should have, they thought my requests were way out of line. They said I'd have to take my brother and sister to school every day, and I wouldn't be able to drive much after school. This is ridiculous —I'm paying for half of a car I can't even drive where I want to go! It just isn't fair." — *Neal, 16*

"Since my parents are paying for my car, I think it's reasonable to run errands for them. After all, my parents have spent a lot of their time driving me places and getting me things. And I have fun just driving around, even if it's only to the store for a gallon of milk." — *Andrea, 17*

"My mom was happy when I got my license because she saw a great opportunity to get help with household stuff. But it hasn't worked out because I hate driving. And even if I liked driving, I don't think it would be fair to expect me to run errands. She might be busy, too, but I'm the one trying to keep my grades up and have a lot of extracurricular activities so I can get scholarships for the college of my choice." — *Amy, 16*

*... about choosing their own church:*

"I switched churches a few years ago because the youth group at my parents' church fell apart. My parents were kind of disappointed that I didn't want to go to church with them, but they understood that I needed to do something different. I'm still attending the new church, and it's been great for me. Plus, when I leave for college and need to find a new church, I'll know how to find one that's right for me." — *Meredith, 17*

"I've been to several churches without my parents. At first they were supportive, but when I told them what denomination my new home church was (it's Baptist and they're Catholic), they got very angry. They've never stopped me from going, but they make it hard to live in the same house with them." — *Erin, 17*

"I want to go to a different church, but my parents won't let me leave. I'm not getting anything from my church spiritually, and I need something more. If I were a parent, I would be proud to let my child grow strong in the Lord even if it meant letting them go to another church. I'd back them 110 percent." — *Nancy, 16*

"When I got to high school, I began to feel like I'd seen everything my parents' church had to offer. I had the whole church service memorized; I repeated the words without thinking about what they meant. So I started seeking God more, and that meant finding a new church. My family was shocked. My mom cried for days, saying I'd betrayed my family and my heritage. But eventually, she noticed a change in my life. Now she's seeking God more, too." — *Wally, 17*

"At my parents' church, the youth group is really small, and I felt like an outcast. Now I go to a different church, where there's a wider range of people I can relate to. My parents were totally against me going to another church at first. But they've seen how much I've grown up in Christ since then, and they're cool with it now."
— *Katelyn, 16*

"My parents' church doesn't teach the gospel, and going there wasn't helping me in my relationship with God, so I started going to a different church. First I just went to the youth group, then my parents let me go there every week for services. My parents still like for me to go to church with them for certain events, and now my mom, who's not a Christian, comes to my church for some events, too. God is really using this situation for his glory." — *Derek, 17*

### ... about risqué clothes:

"I think it's a parent's right to enforce reasonable standards of modesty—understanding that 'reasonable' is a very ambiguous word. But parental strictness can't change the underlying reasons why their children want to dress a certain way. If someone wants to wear certain kinds of clothes badly enough, they'll start wearing them behind their parents' backs, which can lead to worse things." — *Sarah, 15*

"If you watch teenagers in a group, a guy's eyes will always be on scantily clad girls. As a girl, my focus should be on what Jesus wants me to do, and not on getting a guy's attention. We girls have a responsibility to help guys focus on the things of God and not on earthly things—including ourselves." — *Alisha, 16*

"In my own opinion, it should be up to the teens what they wear as long as their values or beliefs do not change due to peer influence." — *William, 17*

"Most styles today aren't that bad—they cover the shoulders and go down to at least mid-thigh. My parents are completely comfortable with what I wear. Every once in a while I'll wear something tight, short, or showing my bra strap, but they usually don't say anything because I don't wear those styles too often."— *Lindsay, 16*

"As a Christian, I strive to portray myself as a person with high morals. That goal cannot be met if I'm sending the message: 'Look at my body—don't bother to invest in my mind, because I obviously don't have one if I'm dressed like this.'" — *Ashley, 15*

"Parents should definitely play a large role in what their children are allowed to wear. But it's important for the parents to follow their own advice. It's disturbing to see what many teenage girls wear, but then if you see their parents' clothes, it's easy to figure out why they dress the way they do." — *Nicole, 17*

### ... about family vacations:

"My parents have never given me a choice of whether or not to go on a family vacation. I've always wanted to go. However, by the end of the vacation, I can't wait to get home. My brother and I always end up fighting, which makes my dad mad, and no one is in a good mood." — *Megan, 17*

"We are going on a vacation soon, and I don't want to go. My mom isn't giving me a choice about going, and we fight about it every day. She doesn't care what I want or say." — *Ryan, 15*

"I choose to go on vacations with my family because I lead such a busy life that not only is it great to get away, it's also good to spend time with my family. Vacations are good because you get to spend time together without having to worry about things like work and stress." — *Sandy, 17*

"We always go somewhere during the summer, whether I like it or not ... usually not. I'd rather stay home and have time alone with God and my friends than be away somewhere I'd never choose to go. I'm at the age when I should be able to make my own decisions. I want my freedom." —*Tammy, 17*

"My parents are divorced, so I get to decide which parent I'd like to spend time with. I chose to go on vacation with my mom and stepdad because this is my last summer before college and we won't get to go on vacations like this again." — *Rebecca, 17*

"My family's about to go on what my parents consider a vacation. Of course I didn't get to have a say in where we're going, because we go to the same stinking place every year. I've been there for 18 years straight (including the summer Mom was pregnant with me). My dad's been there every summer since he was 12. That's 40 years! My parents are just crazy." — *Travis, 17*

### ... about being busy:

"I hardly ever have free time. I mostly write reports and study. I also have soccer practice, clubs, and other volunteer work. My parents are usually OK with my schedule, but they get pretty annoyed with all of my activities—even though it was their idea for me to get involved in them! I would be happy just to do school, but my parents want me to be well-rounded." — *Amy, 17*

"I'm involved in tons of clubs, sports, musicals, and volunteer work. My parents think it's good for me to be as busy as I am, but it has taken a toll on my health. I also don't get much family time at all. Either I'm busy, or they're busy. I really wish I got to spend more time with them, but even if I wasn't as busy, they would probably be too busy to do something with me." — *Brooke, 17*

"I am way too busy! My parents, however, do play an active part in helping me prioritize my life. They encourage me to participate only in activities that are important to me and to not get so involved that I never have free time. They also do the most important thing any parent can do: They are my cheerleaders!" — *Lauren, 17*

"My family eats dinner together every night. After that we don't see much of each other, unless one of us needs to talk. I think I spend enough time with my parents, though I know I will realize when I'm older that I probably took them for granted." — *Stephen, 16*

# The Older TEEN

## Ages 18-19

by Dave Veerman

# The Older TEEN
## Ages 18–19

Perhaps the most important words to remember during the teen years are *change* and *transition*.

During all the stages of adolescence (early, middle, and late), children change dramatically, in every area of life. Physically, little children morph into large adults. Intellectually, they move from thinking in concrete terms to thinking conceptually and analytically (and, thus, they begin rationalizing and arguing). In the social area, they go from having playmates to needing friends, dates, and marriage partners. And spiritually, they transition from learning facts about the Bible, God, and Jesus, to having a vital, personal relationship with their Creator and Savior. These changes bring tremendous stress and strain on individuals and their families.

We parents are much more comfortable observing either end of this process, but not the middle. But that's precisely where we find ourselves during these tumultuous teenage years.

One of the biggest changes in children and their families occurs soon after high school graduation. The grand ceremony with the speeches about being the "leaders of tomorrow" and "the first day of the rest of your life" are soon followed with a grand push to make decisions and to choose life's direction. And this movement brings a new tension to parent and child relationships.

Some kids can't wait to break away from home and be on their own; others fear separation and want to live at home forever. Some kids excitedly embrace the challenge of higher education; others settle for entry level employment and minimum wage. Some kids question the theology of their childhoods and seek to find their own faith; others hang back, threatened by doubts and change. And, like snowflakes, each teen is unique—no two are alike.

During all this turmoil, parents wonder when to push and when to back off. They know their children well and think they know what's best for them. But they also realize that eventually, their children must make their own choices and find their own way.

It's not easy being the child in transition from teenager to adult.

It's not easy being the parent in transition from Mom or Dad to peer.

This section focuses on kids right out of high school. And the questions reflect the tensions and parental ambivalence mentioned above. The answers aren't perfect, of course, because only God knows each parent, child, and relationship. But I have tried to answer each question with sensitivity to the concerns of the parents and the needs of the child.

Along with the answers to specific questions, the best advice I can give is to hang in there with your teen and look for allies—books, pastors, other parents who are going through the same passage. Trust yourself, trust your kids, and trust the Father.

—*Dave Veerman*

"I rarely come home from college during the school year, so it has been different getting used to living at home for the summer after being on my own. I feel like I take a lot of liberties with my freedom, like telling my mom where I'm going instead of asking her, which I kind of feel is disrespectful. I think I just got used to making my own decisions." — Mary, 18

# ENJOYING COLLEGE

*Now that our son is about to start college, we've been reminiscing about our own wonderful college days. How can we help our son get the most out of college?*

You're asking a very important question, and it shows that you care about your son and his college experience. The first point to remember is that the primary purpose of any school is education. In other words, in the middle of all the fun, friends, and extracurricular activities, your son should focus on academic achievement. In this regard, he should choose a course of study that will help him grow mentally and spiritually, as well as help him find a career in which he can use his gifts and abilities.

With that understanding, the key word for the rest of the college experience is balance. Brainstorm with your son ways to develop himself in all the areas of his life: physically, socially, mentally, and spiritually. Some kids go off to school and get so caught up in the social life, parties, and dating, that they flunk out. Others are so involved in sports and the physical area that they take easy courses and make few friends outside of the PE Department. Others hit the books so hard that they graduate with highest honors but with no friends or fun memories.

His spiritual growth on campus is essential as well. In this regard, talk with him about plugging into a good church, getting involved in a campus ministry, and finding an area of Christian service.

Your son will get the most out of college if he keeps his eyes on Christ, remembers the importance of getting a good education, and works at maintaining balance.

**ACTION STEPS:**

1. **Stress the importance of academics.**

2. **Brainstorm ways for your son to maintain balance between the physical, social, mental, and spiritual aspects of college life.**

3. **Remind him to keep his eyes on Christ.**

"I think a teen should be able to make her own college decision, because she's the one who has to actually attend the school. If she's forced to go to a Christian college, she might not even succeed because she'll be so caught up in how much she wanted to go to a state school. It's unfair for parents to insist on making that decision, because choosing a college is a very important part of beginning adult life." — JoAnne, 19

# COLLEGE CHOICE

*We want our daughter to attend a Christian college, even if it's only for a year. But she really wants to go to a big secular university in our area. We have good reasons for wanting her to go to a Christian college, and we're not choosing a specific one for her—but she still says we're controlling her life. What do we do?*

Have you told your daughter how you feel and your reasons for wanting her to attend a Christian college? That's an important first step. She needs to know that you care about her, want the very best for her, and are trying to look at the big picture for her education and her life.

This is an important transition time in your daughter's life, and in your relationship with her. She's moving toward independence and probably pushing for more freedom right now than you want to give. Let her know that you also want her to become an independent adult, but your timetables seem to be different. Talk about how you and your daughter can help the transition from dependence to independence go as smoothly as possible.

This would also be a good time to discuss your daughter's reasons for wanting to go to the big secular school. Check her motives and values. If possible, instead of comparing "her choice" and "your choice," discuss her specific concerns: variety of academic programs offered, athletics, student life, proximity to friends—whatever is important to her. Maybe your daughter's aversion to Christian colleges stems from a minor hang-up or a misperception. If so, her misdirected thinking could be corrected by reading some literature about Christian colleges, talking to a recent grad, or visiting a local Christian college campus.

As you talk with your daughter, brainstorm possible compromises. Maybe as you suggested, she could agree to attend a Christian college for at least one full year, then determine her next step. Or possibly she'd be willing to attend special visitor's weekends at three Christian colleges before making her final decision. You all need to be open to at least discussing a range of alternatives.

**ACTION STEPS:**

1. **Let your teen know that you have her best interests in mind, and talk about the transition you're all going through.**

2. **Assess her reasons for wanting to go to a secular university.**

3. **Be willing to compromise, but be clear that if you are expected to pay for college, you will have a voice in the decision.**

"Leaving home and becoming self-reliant forced me to examine my heart and life. I have become a much stronger Christian and have grown so much closer to my best friend—God. I think when you go through a life-changing experience like this, your parents have to just let you go and trust God to take care of you."

— Tina, 19

# LETTING GO

*We've just sent our oldest child off to college. We're thrilled for her, but we can't help feeling like someone has died. Why are we so sad about this?*

What you are feeling is very normal, especially when parents have a good relationship with their kids. When you left your daughter at college, kissed her good-bye, and drove slowly and tearfully away, you realized that you were letting go and that your family would never be the same again. From this point forward, your daughter will be a visitor at your home, not your "little girl."

It's not easy to let go of children. Parents begin this process early—remember how you felt when your daughter began her first day of school? Yet good parents realize that the goal of parenting is to produce physically, emotionally, and spiritually mature individuals who can function quite well on their own ... without depending on Mom and Dad.

When a child enters college, it's a major passage in life for her and for her parents. It's exciting, happy, and sad, all at the same time. This passage also stretches your faith because you will have to depend on God and be confident that you have prepared your daughter well for this next stage in her life. At times like these, Jeremiah 29:11 is a great promise for the whole family to remember: "'For I know the plans I have for you,' declares the Lord, 'plans to prosper you and not to harm you, plans to give you hope and a future.'"

Of course, sending your daughter off to college does not mean the end of your relationship with her. In fact, you may find yourself relating more to her as a peer over the next few years. And at the next few stages of her life—her first job, marriage, parenthood—you'll probably see her gain a whole new appreciation for you and your parenting skills.

**ACTION STEPS:**

1. Try to view your child's growing independence as a mark of your success as parents.

2. Take confidence in God's promises for her future.

3. Start relating to her as a peer and prepare yourselves to support her through the other big changes on the horizon.

# TEACHING "STREET SMARTS"

*How can we help our daughter prepare for college life? She's a very sweet, rather naïve girl, and we're concerned she's not ready for life on her own. What can we do to help her gain some "street smarts"?*

College is a time of transition, and college students are not entirely "on their own." Some colleges and universities are much more open and unstructured than others, so together you should choose one that is more sensitive to the needs of its students and watches out for them. These schools will have reasonable rules, resident assistants (older students in the dorms, each of whom is responsible for a group of students), and a counseling and care system in place (including faculty advisers, chaplains, counseling services, and so forth).

If your daughter has never been away from home, and you think she would have great difficulty adjusting to college life at any school, you can begin right away to prepare her by giving her independent living experiences. During the school year, she could spend a long weekend with relatives in a distant city and another weekend with a college age friend at her friend's college campus. In the summer, she could go away to camp or travel on a church mission trip. You can start slow and then add to her experiences.

You should also supplement these experiences by having your daughter talk with young people from your church who are upper-classmen in college or who have just graduated from college. They can tell her what to expect, both of college life and of being away from home.

ACTION STEPS:

1. Look for a college that has a strong support system to help students adjust to life away from home.

2. Start giving your child on-her-own experiences, such as weekends away from home or a summer mission trip.

3. Put your daughter in contact with a college upperclassman or graduate who can tell her what to expect.

# MISSIONS OR COLLEGE?

*Ever since he went on a mission trip his junior year of high school, our son has been convinced that he's called to overseas work. He's very excited about it, which is great, but he wants to go right after high school. We'd really like him to go to college first. It has become the biggest fight we've ever had with him, and we're just stuck.*

It sounds as though your son wants to work overseas because of his relationship with God. So that's good. But you should also explain, in love, that God's Word says that children should honor their parents (Deut. 5:16). The One who calls him to the mission field also calls him to submit to the authority of his mom and dad. So it certainly doesn't make sense to "fight" over this issue. Let your son know that you support his desire to be used by God in another country. You just question the timing, not the goal or desire.

Explain that most mission agencies want their representatives to be college graduates; many also require post-graduate work. Help your son see the long view—to consider where he will be and what he will be doing 20 or 30 years from now. It's important to prepare now for the future. College provides a great opportunity to grow spiritually, mentally, and emotionally, and to learn valuable information and skills that God can use for his glory. And this preparation time can be mission time as well. Your son can serve God now, as a witness to his friends at home and at college. He doesn't have to go to another country to be a missionary.

Work with your son on finding a Christian college that offers a major in missions or has several mission options. Most Christian colleges have overseas programs as well as short-term mission trips. Another option to consider would be a Bible college education, which would help prepare him for full-time Christian service.

Pray together about this matter. And pray for your son that he will submit to your authority and listen to your counsel.

**ACTION STEPS:**
1. **Explain the importance of college as a preparation for lifelong service to God.**
2. **Help your child find a Christian university or Bible college with many missions opportunities.**
3. **Pray with him about his future and about your family relationship.**

# INDEPENDENCE

*Our daughter, a high school senior, will graduate near the top of her class and could get into just about any college in America. But she doesn't want to leave home, and she says she wants to go to college in our town. Unfortunately, the only choice is a community college without much academic reputation. How can we spur her on to more independence?*

Look for an opportunity to have a heart-to-heart talk with your daughter about her future. (You may want to go out to breakfast together, or something similar, to provide this opportunity in a neutral setting.) During that talk, ask about her long-range goals for her life (career, marriage, and so forth) and discuss how she might be able to reach those goals. Share your own story of when you left home, the lessons you learned, and the steps you took to meet your goals.

Next, explain to your daughter your goals and dreams for her, focusing on the idea that you want her to be an independent, self-supporting, and self-reliant adult. Also explain that having her grow up and leave home is difficult for you, too. Empathize with her desire to stay at home (in some ways, you would like that as well), but stress the importance of her leaving—because eventually, she will have to.

If your daughter is not ready to leave home because she needs to mature in certain areas, you could work out a plan for her to stay home for a year after high school, working and taking a few courses at the community college. But she should see this year as a time of transition and preparation to become more independent. During the year she could go on a short-term mission trip, work at a camp, or visit distant relatives. Trips like those will help her feel more confident about living in a new community. A year at home may also serve to open her eyes, especially when she sees her friends move on in their education and careers.

Find options that are still safe and comfortable during the year as, together, you choose the right college for her in another city.

## ACTION STEPS:

1. Talk to your teenager about her long-range goals and your goals for her life.
2. Consider letting her stay at home for a year as she explores safe options for gaining greater independence.
3. Search together for a college in another city.

"LOOK, MOM AND DAD. ALL I WANT IS A LITTLE MORE INDEPENDENCE. IS THAT TOO MUCH TO ASK?"

"I still live at home while I attend community college. I don't have a curfew or pay rent, but I have to run errands like taking my younger sister places and occasionally buying the groceries. I think our arrangement is fair, because I know I'm saving a lot of money by living at home. And I can think of no better roommates than my great family!"

— Courtney, 18

## NOT READY TO GROW UP

*Our daughter will graduate from high school this year, and she's very upset about it. She says she's not ready to leave her friends or start all over in college. She just seems so depressed about growing up. What can we do to help her?*

Although the opposite is usually portrayed, not all young people want to leave home as quickly as possible and move out on their own. Often this is the case with a child who has grown up in a loving and safe home. As she becomes increasingly aware of how fast time is passing, she might become fearful and insecure.

You can remind your daughter of God's wonderful promise in Jeremiah 29:11: "'For I know the plans I have for you,' declares the Lord, 'plans to prosper you and not to harm you, plans to give you hope and a future.'" Assure her that God will be with her every step of the way. In fact, she can never be out of his presence or lost to his love (see Romans 8:38-39).

Encourage her to take one small step at a time instead of thinking way ahead. Three or four years can seem like an eternity to an 18-year-old, and imagining marriage and/or a career in a few years can be very intimidating.

Ask her to think of a similar passage in her life, perhaps when she began high school. As she stepped onto that campus, she probably knew few of the students and none of the teachers. For a while, she probably had trouble just finding her way between classes. But she learned her way, made friends, got involved in activities and studies, and had a great experience. And God was with her. That will happen in college, too. Surely she'll miss you and the rest of the family, but she will be embarking on another exciting adventure.

**ACTION STEPS:**

**1. Remind your daughter of God's promises to guide and protect her.**

**2. Encourage her to think in small steps instead of huge leaps.**

**3. Ask her to remember another major passage in life, recalling both the initial difficulties and the ways she adjusted successfully.**

# COLLEGE COSTS

*Our daughter wants to attend a Christian college, but we can't afford it and would hate to see our daughter go into debt for her education. We'd rather send her to a less-expensive school. How can we share our concerns while still letting her make her own decision?*

Although your concern about debt is valid, it's important to keep in mind that some things—like a good education—are worth the cost. This doesn't mean you have to spend tons for your daughter to get a good education, even at a Christian school. Christian colleges come in a variety of costs (for example, at Moody Bible Institute in Chicago, tuition is free). That said, however, you're right in assuming that most private Christian colleges are more expensive than public schools.

Talk to your daughter and find out why she wants to attend a Christian college. You might learn that she's got some legitimate concerns about being on a large campus, or that she likes the idea of learning in a solidly Christian environment. Those feelings are an important part of the college selection process and can't be dismissed.

If a Christian school is the right choice for your daughter, there are a number of ways you can find the money for her education. Encourage her to apply for scholarships and learn more about government loans and grants (her high school counselor and the college admissions office will help). Help her find a good part-time job where she can earn part of her tuition. Research the schools' financial aid options as well—a good package can sometimes make a school with a high sticker price more affordable than a "cheaper" school. You could also talk to your bank about low-interest loans. Whatever steps you plan to take, talk them through with your daughter and the financial aid officers at the college.

As another option, your daughter could spend her first year or two at a community college, then transfer to a Christian college. She could also take a year off to work and save money before starting at the Christian college.

Pray about this together, asking God to direct you to the right college and funding sources. Your daughter might end up at a less-expensive school in the end, but make sure that she's there because it's the best choice for her, not because it's the cheapest.

**ACTION STEPS:**

1. **Find out why your daughter wants to attend a Christian college.**
2. **Explore scholarship and financial aid options.**
3. **Pray with her, asking God's guidance in her search process.**

"Ultimately, college should be the teen's choice, but she should seriously consider her parents' opinions. She should listen to them and discuss the pros and cons of each choice. And the whole family should spend time in prayer to see where God is leading." — Jennifer, 18

# UNREALISTIC DREAMS

*Our youngest child is about to graduate from high school. She wants to be an actress instead of going to college. She is very talented, but we aren't sure she can make it in such a risky profession. How can we find the balance between encouraging her to follow her passion and helping her be realistic about her future?*

Many professions are very competitive and, thus, risky. It's good that your daughter wants to follow her dream, but the chances of her making a living as an actress are very slim, even if she is loaded with talent.

Help your daughter see that she can work at becoming an actress *while* going to college, not instead of. She can find a college or university with a good drama department and focus on theater or a similar major. Then, armed with her college degree, she will have a variety of career options: acting, teaching drama, or pursuing any other career for which a degree in theater or communications would be beneficial.

In addition to participating in collegiate theater productions (which are much more plentiful and easier to get into than professional productions), your daughter can also become involved in community theater. She may even be able to gain experience by being an extra in a film that is being shot in your area. There are plenty of opportunities to act and ways to learn about theater while she's getting her college education.

If your daughter is idealistic about her chances of success, that's probably because she has heard or read stories of celebrities who were "discovered." For every one of those, however, thousands go undiscovered. And those who have no educational foundation or other job skills often end up waiting tables instead. To give her a taste of reality, have her talk with college drama professors and others in the profession. They'll back up your insistence on getting an education first.

**ACTION STEPS:**

1. **Help your child see that college is an important step toward, not a distraction from, following her dream.**
2. **Point out the opportunities she'll have to act while she's in school.**
3. **Put her in contact with drama professors and others in the profession to provide a taste of reality.**

"When the Bible tells us to honor our father and mother, it doesn't mean to stop honoring them when we finish high school. Our parents love us and want what's best for us, so we should respect that."

— Luke, 18

# ENCOURAGING TALENTS

*Our 18-year-old son is a fine student, an excellent musician, and a strong leader. What can we do to help foster these gifts in him?*

You'll want to start by assessing the quality of opportunities that are readily available to him. Since some schools are stronger than others in specific areas, talk to your son and a trusted school administrator or teacher to see if there's more he can be doing at his high school to develop his gifts. Maybe he could take tougher classes, get involved in additional music groups or programs, or take on a more challenging leadership role, like student representative to the school board. However, it's also possible that he's exhausted his high school's possibilities, in which case you'll have to be more creative in finding opportunities for him to grow.

For an added academic challenge, see if your son can take a class or two at a local college. Often, these classes count for both high school and college credit, which makes them doubly appealing.

You have several options for fostering your son's musical talent. If he isn't already taking private lessons, sign him up with the best teacher in your area. If he's already taking lessons, ask his teacher about contests or camps he might participate in. Also encourage him to share his talent with your church and community by performing regularly.

You also mentioned leadership. Besides the usual opportunities in school, your son can find other places to develop his leadership abilities. In this regard, remember two important words: service and mentor.

The biblical model of leadership is servant-leadership (see Mark 9:35; 10:43). Your son should look for ministries and programs where he can become involved in serving others. This will help him learn the most important lessons for becoming a strong leader.

A mentor is someone who will guide and coach your son in a particular field and in life. A good mentor provides a positive role model and wisdom. So help your son find an older, wiser Christian man who will agree to be his mentor. It could be a teacher, someone from your church, or a relative your son admires. This kind of relationship was the apostle Paul's method for training future leaders, like Timothy (Phil. 2:22). Your son could meet regularly with his mentor to receive insight, counsel, and guidance.

## ACTION STEPS:
1. **See if there are more opportunities (academics and extra-curriculars) that your child could be pursuing at his school.**
2. **Consider signing him up for a college class and/or private music lessons.**
3. **Encourage him to learn leadership skills through service.**

# Thanks...

As I was growing up, graduating from high school, going to college, getting married, starting a career, I began to realize that all the advice my parents had given me was true in their own lives. It wasn't just talk. They really lived it. That consistency was vital in instilling in me a seriousness about Christian faith—to which they ultimately led me.

If along the way, I had sensed they were telling me one thing, but living a different life altogether, I'm not sure I could have believed the sincerity of their faith commitment. And quite possibly, that contradiction in words and lifestyle would have pushed me away from faith.

I'm so thankful my mom and dad were, and are, the "real deal." My prayer is that my wife and I will be just like that for our children.

Clay Crosse—recording artist

# PASTORAL PREPARATION

*Our 18-year-old son has a deep desire to be a pastor. What can we do to help him prepare for that kind of ministry?*

Affirm your son in his calling and remind him of 1 Timothy 3:1: "It is a true saying that if someone wants to be an elder, he desires an honorable responsibility" (NLT). But also explain that this choice should not be made lightly (see James 3:1).

In helping your son prepare for the ministry, encourage him to consider two time periods: the present and the future. Sometimes individuals who express a desire to have a future ministry have little or no ministry involvement in the present. That doesn't make a lot of sense. Someone with a real heart for ministry will want to minister now. So help your son find a place to serve Christ in the church, on his campus, or in the community. This will help him hone his gifts and learn more about what it means to serve people.

Also, make sure your son is practicing some key spiritual disciplines—prayer, fellowship, worship and time in God's Word. He not only needs these practices to be a good pastor someday, he needs them right now as he makes decisions about his future. Following God's plan for his life will take discernment, counsel, and wisdom—things he can only get through a close relationship with God and other Christians.

The second, and more significant, time period is the future. You and your son should map out a possible course of study and experience that will best prepare him for the pastorate. This will involve undergraduate and graduate studies. Your son will need to study the Bible and learn theology, ecclesiology, missiology, and other specialized content and skills. This happens best at the graduate (seminary) level. Check out a variety of seminaries and see what they require for admission, including the preparatory college courses they recommend.

Your son might want to attend a Christian liberal arts college, where he could also take courses in biblical languages, Bible, Christian education, and so forth. Bible college might also be an option.

Of course, keep in mind that your son is only 18. He may change his career plans, and that's OK. Your role is to help him along the path he chooses, not necessarily to steer him in the direction that seems right at this moment.

ACTION STEPS:

1. Take your child's "spiritual temperature" to see whether he is seriously preparing now for a career in ministry.
2. Map out a course of study and experience that will best prepare him for the pastorate.
3. Keep in mind that your son may change his plans.

"I took two weeks off work to be a counselor at a Bible camp. It was an extremely profitable experience because I'm now attending a Bible college and plan to be a youth minister when I graduate." — Jeremy, 19

# CHOOSING A MAJOR

*Our son is a sophomore in college and still hasn't decided on a major. We don't want to pressure him, but it's frustrating to watch him float from one thing to another. How can we encourage him to make up his mind?*

College students tend to change majors every few months during their first couple of years at school, so your son's experience is typical. More important than the fact that your son hasn't chosen a major is the reason for his indecision. He is maturing and changing (remember, he's still an adolescent); thus, his interests may also be changing. As he discovers more about himself, he may gravitate away from one field of study and toward another. If this is the reason for his change of heart, relax and encourage him to do his best in the new area.

If, however, your son changes his mind when he finds a particular course boring or difficult, you probably should take a harder line. Every major will require some boring and difficult courses. Your son shouldn't think that he can slide through school without doing much studying or sitting through more than a few long lectures.

If your son is confused because he really doesn't know himself or what career path he wants to take, encourage him to take some tests that measure his abilities, aptitudes, and interests. (Most colleges have career counselors who administer these tests.) You can also encourage him to talk with caring Christian adults who know him well. These friends can share what they see in him, affirming his abilities and gifts. After all of this, you should sit with your son and analyze the test results and friends' insights together. This will help him select the appropriate courses and major.

**ACTION STEPS:**

1. Try to determine your son's reasons for being undecided—to find his interests and strengths, or to run away from boring or difficult classes.

2. Encourage him to get a better idea of his aptitudes and abilities by taking a test and/or talking with Christian friends.

3. Using the results of these tests and discussions, help your son choose a major.

# RELIGION MAJOR

*Our son is about to go away to a secular university. He wants to be a religion major, but we've been informed by other parents that this school's religion department has notoriously liberal faculty members who deny the Bible's inerrancy. We can't help but imagine him coming home over a break and informing us that he doesn't believe in the Bible or God anymore. What can we do?*

You raise a very important concern. Certainly you don't want professors, especially those who teach religion and theology, to undermine your son's faith. To keep this from happening, first discuss the situation with your son, affirming his faith and sharing your concerns. During this discussion, you may want to suggest that he choose another major and then focus on Bible and theology in post-graduate studies. You may also want to share your own spiritual journey and how you came to believe in the inerrancy of Scripture, the deity of Christ, and so forth.

For outside perspective, talk with your pastor or another Christian you trust. Ask this person for resources that will bolster your son's faith and help him know what he believes and why. These will get you started: C.S. Lewis (*Mere Christianity, The Great Divorce, Miracles*); Paul Little (*Know Why You Believe, Know What You Believe*); Josh McDowell (*Evidence that Demands a Verdict, More than a Carpenter*); and R.C. Sproul (*"Choosing My Religion"* videos and many books).

Also encourage your son to get involved in a solid campus ministry. In addition to denominational ministries, InterVarsity Christian Fellowship, Campus Crusade for Christ, and The Navigators offer fellowship, apologetics, and outreach, usually guided by a trained staff person.

If your son expresses doubts about his faith, now or after a few classes in college, be careful not to argue with him. Instead, affirm his thinking where you can and encourage him to keep looking for answers. Remember, it's important for your son to make his faith his own, and he may have to ask serious questions on the journey.

## ACTION STEPS:

1. **Discuss your concerns with your child, and suggest waiting until postgraduate study to focus on religion and theology.**

2. **Offer resources to bolster his faith, including Christian books and media and involvement in an evangelical group on campus.**

3. **Understand that doubts and questions are often part of a young person's journey to making his faith his own.**

# LACK OF AMBITION

*Our son is graduating from high school this year, but he has no goals or ambition—college is definitely out, he says. Instead, he plans on working some minimum wage job and hanging out with his high school buddies. Any advice on what to do?*

Could your son go to college if he wanted to? That is, does he have the academic capability? If not, another type of vocational training could be his best option. Or maybe he needs to get a taste of the real world for a while—that might motivate him to further his education and seek meaningful employment. You need to talk through this issue with your son, listening carefully to his views, and calmly explaining your perspective.

Let him know you believe that God has given him unique gifts, talents, and abilities that can make a difference in the world. Offer to help your son identify his strengths through testing and counseling. You could also encourage your son to volunteer with a ministry or community service organization.

The next step is to talk to your son about his goals for the next few months, for a year from now, and for his life. Then you and your son need to develop a schedule for him to follow as he moves toward independence and reaching his goals. You should also determine what type of support you will offer as he pursues his goals. Let him know how much financial assistance you are willing to offer toward a college or vocational education, If he chooses either of these options.

If his plan is just to live at home and "hang out" indefinitely, take a firm stand. Tell him that you will charge rent, and talk through your expectations for him as a renter/son.

In all of these discussions, look for solutions that allow for compromise. You should also be prepared to make mid-course corrections. For instance, your son claims he wants to just stick around home and hang out with his old buddies. Before long, however, those old buddies may decide that they want more from life than what your hometown has to offer. They may go to college or get married or move out of town. While your son may not be ready to accept this possibility, you can certainly take it into consideration as you think about future options for your son.

**ACTION STEPS:**

1. **Explore a range of options, including vocational training.**
2. **Discuss your teenager's goals, a schedule for reaching them, and the amount of support you will offer for each stage.**
3. **Have alternate plans in mind.**

# MOTIVATION

*Our son was doing great at the beginning of his senior year of high school, preparing to go to his dream college. But the college didn't accept him. Now he's given up on his schoolwork and refuses to think about his future. How can we get him motivated again?*

Losing a dream is quite a blow for anyone, so empathize with your son and help him grieve his loss. Then, at an appropriate time, help him see that his experience is not unique; it happens to thousands of high school seniors every year. That's why guidance counselors encourage students to apply to a "safety" school, where they know they will be admitted, along with the "dream" school. Also explain to your son that he might still get into his dream college by transferring after a year at another institution—it's often easier to get accepted that way.

You may want to check with the college to make sure that everything in your son's application was correct. For example, is his high school transcript accurate and up-to-date? Perhaps he could submit additional information or recommendations to get him placed on a waiting list.

To help your son find other options for next year, it would help to find out why the original college is his dream school. Is that where he has always wanted to attend? Is his girlfriend going there? Does he like the football team? Did he dream of being in one of their prestigious programs? Pinpointing the main reason will help you narrow your search for the best alternatives.

Also, help your son look at this situation from God's perspective. Perhaps this is not the right school for him. Explain that he can learn valuable lessons from this setback. In fact, he's already learned one—that's the way life is sometimes. But he doesn't have to be defeated.

This would be a good time to enlist the help of other adults whom your son respects. They can share their stories of personal disappointments and how they bounced back and then moved on with their lives. Your son needs to know that God wants to work everything for good in his life (Rom. 8:28), and that no matter what happens, he can never be lost to God's love (Rom. 8:38-39). That's a lesson that will serve him well throughout his lifetime.

**ACTION STEPS:**

1. **Allow your child to grieve his loss.**

2. **Explore his options for attending another college and/or eventually enrolling at his "dream school."**

3. **Help him see this as a life lesson in trusting God's plan.**

# DISAPPOINTED HOPES

*We want the best for our kids, but we're not sure when to push them and when to lay off. Of course we don't want to be overbearing, but we want them to realize their own potential. What should our role be, and how can we deal with feelings of disappointment when it seems like our kids just aren't trying hard enough?*

At every parenting passage, it's important to affirm your children and reassure them of your never-ending love and blessing. They need to know you're their biggest cheerleaders, even when they struggle in school or don't take the career paths you hoped for them.

You still can push your kids to excel and encourage them to explore alternatives, and you certainly can let them know where you think they have potential. Eventually, however, they'll have to make their own way, and you'll have to accept that.

During these times, it's also important to ask, "Whose needs are being met?" Many parents, under the guise of "wanting the best for my child," push their children into certain activities and involvements (and even careers) in order to enhance their own self-esteem.

Don't allow yourself to get so caught up in all of this so that you lose sight of each individual child. Instead, focus on loving your kids unconditionally and turning them over to God.

**ACTION STEPS:**

1. Affirm your teenagers for who they are, even if that's not exactly who you hoped they'd be.

2. Keep your teens' needs, and not your own, in the forefront.

3. Release your teens to God's care and guidance.

# RISKY MINISTRY

*Our son has a real heart for the poor and wants to take part in a summer program in the inner city. We're concerned for his safety. He's an adult now and doesn't need our permission to go, but do we have any right to ask him not to?*

It's understandable that you're concerned for your son's safety, and you have the right to express your concerns. How you talk with him is the important issue. If your son is of age but still under your supervision (he lives at home or he's at college), you still have authority over what he does during the summer. If he is totally out of the house and on his own, then he can make his own decisions, hopefully taking into account your valuable counsel.

In either case, do not issue strong statements, generalizations, or demands. Instead, look for a good opportunity to discuss the situation. Begin by affirming your son's heart for the poor and your delight in his desire to serve Christ. Next, explain that your concerns arise from your love for him. Express those concerns and listen to his thoughts and ideas. If this discussion is done in the right spirit, you probably can come to an agreement about what safeguards should be in place before he is allowed (or he decides) to go.

Let your son know that you want to contact leaders of the inner-city ministry to find out more about the program. Those leaders are probably very concerned about safety and will allay many of your fears.

Close this time by praying with your son about this decision. If he eventually goes, remember David's words in Psalm 27:1-3: "The Lord is my light and my salvation—whom shall I fear? The Lord is the stronghold of my life—of whom shall I be afraid? When evil men advance against me to devour my flesh, when my enemies and my foes attack me, they will stumble and fall. Though an army besiege me, my heart will not fear; though war break out against me, even then will I be confident."

**ACTION STEPS:**
1. **Express your concerns in the context of a calm, open discussion.**
2. **Ask ministry leaders for concrete information about the risks and safety precautions taken by their groups.**
3. **Pray with your son about this decision.**

# SUMMER PLANS

*Our daughter is a freshman at college and has the chance to work as a counselor at a Bible camp during the summer. While it would be a nice experience for her, she wouldn't make much money. Undoubtedly, we'd have to pay more for her next year of college than we'd planned. So how much say should we have in this decision?*

You should have lots of input in this decision. After all, she's only a freshman, and you are paying the bills. Instead of declaring and demanding that she earn more money, however, use this as an opportunity to build your relationship with your daughter and to teach her a valuable life skill.

Set aside a time when you can discuss the situation for a couple of hours without interruption. Begin with prayer, thanking God for your daughter and asking for his guidance. Then let your daughter know how proud you are of her and her desire to serve the Lord. Listen carefully to her ideas, proposed plans and reasoning, without interruption. Young college students can be very idealistic, so your daughter may make statements that you consider totally unrealistic or even outrageous. But resist the temptation to interrupt or refute her reasoning.

After your daughter has finished, you should explain the realities of financing her college education. Let her know that money is not the most important consideration, but college is expensive and the money has to come from somewhere. Be honest as you outline the choices and sacrifices that will have to be made. Next, and this is the hard part, ask her to suggest a solution that would respect the needs and concerns of everyone involved. How would she resolve this issue? What would she do if she were you?

Then see if you can come to a compromise. For example, maybe your daughter can work at the camp, but plan to find part-time work on campus during the school year to make up some of her expenses. Or perhaps she can wait a year and work at the camp between her sophomore and junior years in college. If this is too much to decide right now, suggest that you all think about this for a few days and then discuss it again.

**ACTION STEPS:**

1. **Set aside a time to discuss this with your teen, and open the discussion with prayer.**
2. **Listen carefully to her ideas, resisting the temptation to interrupt her or refute her reasoning.**
3. **Ask her to propose a compromise, and keep talking about it until you can all come to a resolution.**

"I had the opportunity to work at a Christian camp for the summer, which would have been fun but wouldn't pay anything, or get a job. Since I start college next year, I need the money, so I had to decline the camp's offer. Instead, I decided to go on a mission trip before I had to start working." — Josh, 18

# LEAVING YOUTH GROUP

*My daughter just graduated from high school. She should be attending the college class at church, but she keeps hanging around her senior high youth group. What can I do to encourage her to let go of the past and get on with her life?*

You're right to expect your daughter to move away from the high school ministry. Actually, your church's youth director probably shares your feelings. They want the new youth group to find its own identity and for the new upperclassmen to assume leadership in the group.

At the right time (not at church or while another issue is causing tension in the house), talk about your feelings with your daughter. Use an example from her past to communicate your point. For example, if she played a sport in high school, you could ask how she would have felt if the recent graduates had continued to hang around practice or had been allowed to play in the games.

Let your daughter know that it's all right to spend time with her friends who are still in high school. But that time should be spent outside the youth group. Your daughter can have those friends over to the house, go out for pizza with them, or just hang out. Leaving the youth group doesn't have to mean leaving those friends behind.

If your daughter will be going away to college in the fall, you'll probably see a change in her desire to hang around high school students. She'll realize she's moved on. And when she comes home to visit, she'll sense that the group has changed as well.

If your daughter stays in the area, however, the temptation to stick with the old group will be much stronger. In this case, encourage her to get involved with activities and ministries targeted for college students. You might also want to help her find a place to minister (for example, teach Sunday school, sing in the choir, or help with Vacation Bible School). Seeing that "adult" life is full of activities and opportunities will keep her from pining away for the good ol' days of high school.

**ACTION STEPS:**

1. **Explain to your child that this transition time is important for her and for the younger students who need their chance to shine.**

2. Encourage her to spend time with her high school friends outside of church.

3. If she's staying in the area, help her find new ways to get involved in "adult" life.

"I rededicated my faith when I was 17, and this past year I've been growing a lot. When I question my faith, it's about how to live and make choices as an adult. My dad helps by pointing me to the Word of God, helping me understand it and praying with me." — Suzi, 18

# MINISTRY MOTIVATIONS

*Our 19-year-old son wants to be an adult volunteer in our church's youth group. We're glad he wants to be involved, but we suspect he's more interested in the girls than in actual ministry. Should we talk to him about our suspicions or let the youth pastor deal with it?*

Even if volunteers are very difficult to find, your youth pastor would not want a 19-year-old with suspicious motives. So the first thing you should do is talk directly with your youth pastor, in secret and in confidence. Don't accuse your son, especially since you aren't absolutely sure of his reasons for wanting to be involved in ministry. Instead, just share your observations and suspicions. Then, together, you and the youth pastor can decide on a course of action.

The youth pastor, for example, may feel that your son could prove to be a reliable volunteer and could establish some good relationships with underclassmen guys. The youth pastor might feel comfortable giving your son an unspoken probationary period to find out if your son is a good fit with the group.

On the other hand, the youth pastor may have picked up some signals from your son's behavior that your conversation confirms. In that case, the youth pastor probably should inform your son that he cannot help with the youth group for at least another year, and explain why.

Sometimes recent graduates have a difficult time moving away from high school and getting on with their lives, especially if they still live at home and have enjoyed the youth program. These young people usually need at least two years of separation to mature and to avoid problems like the one you suggest. Encourage your son to find a Sunday school class or youth group for people his age. And help him find other ways to minister in the church.

**ACTION STEPS:**

1. Meet privately with your youth pastor to discuss your concerns.
2. Determine whether it would be best to stop your son's youth group involvement or allow it to continue under close supervision.
3. Encourage him to find a church group for people his age and/or to find other ways to minister.

# VISITING AT COLLEGE

*I want to visit our son at college, but I'm not sure how often I should do it. What's a good rule of thumb?*

All universities encourage some visits. These can include parents' weekends, Homecoming, concerts, and special events. So don't feel guilty about visiting at those times. But you should be careful not to visit too much, especially the first semester or year. Remember that the college years form the bridge between adolescence and adulthood. The Apostle Paul wrote, "It's like this: When I was a child, I spoke and thought and reasoned as a child does. But when I grew up, I put away childish things" (1 Cor. 13:11, NLT). Your son needs time to grow up.

Here's a rule of thumb—let your son call home anytime, but don't call him during the first semester. Give him time to move on with his life, distance himself from high school, and get established at college.

Next, determine the level of contact he wants. Don't smother him with frequent visits and calls. After all, you don't have to see your son to be able to communicate with him. You can send letters, cards, and e-mail on special occasions, and you can send care packages from time to time. College students love mail and packages—especially food.

**ACTION STEPS:**

1. **Give your child time to establish himself at college by letting him take the lead on phone calls and visits.**
2. **Determine the level of contact he wants.**
3. **Communicate with him in other ways, like sending care packages.**

"If parents are around too much, their kids get too attached and dependent. Then what would happen when the kids start working or get married—would they still rely on their parents for everything? A visit every three or four months seems about right to me."

— Christine, 18

# VISITING HOME

*Our daughter just started college, and doesn't seem interested in seeing much of us. We miss her, and wish she'd come home more often. We know this is part of her growing up, and don't want her to visit out of obligation, but we'd like her to know how we feel.*

First of all, remember that fall is a very busy time of year. Your daughter's schedule is packed with new classes, social plans, sporting events, and other activities. She most likely has little time to write or call, let alone come home. Although you wish she would show more interest in life at home, her busyness is probably a good sign. Many young people have a very tough time leaving home; homesickness is common during that first year at college. So it's good that your daughter wants to grow up and get settled in her new life.

Of course, parents, like you, who have good relationships with their kids and enjoy being with them, usually find it difficult to let go. But you must. Your daughter needs to know that she has your blessing and approval for this next stage of her life. In the Bible, giving the blessing was an important part of rearing godly children (see Genesis 14:19; 24:60; 48:20; 49:28). So tell your daughter how proud you are of her; encourage her to make the most of her special gifts and talents; express pleasure in seeing God work in her life.

As far as sharing your feelings about this subject, let her know she is missed, but avoid making her feel guilty. And remember, you can still show your love and concern for her in other ways—by visiting for weekend events, for instance. On holidays and other special occasions, you could send her a card with a note that expresses your love. Occasional calls and e-mails are all right, too. Every six weeks or so, you could send a package of goodies (Christmas cookies, "Final Exam Preparation Kit," "Spring Surprise," and so forth).

When your daughter does come home, make sure you show a genuine interest in her life at college. Spend your time together catching up and enjoying her company so that those moments will carry all of you through until the next time you see each other.

**ACTION STEPS:**

**1. Remember that college students are busy—and that's a good sign!**

2. Give your blessing to her as she establishes herself at school.

3. Show your love and concern in creative ways.

"My parents don't visit me much at all. Actually, I prefer to go home and visit them. But I think it would be nice for them to come up and see me a couple times each semester, because I'd love the chance to talk about college life and have a break from the 'luxurious' school food!" — Jennifer T., 19

# FLUNKING OUT

*A few weeks ago, our 19-year-old son called us from college and asked us to come and get him. He was on academic probation and had finally flunked out of school. He's home with us now, but we really want to encourage him to give college another try. How can we help him be better prepared the next time?*

By asking how you can help your son better prepare for college, you're on the right track. He needs to realize that his education hasn't stopped just because he flunked out of college. In fact, you expect him to learn and grow while he's at home, with the goal of him returning to school.

The truth is, some young people aren't ready for college. They might be emotionally or intellectually immature, and they need a year or two to grow. Some can't handle all the freedom that college presents—they stay up too late, skip classes, put off doing their assignments, and flunk out. Some have never learned to study on their own because Mom or Dad made sure they got their high school assignments done and turned in on time. Away from the enforced discipline of their homes, they're unable to buckle down and make the grade.

Whatever the reasons for your son's academic struggles, right now he probably needs a dose of the real world. Insist that he get a job and learn to budget his money and time. Teach him how to make a "to-do" list and how to prioritize everything on it. Then, together, check out the catalog for a local community college and see what courses he can take. You probably will find a few basic college-level courses offered at night. Or you might find that the park district offers a class in study skills or speed-reading that would be good for him. Have your son take a course or two each semester.

Given the fact that he chose to go to college in the first place, I assume he's willing to give it another try. If his confidence is shot, finding some success in these other classes will help. In time, he'll likely want to return to college. This time, he'll be ready.

**ACTION STEPS:**

1. Insist that your son get a job while he's home.

2. Help him build time-management skills by working on "to-do" lists.

3. Encourage him to enroll in classes at a local community college or park district.

# NOT QUITE AN ADULT

*Our 19-year-old son is a sophomore in college and insists on being treated as an adult. He gets angry if we offer him advice or "meddle" in his life. At the same time, he often asks us for money and other kinds of help when he's in a tight spot. How can we treat him as an adult when he doesn't act like one?*

Picture your relationship with your son since high school as a continuum. During high school, he lived at home and was expected to submit to your house rules and respect your wishes. And because he lived at home, you could monitor his behavior and enforce a wide variety of consequences for misbehavior. At the other end of this process, after college graduation, your son will be totally on his own. That is, he will support himself by being gainfully employed, and he will choose a place to live.

Right now, he's in the middle, moving toward independence. To help him grow up, here's a rule to follow: Don't do anything for him that he can do for himself. This means letting him wriggle out of his own tight spots. At those moments, you can ask how he intends to solve the problem or get more money, and you can offer suggestions for possible courses of action. As long as the situation isn't life threatening, lovingly let him know that this is something that he'll have to do for himself.

To help your son prepare for post-college life, set up a system of providing him money for personal expenses. Put an agreed-upon amount in his account on a regular basis, much like a paycheck, and get in the habit of denying his requests for additional money unless

"ISN'T THAT CUTE? TOMMY'S BUILDING A TREE HOUSE."

he can demonstrate a genuine, immediate need. When you do give him extra money, hold him accountable for how he spends it, until he demonstrates responsible spending habits. He will probably accuse you of "meddling," but if it's your money, it's perfectly acceptable for you to know—and, to an extent, control—how it's being spent.

In finances and in other areas, you can keep giving him advice and counsel, but choose the right times and the right approach as you do. When he struggles or makes mistakes, avoid saying or implying "I told you so" or "You should have asked me .... " Begin to treat your son like a friend, and he'll soon grow into the role.

**ACTION STEPS:**

1. **Don't do anything for your child that he can and should do for himself.**
2. **Start giving your son money on a regular (not an as-needed) basis, and hold him accountable for how he spends it.**
3. **Give advice as you would to a friend, being careful not to sound sarcastic or condescending.**

# MONEY MANAGEMENT

*We thought we'd taught our daughter to manage her money well, but now that she's at college, she's always asking us to send money. She doesn't have a job, and we're already paying her tuition and other college expenses. How can we help her be more financially responsible?*

The best way to help your daughter manage her money is to design a budget with her and then insist that she stick to it. If she's providing her own spending money, let her know that you will not supplement it. On the other hand, if you're providing those funds, you may want to give her a set amount on a monthly or bimonthly basis until she demonstrates maturity in her spending habits.

As you discuss this budget, work hard at listening carefully to her and taking seriously her list of "necessities." Share your expectations for her saving and spending habits, describe what you consider to be necessities, and encourage her to be responsible in her use of the funds you are entrusting to her. You may want to discuss the parable of the wealthy man and his stewards (Matt. 25:14-30).

Parents who love their children find it difficult to say no to them, especially when they are far away and seem so needy. But no is often the best answer to give. Your daughter will learn the invaluable lesson that she can't get whatever she wants whenever she wants it. Life just doesn't work that way. If she spends her money unwisely and runs out, you may have to say something like: "I'm really sorry, dear, that you made that choice. What will you do now?" Let her know that her actions resulted in the problem, and that she needs to solve that problem herself.

## ACTION STEPS:

1. **Sit down with your daughter to draw up a budget.**

2. **Discuss what financial responsibility means to you and why it's important for her to learn good stewardship.**

3. **Stop bailing her out; instead, let her find ways to solve her own problems.**

"Next year at school, I'll have an apartment and a car—both huge financial responsibilities. So this summer, I'm working temp jobs that pay good money. I had the option of working for the civic theater, which is my major, but I had to turn it down. My parents are so proud of my decision!" — Erika, 19

# CREDIT CARDS

*Our son will head off to college in a few months. We've read some horror stories about college students and credit card problems. What can we do to instill a sense of financial responsibility in our son so he can avoid these kinds of pitfalls?*

You're right to be concerned about your son and potential problems with money, especially since credit companies are notorious for flooding students with card offers. Fortunately, you still have some time to help him understand how to set up and live by a budget. If you haven't done this already, you could show him your family budget and explain how you set aside specific amounts of money every month for tithing, savings, food, mortgage, and other expenses.

Explain to your son how money and materialism can be a terrible trap. The Bible says, "For the love of money is a root of all kinds of evil, and by craving it, some have wandered away from the faith and pierced themselves with many pains" (1 Tim. 6:10; see also Proverbs 22:3,7). Give examples of people you know who have struggled with debt—even stories from your own past, if they apply.

Discuss with your son how much money he thinks he'll need for school expenses, social life, emergencies, and so forth. (Experts estimate $150 per month for personal expenses, on top of tuition, room and board, fees, and books.) Next, discuss the sources of your son's spending money—how much you'll give him, whether he needs to find part-time work to earn more. If you'll be providing the bulk of his spending money, you could parcel out the funds, sending him a portion every few weeks until he demonstrates good stewardship (see Matthew 25:14-30 and Luke 12:41-48).

Instead of a credit card, your son probably should use a debit card. This would allow him to be prepared for emergencies without having to carry a lot of cash, and it would keep him from going into debt. Tell him to throw away all the credit card offers he receives. In a year or two, you might want to reopen the credit card discussion, because he'll eventually have to establish a good credit rating for himself. But for now, he's definitely better off without one.

**ACTION STEPS:**

1. Help your child understand the importance of budgeting and good stewardship.
2. Create a budget that includes his expected college expenses and details of where the money will come from.
3. Start him off with a debit card.

> "While I appreciate the love and concern my parents have for me, I'm really annoyed at being home for the summer. During school, I live 120 miles from my parents, and they don't stay up all night listening for me to come home. Now that I'm here, if I go visit a friend, they lay guilt on me for staying out late. I wish I could afford to get summer housing elsewhere."
>
> — Kirsten Marie, 18

# HOUSE RULES

*My son is a freshman in college and is living at home. He stays out all hours of the night, which of course keeps me awake worrying. I say that as long as he lives under my roof, he needs to be in by midnight. He says he's an adult now and can do whatever he wants. Who's right?*

Even though your son might technically be an adult, he needs to realize he's not entirely ready for complete independence. If he was, he wouldn't be living at home. On the other hand, you also need to recognize that your son is no longer a high school student. Instead, he's in the fuzzy transition time between adolescence and adulthood, which makes it tough to know where to draw the line.

You do have the right to insist on certain guidelines and rules for your house. But instead of making this a question of who's right, it needs to be a matter of how you'll both live at peace in the house. So while it's important to be assertive, don't let this issue escalate to an angry confrontation.

Find a time when you can sit down and talk with your son. The goal is establishing and agreeing upon a reasonable set of house rules. Let your son know that living with other people means showing mutual respect, and that's true whether he's living at home, in a dorm, or in an apartment with friends. Stress that what you're asking for isn't just honor as parents (though you certainly deserve that), but common courtesy. The more you can disentangle this discussion from the complex politics of parent/pre-adult son, the better.

Since curfew seems to be a major issue, make sure to set clear guidelines. At the same time, however, explain that you will try to be flexible and compromise with your curfew times, especially on Friday nights. As your son shows that he can handle additional freedom and responsibility, you will give it to him. Help him understand that you are looking at the bigger picture, trying to guide him toward total independence in a few years. His freedom is your goal, too.

This would be a good time to discuss trust. Explain that you really want to trust him and will try to give him the benefit of the doubt (you don't enjoy worrying, and worry doesn't help much—see Matthew 6:25-27). But you should also explain that trust is fragile, and once it's broken, it's difficult to put back together. Close this time by thanking him for being a good son, and then pray together. Ask God to help you both adjust during this time of transition and to strengthen your relationship with each other and with him.

**ACTION STEPS:**

**1. Explain to your child that you do still have a right to establish**

rules for your house, while he has a responsibility to show common courtesy.

2. Set clear guidelines, but leave room for flexibility.
3. Ask God to help you both adjust to this new stage in your relationship.

"College is supposed to give you the experience of living on your own, while still having some supervision to help you if you fall. How can you even start to experience living on your own if your parents are keeping you tied down with a bunch of rules and treating you like they did when you were in high school?" — Adam, 18

# SKIPPING CHURCH

*My daughter goes to a Christian college, but we can tell from talking to her that she's become pretty lax about church attendance. Should we talk to her about this?*

Take a minute to consider your ultimate goal for your daughter in this area. Which is more important to you: your daughter's church attendance or her spiritual growth? Certainly involvement in church is important for worship, instruction, fellowship, and service. But even more important is a person's relationship with God. And not attending church isn't significantly worse than going for the wrong reasons —because everyone else is going, out of duty, or to meet guys.

Most Christian colleges discuss this phenomenon with students, encouraging them not to allow Bible classes to take the place of personal devotions or to let chapel become a substitute for church. A phone call to the college chaplain could give you a chance to express your concerns and get an insider's perspective on the issue.

Don't assume that your daughter's non-attendance is a symptom of a deep spiritual problem. Other factors may be involved. For example, she may have difficulty finding a good church that's close. Or she may be adjusting to life on her own and has trouble getting up on Sunday morning.

Remember, too, that this is a time of transition. Maybe this is her way of asserting her independence. It would be good to discuss this issue with your daughter, but don't let it escalate into an argument. She needs to know that you're concerned, but that you trust her to make the decision.

Finally, give her the freedom to try churches other than those of your denomination. Now is a great time for her to learn about new traditions.

## ACTION STEPS:

1. **Calmly express your concerns to your daughter and, possibly, the college chaplain.**
2. **Try to discern her reasons for not attending church, whether they're spiritual or merely logistical.**
3. **Affirm her freedom in this area and encourage her search for a church she likes.**

"I think the most beneficial thing parents can do is be open to our doubts and realize that it's natural for us to question things. Part of faith is figuring out exactly what you believe, not what your parents, your peers, or your church want you to think." — Emily, 18

# DOUBLE LIFE

*Our 18-year-old son was raised in the church and says he's a Christian. But he doesn't seem to live out his faith. He's started drinking at parties and is dating girls who don't have strong morals. We want him to see that being a Christian involves some lifestyle changes—he can't live a double life. What can we do?*

If your son is still living at home, you can curb the drinking by letting him know you won't tolerate it and explaining the consequences. You can also let him know that you don't approve of his new lifestyle choices, including the type of girls he's dating. Be sure to do this firmly and quietly. In other words, don't allow the conversation to escalate into a shouting match.

If your son learns that you know about his "double life," then his cover is blown. Knowing that you've found out his secret might cause him to take an honest look at himself and how he's living.

It sounds as though your son is trying to break away from his past and exert his independence. You state that he was raised in the church, so he may have been acting as a Christian up to this point without really making his faith his own. This is a deeper problem than the lifestyle choices he's making. To get at this root cause, encourage him to look for answers to his questions about Christianity and find the truth for himself. If he doesn't agree with the Bible's prescriptions for living, why not? Why does he find it so important to assert his independence from God?

You can also talk with a youth minister or trusted Christian friend whom your son respects. Describe, in confidence, your son's behavior, then ask this person to come along side your son and help steer him in the right direction.

Throughout all of this, keep praying. Remember, James 5:16 says, "The prayer of a righteous man is powerful and effective."

**ACTION STEPS:**
1. **Calmly confront your son with what you know and communicate your disapproval.**
2. **Help him identify the root cause of his rebellious spirit, encouraging him to seek God's answers for the questions he's struggling with.**
3. **Keep praying.**

# Thanks...

My dad was the son of a Swedish immigrant to America, and he was a very, very hard working man. In the depression years, he held down a job to keep us fed while he went to both accounting and law school at nights. He went 12 years and became both an accountant and a lawyer. My dad had a tremendous work ethic, and a great sense of duty. He would tell me as a kid, "You should always do your duty, whatever your duty is." I had a great close relationship with him.

I can remember my freshman year in college when I decided to go into the Marine Corps. I knew my dad would be jolted, because they were bringing back bodies in pine boxes from Korea at the time. And he just looked at me and then he finally said, "You have to make your own decisions, and I'm not going to interfere. I'm not going to be the one to try to influence you." He was really a wonderful person to be able to talk things through with.

Most significantly, my dad was a great moral teacher, though he was not, as I would understand it, a Christian. I can remember him always telling me never to lie, always to tell the truth. And interestingly, of all the people involved in Watergate, I was the only person not charged with perjury.

Chuck Colson—President,
International Prison Fellowship

# WILD PARTIES

*Our college-age son has been attending parties at his school where people are drinking. He's assured us that he doesn't drink and just wants to be with his friends. Is it OK for him to go to these parties if he's not drinking?*

Not too long ago, most of the parties at universities featured drinking. Recently, however, many schools have been cracking down on the practice because of the problem of underage drinking and the number of alcohol-related accidents and deaths. In fact, some fraternities and sororities prohibit alcohol at their social events. So it is possible for your son to find dry parties.

Even in the midst of this trend, though, a high percentage of college students drink or use drugs like marijuana. So it will be virtually impossible for your son to totally isolate himself from those who indulge. It would be good, therefore, to discuss how he should react in certain situations when alcohol and drugs appear. For example, he should never ride with a driver who is under the influence—advice that should be obvious but is always worth repeating.

Also, encourage your son to take the social initiative with his friends, suggesting fun activities that don't involve alcohol. A social occasion that revolves around drinking takes very little creativity, so it's easy to just go to the party or bar. Your son and his friends will have a lot more fun if they can be creative in their dates and other activities.

As another option, most colleges and universities have Christian ministries. These ministries will sponsor concerts, talks, receptions, parties, and other events that don't involve alcohol. Encourage your son to get involved and make friends there.

Finally, make sure your son actually has the moral strength to resist the temptation to join his friends. Talk to him about his reasons for saying no. If he's got some solid reasons, such as he believes it's wrong, or that he knows he can have fun without alcohol or drugs, he's probably made a choice he feels good about and will stick to. Just the same, encourage him to always bring an abstaining buddy with him if he goes to these parties. He'll be much more likely to stay away from temptation if he's got a friend there to keep him accountable.

**ACTION STEPS:**

1. Remind your son of the dangers associated with drinking and drugs, even if he's not under the influence himself.
2. Urge him to take the initiative with social planning so he can propose alcohol-free alternatives.
3. Encourage him to get involved with a Christian group on campus.

# DRUGS AND ALCOHOL

*My son is ruining his life with drugs and alcohol. My husband and I have tried everything to get him to stop, but nothing works. We want to show him our love, but we don't want to act like we think what he's doing is OK. We just don't know what to do anymore.*

It must be very painful to watch your son destroy his life through alcohol and other drugs. I'm sure you've spent many agonized hours in prayer about this, and I encourage you to keep praying.

You say that you have "tried everything," but what does "everything" mean? Does "everything" include working with other people in your son's life, going to counseling or using intervention? If not, that's where to begin.

"Intervention" is a term used by those who work with families of substance abusers. It involves confronting an individual with his or her self-destructive behavior. An individual who abuses drugs or alcohol tends to live in denial and make excuses. When you try to confront him in private, he may try to convince you that nobody else thinks he has a problem. But when several people do the confronting, then he may get the message. So you might want to have several family members and friends meet together with your son to confront him about his problem.

Drug and alcohol use may be symptomatic of a deeper problem that could be uncovered through professional counseling. Whether or not your son goes to counseling, you need to see a professional counselor who can give you other practical steps to take, as well as give you strength and hope. Ask your pastor for the names of Christian counselors who can help. Also seek out Christian friends who will listen, offer counsel and pray for you and your family.

Your son needs to know that, while you love him deeply, you do not approve of his lifestyle choices. If he continues to use drugs and alcohol despite your feelings, concerns, and counsel, you should use tough love. This means that if your son is under 16 years of age, you may have to turn him over to the civil authorities. If he is over 18, you could consider cutting off financial support.

When you communicate these realities to your son, explain your point of view and your decisions very firmly and seriously without name-calling and anger. You and your husband may feel like failures, but you need to take this strong action. Your son needs to see that his actions impact the lives of others.

## ACTION STEPS:

1. Confront your son with the reality of his problems.

2. Seek counseling—for you and, if he's willing, for your teen.

3. Consider a "tough love" approach to force your son to face the consequences of his choices.

# SUBSTANCE ABUSE

*Our 18-year-old son openly admits to drinking and even doing drugs. We don't know how to handle this. How can we show him unconditional love but still enforce the rules of our household?*

Unconditional love means loving without strings attached. So your son should know that nothing he does will stop you from loving him. But he should also know that this does not mean that you accept and approve of everything he does. Love does not mean approval. In fact, sometimes love has to be very tough. That's how God loves us. God wants what's best for us, so he disciplines us accordlingly (Heb. 12:5-11). But he loves us so much that he sent Jesus to die on the cross in our place (John 3:16).

As soon as possible, sit down with your son and calmly, yet firmly, explain your stance. Let him know of your unconditional love for him and of your disapproval for his actions. Explain how love often means making tough decisions and taking strong action. Tell your son how loving parents don't allow their young children to make choices and go places that will hurt them. They don't allow their baby to play in the fire, eat poison, or put a finger in an electrical socket. No matter how much the child persists or cries, they don't let him have his way.

Next, say that you realize your son is not a small child, but you see him making immature, self-destructive choices. And because you love him, you will do everything in your power to stop him from hurting himself and others.

Then you can outline your rules and the consequences for breaking those rules. For instance, if you catch him with alcohol on his breath, take away his driving privileges for a month or do whatever it takes to let him know you're serious about this. Be sure to enforce your rules and follow through on the consequences, even if your son seems genuinely sorry for his actions and promises to do better. If he persistently disobeys the rules or can't seem to break himself out of his destructive cycle, he needs more help than you can give him alone and should be enrolled in a treatment program. Tough love at home is an effective way to counteract rebellion, but it might not be the best solution if your son's problems run deeper.

**ACTION STEPS:**

1. Explain to your child that love does not mean approval—a firm "no" can sometimes be the most loving response.

2. Outline rules and consequences, making it clear that their purpose is to keep your son safe.

3. Consider an outside treatment program if he is unwilling or unable to abide by your rules.

# GAMBLING

*We've learned our son has been gambling. He says he only bets on a few football games and has gone to the racetrack once, but we suspect this is more of a problem than he's letting on. How can we confront him with our concerns, and how can we find help for him?*

Gambling is a growing problem in the United States. Legalized gambling has increased tremendously, with the number of casinos and state-sponsored lotteries increasing at an alarming rate. In addition to being very addictive, gambling brings a host of problems to communities and individual lives. Studies have consistently shown, for example, that when casinos arrive, crime levels increase.

Perhaps the biggest problem with gambling, however, is that it promotes the idea that a person can get something for nothing. The message is, "Get lucky, and you'll have instant happiness—no problems, no sweat." That philosophy is wrong in so many ways. And it breeds laziness, greed, and foolishness. So many people have lost all they had in hopes of winning it big. Your son needs to know all of this and recognize his gambling as a real problem.

You need to intervene now, before the problem gets worse. If your son lives at home and is under your supervision, have a serious talk with him and cut off his funds until he can demonstrate responsible behavior. Also realize that many of those most susceptible to gambling have what has been labeled "high-risk personalities." If your son fits into this category, he might need counseling to show him how to focus on safer ways to meet his needs.

If your son is living away from home, look for allies in his church, job, circle of friends, or university. There may be a local chapter of Gamblers Anonymous. Find someone who can find out the truth about your son's gambling habits and who will work with you to help him.

**ACTION STEPS:**

1. **Explain to your child the dangers of gambling.**
2. **If he still lives at home, cut off his funds and consider enrolling him in a counseling program.**
3. **If he lives away from home, seek allies close to him who will help you evaluate and solve the problem.**

"I think the most important thing a parent can do is assure their child that she will be loved—by them and by God— no matter what kind of changes her faith goes through, and that God will always be there to guide her."

— Amanda, 18

# REBUILDING RELATIONSHIP

*We've had to ask our 18-year-old son to move out. He has caused so much heartache and pain in our family, we felt it was best for all of us that he leave. What kind of relationship is appropriate for us to have with him now? Should we try to see him or let him set the pace?*

This tension is not easily resolved—loving the sinner but hating the sin. Your son should know that while you don't love his actions and attitudes (in fact, you disapprove of them completely), you do love him unconditionally.

The phrase "heartache and pain" sounds severe, so your contact with him should be on your terms until he demonstrates a radical life change. You can begin reestablishing contact in small ways, such as inviting your son back to the house for special occasions (a birthday celebration, a visit by a favorite relative, a graduation party for a younger sibling and so forth). But even here, you need to establish the rules for his visit. If he follows your rules while he's home, then he will be making a move back toward the family and, perhaps, toward healing. His behavior and attitude will set the pace.

You can also send your son cards and gifts when appropriate to let him know that you're thinking of him and still care. This will be difficult, but stand firm in holding to your limits and standards, while continually assuring him of your love. Your son should know that he can do nothing to keep you from loving him, but right now your love necessitates some strict boundaries.

**ACTION STEPS:**

1. **Reestablish contact with your child slowly and on your own terms.**

2. **When your son visits, gauge his attitudes and actions to determine whether he's ready for further reconciliation.**

3. **Stand firmly by your house rules, but look for ways to demonstrate your unconditional love.**

# VIOLENT TEMPER

*My 18-year-old son has always had a hot temper, but recently he blew up at my wife and actually hit her. He obviously has a problem, but short of having him arrested for assault, we don't know what to do about this.*

This is a very serious problem that must be confronted immediately. There is no excuse for a child hitting his mother, and it should never be tolerated. In fact, this could be a pathological problem. It's possible this incident isn't the first—and may not be the last—of your son's abuse to women.

If this is the first occurrence and your son is remorseful, then you should explain to him that he needs to go for counseling. A professional counselor should be able to get to the root of the problem— the cause of your son's hot temper. If necessary, you should be ready and willing to take the whole family in for counseling. You can probably find a good Christian counselor through your church.

If your son is not sorry for his actions or if this is a repeat occurrence, you probably should force him to move out of your house or call the police. That will be tough, but it may be necessary to bring him to his senses. If a trip through the court system proves necessary, counseling should definitely follow.

**ACTION STEPS:**

1. Confront your son immediately and determine whether he is remorseful or not.

2. If he is sorry for his action, start him in therapy with a Christian family counselor.

3. If he is not sorry or this is a repeat occurrence, consider asking him to move out or calling the police.

# INTERNET TEMPTATIONS

*The college our son has chosen has Internet access available in each dorm room. He thinks that's great, but we're a little worried. At home, we can monitor his computer usage, but once he's gone, we're concerned he'll have access to Web sites we aren't comfortable with. What can we do to help him resist the temptations of the Internet?*

There are two important issues here. The first relates to your son's freedom at college and your inability to monitor his activities. Concerning this issue, you need to realize that your relationship with your son will be changing by the very fact that he's away from home. Browsing the Internet is not the only opportunity he'll have to face temptation and make bad choices. Hopefully you've built into him character, integrity, and solid values so that he'll stay strong in his walk with Christ and resist those temptations.

The second issue concerns the possibility of unlimited Internet access. You may want to check with the school to see what safeguards are built into the computer network and whether or not anyone monitors the students' use. Many schools, for example, have installed software to block pornographic sites.

Find a time to talk with your son about his new freedom, the Internet, and other related topics. Assure him you have faith that he'll make the right decisions. Also, remind him of 1 Corinthians 10:13: "But remember that the temptations that come into your life are no different from what others experience. And God is faithful. He will keep the temptation from becoming so strong that you can't stand up against it. When you are tempted, he will show you a way out so that you will not give in to it" (NLT). Facing temptation is never easy, but God is faithful.

**ACTION STEPS:**

1. Express your concerns to your son, but also stress your confidence that he'll make good choices.
2. Talk to someone at his college to see what computer safeguards are in place.
3. Remind him of God's promises to help Christians resist temptation.

# SPRING BREAK

*Our daughter is a freshman in college and wants to go on a trip for spring break. It's hard for us to picture our daughter, who just last year still had to have permission to stay out past her curfew, off on a one-week vacation with no adult supervision. We trust her, but we don't know anything about the other students going on the trip. She's willing to pay for the trip herself, so it doesn't seem like we have much leverage to ask her not to go. What can we do?*

Your question highlights two important issues. First, there's the matter of your daughter growing up and leaving home. It sounds like this is a difficult transition for you, and you're struggling with her becoming an independent adult. This is normal. Most loving parents who have good relationships with their children wish they wouldn't grow up so fast, because they've enjoyed their kids and love them deeply. But these same parents want their sons and daughters to mature, to leave home, and to become adults themselves. There's the tension.

You should talk this through with your daughter. Describe your mixed emotions—that you want to trust her and give her freedom, but you're a bit unsure of how to do this and how much freedom to give. After all, she's never been this age before. If this trip seems like too much, too soon, let her know how you feel, and be ready to propose an alternative. She should definitely be allowed to do something to let off steam during her break.

The second issue relates to the trip itself and your "leverage." Your concerns about the trip seem to be valid, especially considering the potential dangers for a young woman her age. You have the right and responsibility to know about the other students and the details of the trip, including transportation, housing and tentative itinerary. The source of the funds for this trip does not determine your leverage. You're still her parents and that's all the leverage you need.

So be concerned, ask your questions, and say no if you must. But also look for ways to say yes in order to help your daughter become an independent adult.

**ACTION STEPS:**
1. Share your feelings and concerns with your child.
2. Ask specific questions about the trip to find out more about her traveling companions, logistical plans and itinerary.
3. If you have to say no to this trip, look for other ways to say yes and foster her independence.

# SHYNESS

*Our son started college in the fall and seems to love the academic challenge. But he's extremely shy and bookish. How can we encourage him to come out of his shell and be more outgoing?*

Some people are extreme extroverts—they're motivated by relationships and energized by crowds. Others are quite introverted—they would rather be alone, and they're uncomfortable in groups. Certainly each personality type has advantages in specific settings and jobs, but neither one is better than the other. So don't expect your son to become something he isn't. (In fact, many parents wish they had your problem. They're trying to get their kids to study, but all the kids want to do is have fun!)

On the other hand, you can encourage your son to make friends and to be more sociable. This is best done behind the scenes. That is, you can talk to the resident advisor for your son's floor in his dorm or another adult with whom your son has regular contact. Let this person know your concerns, and find out how he or she can help. This person can inform your son of social events and invite him to join a small group Bible study, an intramural team or another group where he can meet potential friends. And through it all, "Pray continually" (1 Thess. 5:17).

**ACTION STEPS:**

1. **Accept your child's personality type.**
2. **Work with the campus staff to help your son make some social contacts.**
3. **Keep praying that he'll find friends and have fun at college.**

# DATING AT COLLEGE

*When our daughter lived at home, we always got to meet the guys she dated. Now that she's away at college, it scares us to hear her express interest in boys we know nothing about. What can we do to calm our fears?*

It's natural to be nervous about unknown boys dating your daughter. You love her and are concerned for her. And Dad, especially, knows what boys can be like. This is a difficult time for many parents—they know that their family will never be the same again.

When she's home, you should take her aside and talk things over. Begin by letting her know that you trust her, in every area, even though she's many miles away and out of your direct supervision. Then see if she has any questions about college life.

Next, explain your concerns, letting her know that you love her and want only the very best for her, especially when it comes to dating and finding the right man. You may want to remind her that many—but not all—people meet their spouses in college (review how you and your spouse met, if it's appropriate and helpful). Make sure she understands that some guys can be predatory and that date rape is a reality. Give her ideas on where to meet the right kind of guys. A frat party or a bar would not be the best places, for example. In any case, she should be careful.

Besides giving information and counsel, another goal of this conversation is to keep communication channels open. So explain that whenever she has a question or concern, she can come to you. And if she's ever in trouble, you'll drop everything and get to her side as quickly as possible.

If the college is close, you still could meet some of her guy friends. Encourage your daughter to bring them by the house from time to time, or offer to take her and her special someone out to dinner the next time you visit her at school.

This new dating situation can be scary, especially if your daughter is far away from home. But if her values and motives are good, you can trust that they will shine through.

**ACTION STEPS:**

1. **Make sure your child knows that you trust her, even though she's far away.**

2. **Alert her to the potential dangers of dating, then give advice for building good relationships.**

3. **Make an effort to meet the boys she's interested in.**

# Thanks...

Even though our family of six didn't have much money, we had a lot of love and support.

My mother taught my brother Al, my two sisters, Debra and Angela, and me to respect ourselves. She also refused to permit me to date until I turned 18. She wanted me to pay as much attention to my schoolwork as I did to sports. As a result, I graduated in the top 10 percent of my class.

Mom would always tell me, "Jackie, no matter what, always strive to be a good person." From her I learned that whatever you do is a test of character, a test of heart. Will you choose a godly path or your own? That was crucial for me—especially living in the inner city.

Jackie Joyner-Kersee—Olympic gold medalist

# NOT DATING

*Our 18-year-old daughter has never been on a date, but she says she'll start dating when the "time is right." She says she prefers to hang out with her girlfriends instead. Is this normal?*

This is very normal. In American adolescent culture, dating is a big deal, and young people feel pressured to date. Television shows, magazine articles, movies, and just about all things "teen" involve boy-girl relationships. And certainly the pressures are felt on campus, with homecomings, proms and a host of other socials and dances on the school calendar. Parents and other adults often add to these pressures by hurrying their children into the dating scene, hosting boy-girl parties when the kids are young and talking about who the son or daughter "likes." So it can seem as though everyone is dating.

In reality, a small percentage of high school students date often (every weekend), and many date seldom or not at all. By saying she prefers to be with girls, your daughter is probably protecting herself from heartache. She's also asserting her self-confidence by saying, "Look, I don't have to be in a relationship with a guy to have a happy life." Unless you have other evidence, there's no reason to assume that she's abnormal.

Don't pressure your daughter to date, but encourage her to mingle with mixed groups. That way, she can find male friends and, eventually, the right kind of boys to date.

**ACTION STEPS:**

1. **Don't add pressure by echoing the cultural message that "everyone" is dating.**

2. **Affirm your child's self-confidence and identity.**

3. **Encourage her to socialize in mixed groups and build friendships with guys.**

# DATING SOMEONE YOUNGER

*My 18-year-old son is dating a girl who's 14. She's a very nice girl from our church, but it still doesn't seem right to us. He hasn't dated much and seems to be flattered that she likes him. We've told him how we feel, but he insists on seeing her. What can we do?*

Senior guys and freshman girls are often attracted to each other. The girls are attracted to the guys because they are big men on campus, can drive and don't seem as immature as freshman boys. The guys are attracted to the girls because they're young, new to the dating scene, easy to impress and generally not as intimidating as senior girls. As common as this phenomenon is, it still doesn't make it good or right.

My advice would be to set aside some time to talk with your son. Help him understand that while four years' difference in age may not seem like very much to someone who's 40, the difference between 14 and 18 is huge. A 14-year-old girl is changing in virtually every area of life. While she may look mature (and thus attract the attention of older boys), she could be very immature emotionally, socially and mentally.

Ask your son what he likes about this girl. Listen for clues that their relationship does more than make him feel good. It could be that she's actually quite mature and that she and your son really do have a strong, healthy relationship. If that's the case, but you still feel concerned about the age difference, you might want to consider asking him to step back to friendship mode with his girlfriend until she's older.

If this girl is from a solid home, you should be able to talk with her parents and come to an understanding together. They may like your son and the idea that their daughter is interested in a fine Christian young man. But, like you, they're probably concerned about the age difference. When you express your concerns about the relationship, they may feel relieved. Be sure to let them know you're not judging their daughter or your son—you're just not crazy about the two of them being a couple right now.

If your son insists on dating this girl, set some firm guidelines for the time they spend together. Maybe you want to limit their dates to once a week or ask that they spend their time at either your home or hers, with parents present. You might even want to invite the girl and her parents over for dinner and work out a dating plan that all of you can agree to.

Unless you have deep concerns about your son's well being in this relationship, this is probably not something you need to turn into a battle.

**ACTION STEPS:**

1. **Remind your son that while his girlfriend might look mature, she probably still has a lot of growing up to do.**

2. **Share your concerns with her parents and seek their support for your stance.**

3. **Work with your son to set some dating ground rules.**

# FINDING A MATE

*Now that our son is 19, he's thinking about finding a mate, not just a date. What advice can we give him about choosing a godly partner?*

Although some people get married at your son's age, 19 is still a little young. But young people can feel pressured to find "the one" as early as their teens, especially if their older friends are pairing up.

One of the worst ways to find a spouse, however, is to go looking for one. When someone dates in that frame of mind, he or she tends to put way too much pressure on each dating experience and, subsequently, on the other person.

So you should encourage your son to relax and just enjoy meeting and getting to know young women. Instead of approaching dating so seriously, he should just have fun. Let him know that he has plenty of time to find the right person, fall in love, and get married. Marriage is for a lifetime—there's no reason to rush the process.

On the other hand, you should compliment him on his desire to find the right life-partner and help him start taking the steps that will lead to making a good choice. One thing he needs to keep in mind is the importance of marrying a Christian (see 2 Corinthians 6:14). To stay on track for this goal, your son should only date Christians, because any girl he dates could potentially be his future mate. If your son isn't already involved in some kind of Christian fellowship, now would be a good time for him to start. Not only will his faith be strengthened in such a group, but he'll also have the chance to build friendships with Christian young women. As those friendships grow, he'll get a better idea of what he's looking for in a future wife.

If he finds a girl he wants to date, encourage him to get to know her and just be himself. He shouldn't rush the relationship, spiritualize it ("It's God's will for us to be together"), or get serious too quickly. Help him try to *be* the right kind of person rather than trying to get one. In all of this, your son needs to trust in God (Matt. 6:33) and in God's perfect plan for his life (Jer. 29:11).

**ACTION STEPS:**

1. Encourage your son to relax and not try too hard to find "the one" right now.
2. Affirm his desire to find a godly life-partner, and point him to the places where he can meet other Christians.
3. Remind him of God's plan for his life.

"If I was the parent, I'd do my best to keep my kid from getting married till I thought it was right. Marriage is a huge decision. If the two kids really love each other, they should be able to wait for each other, and they should want their parents' approval on this big decision."
— Adam, 18

# MARRIAGE

*We have an 18-year-old son who's been dating the same girl all through high school. Now that they've graduated, they think they should get married and then attend college together. We like this girl, but we think these two are far too young to get married. What can we say to help them rethink this decision?*

You're right to think they're too young to get married. Certainly some people have gotten married at that age and have done well together, but they're exceptions. The divorce rate is much higher for early marriages. And most people who were married at a young age, even those who've had successful marriages, advise against it.

Besides the maturity factor, your son and his girlfriend would begin their marriage with very few resources. Marriage is difficult enough without complicating matters with severe financial and emotional pressures.

The best solution would be a heart-to-heart talk with your son, if he will listen. Unfortunately, however, a person in love is often too emotionally involved and idealistic to listen to reason, especially from a parent. So it would be good to get someone else involved, too—maybe a pastor, youth worker, or relative whom both your son and his girlfriend respect. You could ask this person to intervene and try to convince them to wait a few years.

One of the best arguments you can make is this: Real love lasts. Explain to your son that time will only help him and his girlfriend build a better life together. If their love is the real deal, it will survive a few more years of dating.

By the way, where are the girlfriend's parents in this matter? Hopefully all four of you agree and can present a loving, united front. If talking doesn't work, you'll have to be firm, explaining that you will not pay for college or a wedding until you see specific signs of maturity in both of them. This is a time to be calm, stating your position clearly. Sometimes love has to be tough.

ACTION STEPS:

1. Have a heart-to-heart with your son, explaining the disadvantages of marrying so young.

2. Get other people involved, too—a pastor, youth worker, relative and/or the girlfriend's parents.

3. Calmly let your son know that you won't pay for college or the wedding if he goes through with his plan right now.

"I think 18 is pretty young to get married. I know I'm not ready to get hitched, even though I've had a serious boyfriend for some time now. But if a young couple really wants to get married, their parents should let them—but tell them the parental financial support will be cut off. Married people need to learn to support themselves." — Tiffany, 19

# COED APARTMENT

*My 19-year-old daughter wants to move into a coed apartment off campus. She insists that "nothing will happen," meaning sex, I imagine. But I still think it's a terrible idea. How can I express my concerns without sounding old-fashioned?*

You're right—it is definitely not a good idea for your daughter to live in an apartment shared by men and women. She is being naïve if she really believes "nothing will happen." Look for an opportunity to share your concerns. Explain that human beings by nature are sinful (see Romans 3:23) and that sex is a very powerful drive. Men and women living in the same small area will be drawn to each other sexually—that's the way they're wired.

Even if nothing was to happen, it's still a bad arrangement because of the way it looks and the impression it gives. Believers are to avoid even the "appearance of evil" (1 Thess. 5:22). It will be a challenge for your daughter to be an effective witness when her living arrangement looks suspect.

Don't be afraid of appearing out-of-date. Say no. Be firm. The issue is not old-fashioned—it's a matter of values, morals and the price to pay in the long run.

**ACTION STEPS:**

1. **Remind your daughter of the power of sexual attraction.**
2. **Explain the consequences of a "suspicious" living arrangement, even if nothing sexual ever happens.**
3. **Be firm in your refusal to support her decision to live in an apartment with guys.**

# LIVING WITH BOYFRIEND

*My 19-year-old daughter is planning to move in with her boyfriend. Obviously, that's not what we want for her. We've talked to her about our concerns, but she's made up her mind. What can we do?*

If you have any leverage at all with your daughter, use it. Have a discussion where you state your feelings and point her to God's plan for sex and marriage (see, for example, 1 Corinthians 6:9-20). If she is a Christian, then she should want to know God's plan and obey him. Even if she's not a Christian, this conversation can help her understand where your concerns are coming from.

Be careful not to lose your cool during this talk. In other words, explain how you feel with an attitude of love and concern. If you've decided to impose negative consequences for her proposed action (for example, you will cut off financial support, college payments and so forth), explain these firmly but without malice, sarcasm or anger. Don't be afraid to tell your daughter how much her decision bothers you. She needs to know that you totally disapprove of this move and, though you will never stop loving her, you will be hurt deeply by her choice.

If your daughter is already out of your home and on her own, there's little you can do to stop her from moving in with her boyfriend. Again, however, you should explain how you feel. Make a clear separation between your love for her as a person and your disapproval of this choice she's making. You could also talk with the boyfriend's parents. If they agree that this is a bad idea, you can present a united front.

In all of this, keep in mind how God relates to us as sinful people. God loves us unconditionally, even though we continually reject him and his ways. He lets us know the cost and consequences of sin and allows us to experience those consequences. He hates our sin. Yet when we repent and return, he welcomes us with open arms (see Luke 15:11-32).

## ACTION STEPS:

1. As calmly as possible, explain why you feel the way you do.
2. Talk to her boyfriend's parents and attempt to present a united front.
3. If your daughter goes ahead with the move, continue to communicate both your love for her and your disapproval of her choice.

MR. MELNIK EXPRESSES HIS DISAPPROVAL OF WENDY'S NEW BOYFRIEND.

# LOST VIRGINITY

*A few weeks ago, our daughter was home from college for the weekend. We could tell she was upset about something, and she finally confessed that she had lost her virginity to a boy she'd met at school. It was a one-time thing, but she feels so guilty and awful about it. How can we help her know that God will forgive her? And how can we help her stay sexually pure in future relationships?*

First, be encouraged that your daughter confessed to you. Her honesty reveals what a strong relationship you have with her. Be sure to let your daughter know how much you appreciate her vulnerability, and assure her of your love for her. Remind her that everyone sins (Rom. 3:23), and that God promises to forgive all our sins if we confess them to him (1 John 1:9). He does this because Jesus paid the penalty for sin on the cross, taking our place in death.

Also explain that she feels so guilty about this particular sin because sex is intensely personal. All sins are very serious, but sexual sin strikes at the hearts of the persons involved. Assure your daughter that if she has confessed this to God, she is forgiven, even though she might not feel forgiven right away.

Next, ask what she has learned from this mistake and how she intends to guard against it happening again. Listen, don't lecture. Affirm your daughter's insights, and gently ask questions when she responds too emotionally or idealistically. Help her see that she needs to be very realistic and careful in this area. For example, she should avoid dating certain types of guys and should stay away from compromising situations like wild parties and spending time alone with a guy in a private place. Ask her to confide in a Christian friend at school who can pray with her and help hold her accountable. And if she's still seeing the guy she slept with, you need to stress how extremely difficult it will be for the two of them to abstain in the future. Strongly encourage her to break off the relationship.

Let your daughter know that you will be praying for her, and remind her that God provides a way of escape from every temptation (1 Cor. 10:13). Thus, when she is tempted, she should look for God's way out and then take it. This will be a lot easier if she's thought a lot about the temptations and escape routes before the heat of the moment.

ACTION STEPS:

1. Assure your daughter that God forgives even sexual sins.

2. Ask her how she plans to keep from repeating this mistake.

3. Let her know that you'll be praying for her.

# DAUGHTER'S BABY

*Our 18-year-old daughter got pregnant her senior year of high school. Now she and the baby live with us. We love our grandchild and want to be supportive of our daughter, but this burden feels so unfair. What are our options?*

This is a good question, but it raises many others. The main question is, "What is your ultimate goal?" That's a question you need to answer as a family.

Is your goal for your daughter to become self-supporting and, eventually move out with the baby? If that's the case, it's best for her to finish high school (if she had to drop out), take classes at a nearby college, or get a good job. This will probably place more of the childcare burden on you temporarily, but it's the best step toward helping your daughter make a life for herself and her baby.

Do you and your daughter want your freedom back right away? If so, your daughter can still consider putting the baby up for adoption. Many loving Christian couples are aching to have a child. If this is an option, a Christian adoption agency could help you think through this decision.

No matter what your goal, make sure both your daughter and grandchild know they are loved. While this is a frustrating situation for everyone, it's not something worth losing your daughter over. Now, perhaps more than ever, she needs to know you have her best interest at heart. Communicate that to her clearly.

As you take the next step, talk it out. Pray it through. And seek help from Christian friends who also love your daughter. Your pastor might also be able to suggest local support groups or services that will help you through this difficult time.

**ACTION STEPS:**

1. With your daughter, decide who will ultimately be most willing and best able to care for the child: you, your daughter, or an adoptive couple.

2. Talk through all your options with your daughter.

3. Seek help and support from Christian friends.

# ARROGANCE

*Our 19-year-old has done lots of theological study in college. We're glad he has such a passion for understanding his faith, but he's become rather arrogant about his knowledge of the Bible and Christian history. How can we talk to him about this?*

Believe it or not, it's normal for 19-year-olds to talk that way, especially those who have taken a course or two in a subject that makes them think (philosophy, psychology, sociology, theology and so forth).

Two events are occurring here. First, your son is discovering his mind. He now realizes that he can ponder the questions that have baffled humanity for ages. He's probably never thought this way before, and it's exciting! Second, your son is discovering a new intellectual arena: theology. He's grappling with new issues, and he's challenged and intrigued. For these things, you can be thankful.

Many people who discover something new assume that they are the first (or among the special few) to do so. Thus they can become very condescending as they try to "enlighten" others. And to teenagers, no one is quite as dense as Mom and Dad!

The worst response to this is to argue, especially with sarcasm or anger. The best response is to be patient and listen. Don't try to talk your son out of his ideas and opinions, even if they sound radical. And try not to react negatively to his arrogance. Instead, interact with him, asking questions and agreeing with him where you can. Chances are, this attitude will fade pretty quickly—probably soon after his first debate with a student who knows more than he does.

If your son's arrogance becomes extreme, almost abusive, look for a good time to talk with him about the way he's treating people. Let him know, in love, that his attitude may push others away from him and, in some circles, even turn them off to the truths of God.

**ACTION STEPS:**

1. Realize that your child's behavior is normal, and be thankful that he's discovering the capabilities of his mind.

2. Listen patiently to his new views and don't argue with him.

3. If necessary, take him aside and warn him about the potential consequences of his arrogance.

# CHALLENGING FAMILY BELIEFS

*Our daughter, a college freshman, recently came home for a break. We couldn't believe how much she had changed. Suddenly, she was challenging our family's core beliefs and acting as though her mother and I knew nothing about life. Why is she acting this way?*

Although this is painful to experience, there is an up side to your daughter's behavior. She is undergoing the biggest change of her life and is trying to act like an adult. She is also developing her own values and beliefs. To do this, she probably thinks she must reject (or at least argue with) yours. This is normal, and it's a good process as long as she doesn't do something harmful to herself and others.

When this adolescent swing away from the family's values and beliefs occurs, it's like the trapeze in the circus. The performers swing away, but then they swing back. Statistically, most adult children return to the values they learned at home.

Try not to argue with her, though that may be very difficult. Instead, stay relaxed and listen patiently to her new ideas. Don't take her radical statements personally, even when she challenges your politics, faith, and lifestyle. Ask her questions, and take her seriously. And you never know, she may have important information and insights that could change your life. Be open to the possibility of God working through your daughter.

**ACTION STEPS:**

1. Try to see these changes as a healthy part of growing up.

2. Stay relaxed as you listen to your child's new ideas, and be sure to take her seriously.

3. Be open to the possibility of learning something from her.

# DOUBTS ABOUT FAITH

*Our daughter is a college freshman and has started experiencing doubts about her faith. I guess this is a natural part of growing up, but we don't want her to lose her faith. Is there anything we can do to help her hold on to her beliefs in the face of doubts?*

Being reared in a loving, Christian home is a wonderful blessing for any child. But individuals surrounded by Christianity during childhood may take their faith for granted and just accept what parents, pastors, Sunday school teachers, and youth leaders say without thinking everything through and developing their own beliefs. Often, when these young people go away to college, they "lose their faith." In reality, however, they never had "the faith"; they were merely conforming to their Christian surroundings.

Of course, even very committed Christians experience doubts. If your daughter is attending college in a large city, she may be seeing intense poverty or crime for the first time. Her professors may be raising questions she'd never considered. Or she might be meeting people from other religious backgrounds who are challenging her beliefs in a new way. Dealing with these challenges is a natural part of growing as a Christian.

Doubts, therefore, are not bad, if they motivate the doubter to look for answers and seek the truth. You probably won't enjoy hearing her question much of what you hold dear, but try not to argue or get angry with her. Instead, encourage her to keep looking for answers and offer to look with her, especially when you don't know an answer yourself.

# Thanks...

My mother was a wonderful role model—a woman of prayer and the Word. If I stayed up late to study for an exam and went downstairs to speak to Mother, I'd find her on her knees in prayer. Early in the morning she'd be sitting at her desk reading her Bible. And during the day, if she had a few minutes, she'd slip back to her desk again.

Mother taught me by her example that there's nothing more satisfying than a personal love relationship with the Lord. It's what made her strong. When Daddy would come home exhausted from ministry, my mother's unflagging faith consistently encouraged him. I'm convinced that without a Ruth Graham, there would never have been the Billy Graham the world has come to know.

Her role of ministry to our family was tremendously important then ... and now.

My mother has said, "You can't teach your children to enjoy spinach if every time they see you eating it, you gag." In the same way, you can't teach children to love and serve the Lord if they see you dreading it, complaining about it, or not doing it at all. You have to set an example. My mother had such a joyous love for the Lord that I wanted a relationship with him like she had.

Anne Graham Lotz—Bible teacher and speaker

Classic Christian writers will also help your daughter in this process. Encourage her to read C.S. Lewis (*Mere Christianity, Screwtape Letters, The Great Divorce*); Paul Little (*Know Why You Believe, Know What You Believe*); Philip Yancey; Walter Wangerin; and others. These authors will broaden her perspective and challenge her thinking.

Finally, be prepared for the possibility that your daughter's faith might end up slightly different from your own. As long as she's not espousing something heretical, allow her to build her own relationship with God.

## ACTION STEPS:

1. **Try not to get angry or defensive as your child shares her doubts and questions.**
2. **Encourage her to seek the truth, seeking with her when she asks a question you cannot answer.**
3. **Be prepared for the possibility that her faith could be slightly different from yours.**

"I've gone through a lot of doubting and questioning my faith. My Bible study leader helped by telling me it's a normal part of growth. My parents have been reassuring, too, telling me I'm not a bad person. It's been a rough few years, but God brought me through." — John, 19

# CULT INVOLVEMENT

*Our 19-year-old is involved in a religious group at college that we think may be a cult. He has stopped calling us, and when we call him, he says he doesn't have time to talk. Because the college is far away, we can't visit him very often to check this group out. We feel so helpless. What can we do?*

Most colleges have a chaplain or a dean who can give you information about the group's reputation and can offer suggestions for what you can do. If you don't know anyone in the community around your son's college, ask your pastor or other friends at your church for any possible campus contacts. You might be able to find a local pastor, student pastor or national ministry staff member (such as an InterVarsity leader) to help you figure out what's really going on.

As you talk to these people, you might discover that the group is positive, healthy and Bible-based, and that your son is just trying to discover his faith for himself. If this is the case, and he is sincere about being a closer follower of Christ, then, eventually, he will move toward you emotionally, not away.

Still, you're wise to be concerned about your son's lack of contact with you. One of a cult's best tools is isolation—they encourage members to break ties with family and friends on the premise that those people will try to keep them from seeing the "truth."

If you learn that the group is, in fact, a cult, then you should intervene as soon as possible. If a trusted adult friend, relative or ministry worker lives nearby, ask him to take your son out to dinner and share his concerns for him. The next step would be a surprise visit by you two. During your time together, lovingly and firmly explain that you want him to leave the group.

If your son persists with the group, you might have to cut off your financial support for his education and bring him home. Be sure to enlist prayer support every step of the way.

**ACTION STEPS:**
1. **Enlist the help of a pastor, relative or friend in your child's area.**
2. **Determine whether the group is positive and healthy or, in fact, a cult.**
3. **If the group is a cult, instruct your son to leave it at once or risk losing your financial support.**

# DEVELOPMENTAL DISABILITY

*Our 18-year-old son has a developmental disability and functions at about a fifth grade level. I guess we're not sure about what plans to make for him now that he's no longer in school. Should we find some kind of job for him? Should he continue to live at home? We aren't sure what's best for him now that he's technically an adult.*

School systems are required to help answer these questions. Typically, they will have special meetings with parents to help in these types of transitions. A vocational counselor and a representative from an adult service are usually present at the meetings to answer questions and to describe the opportunities in the area.

The federal government mandates educational responsibility until age 21. This includes classes, job training and community experience. Although 18 is not too late to think about these matters, parents should start planning for the future when their child is 14 because of the long waiting lists for various types of placement. Your school system will help you sort through these kinds of programs as you choose the one that's right for your son.

You also ask about your son's living arrangements. You probably know that group homes offer part-time or full-time residency. Also, respite services are available to provide short-term relief for parents who choose to keep their children at home. Your best option right now is to start looking into group homes where your son might live eventually. That doesn't mean you'd have to send him there—if you want him to remain at home and that seems best for him as well, then there's no reason to make a change. But knowing what alternatives are available can help you make a well-thought-out decision down the road.

**ACTION STEPS:**

1. Discuss your questions with officials at your son's school, a vocational counselor and a representative from an adult service in your area.

2. Determine the best way to provide education until your son is 21.

3. Plan ahead for his permanent home, whether that is your home or a group home offering part-time or full-time residency.

# GRIEF

*Two years ago, our two kids were in a terrible car accident. Our daughter survived the accident, but our son didn't. Since our daughter was driving the car, my wife blames her for the death of our son. How can I show my daughter love and compassion without seeming to "take sides" against my wife?*

Certainly there is nothing more devastating to a parent than the loss of a child. In her grief, your wife is trying to make some sense of this tragedy and looking for someone to blame. By blaming your daughter, however, you may lose your other child as well. Even if the accident was the result of poor driving on your daughter's part, blaming her won't bring back your son. Everyone needs to forgive her and move on.

First and foremost, you and your wife need to work things out, come to an understanding and resolve this issue. This means seeing a pastor or a professional counselor. The inability to forgive is a spiritual problem—Jesus told his followers to love their enemies (Matt. 5:44), and on the cross he said, "Father, forgive them, because they do not know what they are doing" (Luke 23:34). The Bible clearly states that we are to forgive others the way that God has forgiven us (Col. 3:13).

Both of you need to come to the place where you forgive your daughter and grieve with her for the loss of your son. You and your wife need to work together, not against each other.

Eventually, the whole family will need to be in counseling together. Right now, however, while you and your wife are getting your act together, enlist the support of other caring adults who can come alongside your daughter and comfort and counsel her. Talk to a favorite aunt, your daughter's youth leader, a Christian teacher or coach—adults who know her and who can listen, love and nurture.

Throughout this entire process, pray and ask others to pray for your family. Ask God to give you his peace and strength and to bring healing.

**ACTION STEPS:**

1. **Through counseling, resolve this issue with your wife and address her need to forgive.**
2. **Find caring adults who can comfort your daughter.**
3. **Pray for God's peace and strength in this difficult time.**

# LISTENING IN:

*Here's what 18-to 19-year-olds have to say...*

*... about parents visiting them at college:*

"If the parents live in the same state as the college their child attends, I think a visit once every two months or so is sufficient. If the college is in a different state, the parents should just try to visit once a semester." — *Melissa, 19*

"My parents don't visit me much at all. Actually, I prefer to go home and visit them. But I think it would be nice for them to come up and see me a couple times each semester, because I'd love the chance to talk about college life and have a break from the 'luxurious' school food!" — *Jennifer T., 19*

"If parents are around too much, their kids get too attached and dependent. Then what would happen when the kids start working or get married—would they still rely on their parents for everything? A visit every three or four months seems about right to me." — *Christine, 18*

"At the beginning of the freshman year, parents should limit their visits, because seeing your family too much during that time makes the transition harder. But after those first five or six weeks, students have pretty much found their places on campus. Then parents can visit for a weekend maybe once a month." — *Jennifer C., 19*

*... about getting married right after high school:*

"My boyfriend and I have talked about getting married, and we've decided that if we're still in love at the end of college, then we'll do it. Waiting will help us plan out a better future for our home, our children, and even that big wedding I've always wanted." — *Christina, 18*

"Sorry to say it, but 18-year-olds are adults. Now's the time to trust 18 years of child rearing and enjoy the show. If parents don't think marriage is a good decision, then they should say so. But really, what can you say to make someone rethink a decision like this? Probably nothing!" — *Kirsten, 18*

"I think 18 is pretty young to get married. I know I'm not ready to get hitched, even though I've had a serious boyfriend for some time now. But if a young couple really wants to get married, their parents should let them—but tell them the parental financial support will be cut off. Married people need to learn to support themselves." — *Tiffany, 19*

"If I was the parent, I'd do my best to keep my kid from getting married till I thought it was right. Marriage is a huge decision. If the two kids really love each other they should be able to wait for each other, and they should want their parents' approval on this big decision." — *Adam, 18*

"First, the parents should pray about the situation and try to find out if the couple's decision is driven by God's will or by their own desires. Then make sure the young couple gets counseling. A church marriage counselor could tell if their love is the real deal or not." — *Ming, 19*

### ... choosing between a Christian college and a public university:

"I think a teen should be able to make her own college decision, because she's the one who has to actually attend the school. If she's forced to go to a Christian college, she might not even succeed because she'll be so caught up in how much she wanted to go to a state school. It's unfair for parents to insist on making that decision, because choosing a college is a very important part of beginning adult life." — *JoAnne, 19*

"Parents have to realize their college-bound children are capable of making smart decisions. Teens have to realize their parents only wish for the best. But I think it's a good idea for Christians to go to state schools and minister for God there." — *Erica, 18*

"I think it depends on who's paying for college. If the student is paying, it should be his choice, because he has left the household and begun his new life. But if the parents are paying, they get to call the shots because he's still a member of their household." — *Dave, 19*

"I'm a student at a state school. I originally wanted to go to a Christian school, but my parents didn't want me to. Now I'm very active in campus Christian groups, and I've grown more in the past year than I have in my whole life. I'd encourage a Christian teen to go to a state school, because there are so many people there who need Jesus." — *Michaelanne, 19*

"Ultimately, college should be the teen's choice, but she should seriously consider her parents' opinions. She should listen to them and discuss the pros and cons of each choice. And the whole family should spend time in prayer to see where God is leading." — *Jennifer, 18*

### ... about living at home after high school:

"I rarely come home from college during the school year, so it has been different getting used to living at home for the summer after being on my own. I feel like I take a lot of liberties with my freedom, like telling my mom where I'm going instead of asking her, which I kind of feel is disrespectful. I think I just got used to making my own decisions." — *Mary, 18*

"When the Bible tells us to honor our father and mother, it doesn't mean to stop honoring them when we finish high school. Our parents love us and want what's best for us, so we should respect that." — *Luke, 18*

"I still live at home while I attend community college. I don't have a curfew or pay rent, but I have to run errands like taking my younger sister places and occasionally buying the groceries. I think our arrangement is fair, because I know I'm saving a lot of money by living at home. And I can think of no better roommates than my great family!" — *Courtney, 18*

"While I appreciate the love and concern my parents have for me, I'm really annoyed at being home for the summer. During school, I live 120 miles from my parents, and they don't stay up all night listening for me to come home. Now that I'm here, if I go visit a friend, they lay guilt on me for staying out late. I wish I could afford to get summer housing elsewhere." — *Kirsten Marie, 18*

"College is supposed to give you the experience of living on your own, while still having some supervision to help you if you fall. How can you even start to experience living on your own if your parents are keeping you tied down with a bunch of rules and treating you like they did when you were in high school?" — *Adam, 18*

### *... about working for money vs. working for the experience:*

"I had the opportunity to work at a Christian camp for the summer, which would have been fun but wouldn't pay anything, or get a job. Since I start college next year, I need the money, so I had to decline the camp's offer. Instead, I decided to go on a mission trip before I had to start working." — *Josh, 18*

"I'd pick the camp any day. But my parents would disagree, because they think I'm supposed to be working hard and saving money for the coming semester. Then they try to tell me this is supposed to be the best time of my life. How can it be if I'm rushed into adulthood?" — *Lora, 19*

"I took two weeks off work to be a counselor at a Bible camp. It was an extremely profitable experience because I'm now attending a Bible college and plan to be a youth minister when I graduate." — *Jeremy, 19*

"I don't see money as something vital to spend my time getting. I'd rather do something I enjoy than something that pays better. Money can't buy you the emotional dividends a rewarding job pays." — *Michael, 18*

"Next year at school, I'll have an apartment and a car—both huge financial responsibilities. So this summer, I'm working temp jobs that pay good money. I had the option of working for the civic theater, which is my major, but I had to turn it down. My parents are so proud of my decision!" — *Erika, 19*

## *... about spiritual doubts:*

"I think the most beneficial thing parents can do is be open to our doubts and realize that it's natural for us to question things. Part of faith is figuring out exactly what you believe, not what your parents, your peers or your church want you to think." — *Emily, 18*

"I rededicated my faith when I was 17, and this past year I've been growing a lot. When I question my faith it's about how to live and make choices as an adult. My dad helps by pointing me to the Word of God, helping me understand it and praying with me." — *Suzi, 18*

"I've gone through a lot of doubting and questioning my faith. My Bible study leader helped by telling me it's a normal part of growth. My parents have been reassuring, too, telling me I'm not a bad person. It's been a rough few years, but God brought me through." — *John, 19*

"Leaving home and becoming self-reliant forced me to examine my heart and life. I have become a much stronger Christian and have grown so much closer to my best friend—God. I think when you go through a life-changing experience like this, your parents have to just let you go and trust God to take care of you." — *Tina, 19*

"I think the most important thing a parent can do is assure their child that she will be loved—by them and by God—no matter what kind of changes her faith goes through, and that God will always be there to guide her." — *Amanda, 18*

# RECOMMENDED RESOURCES

**Preteens:**

- Campbell, Ross. *How to Really Love Your Child* (Chariot Victor Books, Revised, 1992). If we had to choose a favorite resource for the parents of preteens, it would be this book. Insightful, Christian, practical advice on meeting your child's basic emotional needs.

- Campbell, Ross. *How to Really Love Your Teenager* (Chariot Victor Books, Revised, 1993). The follow-up book to *How to Really Love Your Child*, this covers issues unique to adolescents and has an especially helpful chapter on anger.

- Cook, Bruce. *Choosing the Best: Abstinence Until Marriage* (Choosing the Best, Inc., 1997). This book is designed especially for parents of kids using the Choosing the Best abstinence-based sex ed curriculum in school. It's a candid, thought-provoking resource for any parent. If you can't find it in your bookstore, you can order directly by calling (800) 774-BEST.

- Dobson, James. *Preparing for Adolescence* (Regal, Reprint, 1999). Although it begins with a chapter for parents, this Christian classic is primarily for a teen audience. Topics handled include self-esteem, emotions and physical development.

- Elkind, David. *All Grown Up and No Place to Go: Teenagers in Crisis* (Perseus, Revised, 1997). A classic secular book written by the author of *The Hurried Child*, this describes the dilemmas faced by modern teens and tells why today's world is a uniquely difficult place in which to be an adolescent.

- Hughes, Kent and Barbara. *Common Sense Parenting* (Tyndale, 1996). This book discusses how to develop spirituality in your home and includes an especially helpful chapter on establishing family traditions.

- Kesler, Jay. *Emotionally Healthy Teenagers* (Word Publishing, 1998). This book covers ten parenting principles that include being on your kids' side, not against them; teaching them the consequences of their own behavior; and listening more than you lecture.

- Smith, Michael W. *Old Enough to Know* (Thomas Nelson, 2000). Written for teen readers, this book speaks about sex, fitting in, friendships and more, with the added advantage that it's by a well-known Christian recording star.

**Young Teens:**

- *Brio* and *Breakaway* (Focus on the Family, Colorado Springs, CO). Even non-readers dive into these magazines. *Brio* is for junior high girls and *Breakaway* is for junior high guys, but don't hesitate to order both for your family. For subscription information call 1-800-A-FAMILY.

- *Campus Life* (465 Gundersen Drive, Carol Stream, IL 60188 or Clmag@campus-life.net) While this magazine is targeted at senior highers, your junior high student can find plenty of great stuff here, too—interviews with Christian artists, practucal advice and stories of faith from other teenagers. For subscription information, call 1-800-678-6083, or go to www.campuslife.net.

- Dockrey, Karen. *Facing Down the Tough Stuff* (Lion, 1998). Teenagers face real problems like learning disabilities, cancer, divorce, blended families and friendship woes. When they want advice on these issues, they often turn to their peers, not to adults. This book, written by teens for teens, offers sound suggestions to help sort through these problems. There's also good advice for parents on how to equip our kids and their friends to deal with difficult issues.

- Dockrey, Karen. *Growing a Family Where People Really Like Each Other* (Bethany, 1996). Over and over teenagers lament that they aren't closer to their parents. They want to talk to their parents, want their parents' guidance, and want to live in a happy family. Use the techniques illustrated in this book to build the kind of family your teens yearn for. Full of stories and idea pages, this book reads more like a comfortable conversation than a how-to text.

- Gunn, Robin Jones. Christy Miller Series & Sierra Jensen Series (Bethany House). Twelve volumes in one series and ten in the other satisfy young teens' longing for series fiction. The stories are true-to-life and unashamedly proclaim Christian values. Another good series published by the Bethany House/Focus on the Family team is the Nikki Sheridan Series by Shirley Brinkerhoff.

- Johnson, Kevin. *Why Can't My Life Be a Summer Vacation?* (Bethany, 1994). Kevin Johnson's devotionals are the best I've seen for young teens. They're engaging and true-to-life. Best of all, kids read them. The only problem is, there aren't enough of them to last all the way through the teen years. But more are coming. The other titles in the series: *Can I Be a Christian Without Being Weird?, Could Someone Wake Me Up Before I Drool on the Desk?, Does Anybody Know What Planet My Parents Are From?, So Who Says I Have to Act My Age?, Was That A Balloon or Did Your Head Just Pop?, Who Should I Listen To?, Why Is God Looking for Friends?*

- Stephens, Andrea. *God Thinks You're Positively Awesome!* (Servant Publications, 1997). Young girls in our appearance-oriented society can get pretty obsessed with looks. The changes that hormones bring intensify this obsession. Because God wants us to love others as we love ourselves, this book helps girls enjoy their appearance for the right reason—because they are created by God.

- Shellenberger, Susie and Greg Johnson. *Getting Ready for the Guy/Girl Thing* (Gospel Light, 1991). Anything written by Susie Shellenberger and Greg Johnson is not to be missed. This book is among their best. Your teenagers will be in stitches by the time they finish reading the hilarious stories about talking to the opposite sex. These authors have a unique gift for communicating God's truth to real teens.

## Middle Teens:

- Arterburn, Stephen and Jim Burns. *Parents Guide to the Top Ten Dangers Teens Face* (Tyndale, 1999). An easy reference with real solutions to the problems parents fear most.

- Arterburn, Stephen and Jim Burns. *DrugProof Your Kids* (Regal Books, 1995). Proven, practical ideas for talking to your kids about drugs in a way they'll actually listen to.

- Chapman, Gary. *Five Signs of a Loving Family* (Northfield Publishing, 1998). A terrific resource for families struggling to get along. Even if your family life is great, you'll find some insights to make your good thing even better.

- Cline, Foster, MD, and Jim Fay. *Parenting Teens with Love and Logic* (Navpress, 1990). A favorite among parents who want to guide their teenagers with loving, constructive discipline.

- Cloud, Dr. Henry and Dr. John Townsend. *Boundaries with Kids* (Zondervan, 1998). A wonderful resource for helping kids learn to be responsible, caring adults.

- Cloud, Dr. Henry and Dr. John Townsend. *Raising Great Kids* (Zondervan, 1999). This terrific book offers great ideas for bringing out the best in your teenager.

- Huggins, Kevin. *Parenting Adolescents* (Navpress, 1992). Great insights into the heart and mind of your teenager.

- McPherson, Miles. *The Power of Believing in Your Child* (Bethany House, 1998). If you're having a hard time liking your teenager, this book can help you find the good in your child, no matter what she's going through.

- Rainey, Dennis and Barbara Rainey. *Parenting Today's Adolescent* (Thomas Nelson Publishers, 1998). The Raineys are in touch with today's teen culture. If you feel clueless, this is the book for you.

- Smalley, Gary. *The Key to Your Child's Heart* (Word Books, 1996). This book breaks down major parenting challenges—discipline, character development, communication, and more—into managable chunks, providing ideas you can implement right away.

- Smalley, Gary and John T. Trent. *The Blessing* (Pocket Books, 1990). The power of unconditional love can't be underestimated. This wonderful book can open your eyes to ways you can give your teenagers what they need most.

# Resources

**Older Teens:**

- Bolles, Richard. *What Color Is Your Parachute?* (Ten Speed Press, 2000). Updated anually, this classic book helps individuals identify their strengths and directs them toward meaningful career choices.

- Dobson, James. *Life on the Edge* (Word Publishing, 1995). This book is dedicated to "the generation currently moving out of adolescence and into the arena of adult responsibility." It addresses the defining issues young adults will face in the next decade of their lives. This would be a good resource for parents and their older teens to read and discuss together.

- Hudson, Christopher and others. *Career: Clues for the Clueless* (Promise Press, 1999). All three recommended volumes in this series are compact, easy to use, and easy to read. As the title indicates, this one is packed with practical tips on finding the right career.

- Hudson, Christopher and others. *College: Clues for the Clueless* (Promise Press, 1999). This volume is ideal for college bound students and their parents, providing tons of godly advice, practical hints and entertaining, real-life anecdotes.

- Hudson, Christopher and others. *Dating: Clues for the Clueless* (Promise Press, 1999). This book offers practical help for establishing relationships with the opposite sex and has a ton of ideas of creative dates and dating on a budget.

- Rice, Wayne and Dave Veerman. *Reality 101* (Tyndale House Publishers, 1999). Although written primarily for high school students, this book contains answers to 101 questions about faith, friendship, family, finances and other issues that will be helpful to people of all ages.

- Rice, Wayne and Dave Veerman. *Understanding Your Teenager* (Word Publishing, 1999). Based on the popular seminar of the same title, this book provides insight into the nature of teenagers today, the world in which parents are trying to rear those teens and practical steps that parents can take to guide their kids in the right direction.

- Woods, Len. *I'm Outta Here* (Baker Books, 1999). An intensely practical volume for recent high school graduates, Len describes 50 real-life situations in which ethical choices must be made. These situations are organized in the following sections: ethical, educational, financial, work, sexual, social relational and spiritual.